SOCIAL WORK AND MIGRATION

Contemporary Social Work Studies

Series Editor:
Robin Lovelock, University of Southampton

Series Advisory Board:
Lena Dominelli, Durham University, UK
Jan Fook, University of Southampton, UK
Peter Ford, University of Southampton, UK
Lorraine Gutiérrez, University of Michigan, USA
Walter Lorenz, Free University of Bozen-Bolzano, Italy
Karen Lyons, London Metropolitan University, UK
Colette McAuley, University of Southampton, UK
Joan Orme, University of Glasgow, UK
Jackie Powell, University of Southampton, UK

Contemporary Social Work Studies (CSWS) is a series disseminating high quality new research and scholarship in the discipline and profession of social work. The series promotes critical engagement with contemporary issues relevant across the social work community and captures the diversity of interests currently evident at national, international and local levels.

CSWS is located in the School of Social Sciences at the University of Southampton and is a development from the successful series of books published by Ashgate in association with CEDR (the Centre for Evaluative and Developmental Research) from 1991.

Titles in this series include:

Globalization and International Social Work: Postmodern Change and Challenge
Malcolm Payne and Gurid Aga Askeland

Indigenous Social Work Education and Practice Around the World
Edited by Mel Gray, John Coates and Michael Yellow Bird

Social Work in a Corporate Era: Practices of Power and Resistance
Edited by Linda Davies and Peter Leonard

Forthcoming title:

Professional Discretion in Modern Social Services
Edited by Mel Gray, John Coates and Michael Yellow Bird

Social Work and Migration
Immigrant and Refugee Settlement and Integration

KATHLEEN VALTONEN

University of the West Indies, St. Augustine, Trinidad and Tobago

ASHGATE

Published by
Ashgate Publishing Limited
Wey Court East
Union Road
Farnham
Surrey, GU9 7PT
England

Ashgate Publishing Company
Suite 420
101 Cherry Street
Burlington
VT 05401-4405
USA

www.ashgate.com

British Library Cataloguing in Publication Data
Valtonen, Kathleen, 1944-
  Social work and migration : immigrant and refugee
  settlement and integration. - (Contemporary social work
  studies)
  1. Social work with immigrants 2. Immigrants - Cultural
  assimilation
  I. Title
  361.3'2'086912

Library of Congress Cataloging-in-Publication Data
Valtonen, Kathleen, 1944-
  Social work and migration : immigrant and refugee settlement and integration / by
Kathleen Valtonen.
     p. cm. -- (Contemporary social work studies)
  ISBN 978-0-7546-7194-7 1. Emigration and immigration. 2.
Immigrants--Services for. 3. Refugees--Services for. 4. Acculturation. 5. Social
integration. I. Title.

  JV6035.V35 2008
  362.8--dc22

                                                                2008030124

ISBN 978-0-7546-7194-7

Printed and bound in Great Britain by MPG Books Ltd, Bodmin, Cornwall

Contents

List of Figures

Preface

This book is a response to the challenge of immigrant and refugee settlement which is emerging in many receiving countries. The immigrant settlement and integration field has rapidly become a special province of social work which now plays a pivotal role in its service provision and policy sectors. The integration or so-called domiciling issues that persist into the second generation have brought out even more forcefully the need for deeper understanding of settlement processes, especially among the professional and academic social work body that finds itself at the frontline.

This text is meant to fill a gap in the existing offerings in social work curricula by providing a critical knowledge base for engaging with key issues in the field. The book incorporates conceptual frames salient to immigrant settlement and integration as well as material from studies in the migration field, which are otherwise out of the range of standard social work texts. The reader is offered the opportunity to explore the capacity of the discipline/profession to play a primary role in the course and outcome of settlement, and to influence the integration and multicultural processes taking place at many levels in our modern societies of settlement.

The idea for writing this book sprang from a series of studies on refugee and immigrant integration which I conducted in Finland and Canada from the mid 1990s onward. One of these was a longitudinal study of refugee integration in Finland in the 1990s. However, examples used in the book are drawn more widely from other national contexts. I gained practice experience in refugee settlement services in Finland and valuable insight from the various communities.

I was fortunate in having a period of seven years teaching undergraduate and graduate-level social work at the Cave Hill (Barbados) and St Augustine (Trinidad) Campuses of the University of the West Indies. This work connected me with Caribbean social work programmes which are grounded in social and human development philosophy. Strong emphasis is placed on the potential of social work to fashion change in societal arrangements in the interest of bringing about more equitable life conditions for different social groupings across the society. This structural orientation proved to be very suitable for re-thinking social work approaches with immigrant and refugee communities. I also believe that social workers come to develop unique emic perspectives in the course of working with immigrants and refugees. This is a distinct advantage when embarking on research.

Chapter 1 of the book presents the structure and dynamics of migration flows, different dimensions of refugee movements and other migration flows, and inserts practice with immigrants and refugees into the social work agenda and mandate.

Chapter 2 examines the human rights and citizenship rights approaches for analysis and practice, with a second section focusing on social work theories, concepts and models and their relevance to practice with immigrant and refugee populations.

In Chapter 3 immigrants' engagement with the three overarching institutional systems of society – the state, the market and civil society – is examined, following which the focus is extended to transnational and diasporic links. In Chapter 4 a selection of some of the main theoretical and conceptual frames relating to settlement is presented and discussed in the light of current ideas and debates.

Chapter 5 scrutinizes the politics of inclusion and exclusion. It covers themes of equality, equity and social justice, and examines different forms of existing equity instruments which function as integration facilitating legal and civic mechanisms. Discriminatory barriers to participation and the impact of these for integration are discussed. Chapter 6 examines skill areas which have particular significance for practice with immigrants and refugees. Themes are organized according to the three-tiered category of macro, meso and micro levels. The interrelated strengths, empowerment, resilience and ecological approaches are discussed in this section. In connection with the focus on strengths, the final section looks at sources of power and 'forms of capital' as resources for settlement.

The functions of the family in settlement, its coping systems, its acculturation and its culture-based resources, are presented in Chapter 7. It is argued that the family is the institution that bears the main impact of migration and settlement initiatives, challenges, actions and outcomes. The scrutiny of second generation issues raises some troubling questions about current settlement processes in countries with long experience of immigration, such as France, Germany and Sweden. Chapter 8 looks at intergenerational inequality, identity issues and selected structural aspects of settlement, using Parekh's (1997) parameters of 'equal citizenship'.

Chapter 9 presents different national integration policies and an overview of settlement service components. This is followed by discussion of policy processes and impacting dynamics in organizational and bureaucratic settings. Chapter 10 explores ethical principles in social work with relevance to settlement and integration work. The development of quality features and robust approaches to settlement practice, which is presented in the second section, draws on many of the insights discussed earlier in the work.

Kathleen Valtonen
Turku
October 2007

Acknowledgements

I would like to acknowledge the support of my home institution, the University of the West Indies, St Augustine, Trinidad, for extending special leave for writing this manuscript. Ms Elmelinda Lara and her staff, who were always very accommodating and understanding to a range of requests through the years, are deserving of a special mention here. The office staff at the Department of Behavioural Sciences has been unfailingly helpful and I am also grateful to Tuorla Observatory, Piikkio, Finland, for rendering technical support at times when this was especially critical.

Le Thi My Dung has extended valuable assistance throughout the years. The Centre for Refugee Studies at York University, Toronto, and the Doctoral Program on Cultural Interaction and Integration at the University of Turku, Finland, provided me with opportunities and support for pursuing research in the field.

Finally I would like to thank my colleagues at various universities for the sharing of ideas, discussions and collaboration over the years, all of which have contributed to this work.

To Tuomas, Hannes and Jae Won

Chapter 1

Perspectives on Migration: 'Here and Now' Implications for Social Work

Introduction

The study of migration and settlement calls for us to scrutinize this phenomenon from different angles and within the larger field of action, and to examine the underlying social forces of migration movements. This chapter will focus on the idea of migration as a phenomenon that is embedded in wider national and international events, processes and developments. Factors such as the progression of social and human development affect life conditions in countries of origin, and can act as an impetus for emigration. The economic perspective, for instance, emphasizes income differential between sending and receiving countries, and argues for the importance of this as one of the main migration catalysts. The multifaceted nature of migration, however, is being increasingly appreciated. Migration is moreover a process that evolves with time, regardless of whether we consider the international, societal or personal dimensions. Our conceptual frames can change as we study how processes play themselves out and shape the phenomenon itself.

The initial chapter thus leads the reader directly into the field of migration and settlement, by presenting the structure and context of global-level dynamics and antecedents of migration. Different dimensions of refugee movements and other migration flows are introduced in the second section. The third section situates practice with immigrants and refugees in the social work agenda and mandate.

Migration Today

Migration is an increasingly familiar phenomenon in the societies of today. To migration we owe the cultural cross-fertilization in societies which gives rise to many stimulating and progressive currents of intellectual, social, economic and cultural change. The study of migration is challenging in its complexity. Migration has ramifications both for the migrants themselves and for the societies of settlement. The process of long-term integration requires the involvement of individuals, their families and communities in a demanding period of transition, adaptation and cultural metamorphosis. Personal and social resources must be developed in the first instance to deal with the tasks of settlement.

The style and pace of settlement can be seen largely as a function of the energies, personal and social resources of the settling persons themselves. However, a perspective that takes into account only what settling persons bring to the process would be incomplete, since settlement is qualitatively and decisively influenced by many factors in the receiving societies such as the overall capacity of the latter to incorporate and accommodate newcomers. This is reflected in the arrangements that have been put into place for facilitating integration including formal statutory provisions, specific services and pertinent legislation. The prevailing attitudes in the polity and the public are also significant. Studies provide evidence that the state of the economy in the country, for example, will have an effect on the degree of receptivity to immigrants. Restrictive policies and negative attitudes in the majority are more manifest during economic downturns when citizens struggle with their own contingencies and are sensitive to perceived external threats.

In the public and lay discourse, immigration issues attract attention. Positive press for immigration is generally overlooked or not considered essential when settlement and integration processes proceed satisfactorily. Many aspects of progress in settlement issues and areas remain 'invisible'. When difficulties arise in immigration-related issues, on the other hand, immigrants and refugee groups are vulnerable to being mis-represented and it is not uncommon for perceptions of 'otherness' to surface in covert or overt ways. Immigration issues are also exploited at the level of party politics, at which times the discourse is invariably skewed.

It should be borne in mind that immigrants have an important function in the labour markets of settlement societies. The majority of immigrants belong to the labour force in the countries of settlement, making them important actors in national economies. In a globalized world, contemporary labour markets and economies are becoming increasingly interconnected. These processes feature centrally in economic theories of migration and are presented as a facilitating force in the movement of people across borders. Teitelbaum (1980) points out that extensive international migration is not peculiar to our time, but the enhanced importance of the nation-state in the twentieth century is unique to the modern epoch. Throughout most of human history, national boundaries, where these existed, were far more permeable to the temporary ebb and flow or permanent movement of peoples than they are today.

Van Hear (1998) states that globalization signifies accelerated integration and interdependence of the world economy, the most dramatic signs of which are the mobility of capital, and the liberalization of world trade in goods and services. Ohmae (1990, xii–xiii) refers to the flow across borders of information, money, goods and services as well as greater cross-border movement of people and corporations. With globalization has come the intensification of worldwide social relations which link localities, and allow local happenings to be shaped by events occurring many miles away and vice versa (Giddens 1990). Richmond (1994) observes that the process of globalization has increased the propensity for proactive as well as reactive migration. Whereas improvements in transportation and communications raise awareness of opportunities for mobility in sending and receiving countries, factors such as the global market for arms and superpower intervention in local conflicts have led to instabilities in the world system, with a growth in reactive migration as a consequence of civil war, for example (Richmond 1994).

In most European societies, populations are aging and decreasing. Immigration becomes one strategy that is considered as a way of renewing the labour force and thereby alleviating some social policy problems. In general immigrants make up large percentages of the generation of young adults in receiving countries (Jacobs and Tillie 2004). Immigrant groups tend to consist of a great majority of individuals of prime working age.

With regard to settlement provisioning, state-mandated formally structured measures to accommodate immigrants are seldom a product of brand new initiatives. This brings its own advantages and also some disadvantages. Settlement programmes are likely to be an extension of the existing social service and social welfare system in the country of reception, with a degree of innovation to cater for the particular situation of immigrants. So, for instance, Canada, Australia and several countries of Western Europe have catered for immigrants and refugees within their highly organized welfare systems. In countries where the state is a minor actor in welfare provision, the responsibility for generating welfare and well-being is distributed across the non-public, non-governmental (NGO) and informal sectors, including the family. Immigrants and refugees who are settling into this latter type of system must link into the existing non-state or quasi-state structures, which are heavily grounded in and organized at the level of the community and its collectivities. Settlement processes in some societies thus involve intensive interfacing with the existing range of public services, while in those societies with a wider spread in the 'welfare mix', immigrants and refugees build direct and multiple linkages with the organized services in civil society. The mode in which social services and settlement services are organized and delivered is likely to impact on the nature and profile of individuals' initial contacts with members of the mainstream society. The network-building process and so-called 'bridging' into mainstream society are important priorities in settlement and thus in settlement practice.

Regardless of the type of social service systems and human service arrangements in the settlement countries, social workers have come to be invested with key roles and major tasks in facilitating the integration of immigrants and refugees. Working strategically on the frontline in human and social service provisioning, their engagement with immigrant groups is immediate, ongoing and often intensive. Responses to the short- and long-term challenges facing immigrants and refugees in settlement seem to fall naturally within the professional portfolio.

The parameters of the professional mandate with respect to settling communities are generally more easily identified and defined in contexts where citizens' social rights to social security and welfare are articulated in policy and also institutionally implemented. In less 'mature' social welfare systems, the mandate and specification of professional responsibilities of social work might be much more flexibly and indeed diversely located within the existing service systems. Despite the variation across service provision systems, the social work response to the needs of settling groups has generally been regarded as pivotal. Immigrant and refugee settlement and integration have become established areas of practice. The tasks of immigrant integration lend themselves in a singular way to social work intervention at all levels, including progressive approaches pitched at the structural level.

Within the profession, we are faced with the need to mould strategies that deal not only with short-term practical issues in settlement, but with the long-term questions of integration. The necessity of engaging widely and creatively with the social environment, policy-makers and political agents challenges practitioners to expand their boundaries of practice in the interest of this particular client constituency.

Definitions

'Migration' refers to the movement of people from one settlement place to another. The term 'migrant' can refer to an individual who moves across a national border or to one who moves within national territory. Strictly speaking, the term thus encompasses both international and internal migrants. In international migration circles, however, the term 'migrants' is very often used for persons who cross national borders in moving from their country of origin or habitual residence to settle in another country. Similarly, the term 'displaced persons' may refer to persons who are forced to move across borders but also applies to those who find alternative settlement locations within their own borders (internally displaced persons sometimes referred to as IDPs).

The national policies which guide social services and social work with immigrants are often based on the 'voluntary/forced' distinction. Using the humanitarian circumstances surrounding forced migration as a benchmark, policy-makers tend to address so-called 'regular' immigrants, refugees and asylum seekers as discrete groups with qualitatively different needs in settlement. Entitlements are usually differentiated especially during the initial period. Human service workers and policy-makers vary in their opinions on whether reception and settlement services should cater differentially for these groups. One argument is based on the undeniable existence of basic needs across policy-created categories. Those who emphasize the principle of social justice place need as the central reference point, and argue for greater emphasis on consistency across the provisioning for groups who are 'categorically' distinct but, in reality, in a similar situation. The differentiation between categories signifies differences in entitlements to primary benefits. The disparity can be critical for some groups. For instance, asylum seekers, who await an official decision on their application for refugee status, can be in a precarious situation for long periods. This is due in some circumstances not only to a minimal level of benefit, but to the lack of permission to take up employment, or simply to the lack of employment. Using the examples of the UK and Australia, Briskman and Cemlyn (2005) observe that the harsh public and official climates surrounding asylum seekers have led to a weak social work response. These authors argue for greater recognition of the possible role of social workers in defending human rights and in promoting social justice through macro-level advocacy at national and international levels.

As 'involuntary' migrants, refugees comprise that category of immigrants distinguished by the circumstances of their arrival and the contextual push factors that precipitated their migration in the first place. The United Nations (UN) defines a refugee as someone who has suffered repression or persecution, often at the hands of his or her own government, and who has to flee for personal survival. Refugees flee situations characterized by gross violations of human rights, and of late increasingly from conditions of civil warfare as well as cross-border conflicts. 'Voluntary' and 'involuntary/forced' migration can be conceptualized along a continuum, rather than as two discrete categories. Voluntary migration, at one end, includes, for example, senior personnel in multinational organizations. Individuals who leave their country of origin due to lack of opportunities and precarious economic conditions can be classified as 'involuntary' migrants. Those who are forced to leave by conflict, persecution and human rights violations depart in extreme circumstances and fall at the other end of this continuum.

Under the 1951 UN Convention and Protocol relating to the Status of Refugees, a refugee is defined as follows:

> The term refugee shall apply to any person who ..., owing to a well-founded fear of being persecuted for reasons of race, religion, nationality, membership of a particular social group or political opinion, is outside the country of his nationality and is unable or, owing to such fear, is unwilling to avail himself of the protection of that country; or who, not having a nationality and being outside of the country of his former habitual residence as a result of such events, is unable or, owing to such fear, is unwilling to return to it.

Cox and Pawar (2006) note that the perceived problems with this definition, as they have emerged with time, relate to the exclusion of internally displaced persons and groups; to the focus on persecution, which is not defined here or in other UN conventions, and which may not include, for example, victims of war; and to gender bias in the definition, in that there is a tendency for males to be, or to be seen to be, the direct focus of persecution, despite the fact that women and children inevitably suffer extensively and in particular ways (for example, rape victims or child soldiers).[1] Cox and Pawar (2006) add that the consensus of opinion in the early twenty-first century is that if a new definition were to be sought from the international community, any agreed definition would prove to be more restrictive than the existing one, due to the contemporary concern in many

---

1 See Lyons, Manion and Carlsen (2006).

countries of being inundated by refugees. The criteria embodied in the official definition of a refugee is of decisive importance to those who seek protection outside of their own countries. The right to leave one's country is seldom contested (at least in theory). Yet an individual's right to enter another country is dependent on the national legislation that prevails there. Refugees seek asylum under the auspices of the 1951 UN Convention and Protocol. They fall into a humanitarian category based on criteria that have been determined at supranational level.

'Immigrants' is used in this text as a general term referring inclusively to voluntary or regular migrants, and to involuntary migrants. I use the term 'refugees' in specific reference to those who arrive in the context of involuntary or forced migration. When it is necessary to be more specific in the case of 'forced' migration types, 'asylum seeker' designates persons who start their asylum application process upon arrival in the destination country. In the European Union, for example, asylum seekers are defined as persons who consider themselves to be refugees and who seek, therefore, asylum as well as recognition of their refugee status in the territory of another state. Alternatively the process of determining refugee status can take place in United Nations High Commissioner for Refugees (UNHCR) camps, for example. Refugee status determination (RSD) is the procedure by which refugees are identified and distinguished from other migrants. The procedure can be conducted on a group or an individual basis. Individual procedures are much more resource-intensive and considered to be riskier for refugees, since an individual might be incorrectly rejected. Individual RSD is normally handled by a government, but in many places it is conducted under the auspices of the UNHCR.

Cox and Pawar (2006, 271) comment that in practice a distinction is being made between those who claim asylum in a developing country and those who reach a western country before making an application for asylum. In western countries of reception, the former population tends to be regarded as genuine asylum seekers, presumably because they claim asylum in the first possible country after fleeing. The distinction between genuine and non-genuine is seen as part of the reaction of western governments to the large increase in asylum seeker numbers from the 1970s to the early 2000s (Cox and Pawar 2006).

'Immigrants', 'migrants', 'newer citizens' or 'settling persons' are terms used in this text to refer to both voluntary and involuntary migrants. 'Immigrant communities' and 'ethnic communities' are also referred to as 'settling communities'. 'Settlement' is a term that captures the concrete activities and processes of becoming established after arrival in the country of settlement. 'Integration', on the other hand, includes settlement but puts weight on a goal-oriented dimension of settlement, and indicates that migrants are seeking full participation in the social, economic, cultural and political life of a society, a process which is understood to be compatible with retention of their cultural identity and vital aspects of their culture. Integration is seen thus as the process in which a migrant engages in settlement-related goal-directed activity, and establishes roles, relationships and status in the receiving society. Integration is also seen as an outcome – that stage at which an individual has actually attained equitable, satisfying and meaningful status, roles and relations to the formal and informal institutions in the society of settlement (see Breton 1992). In this book, the central emphasis is on the situation of persons settling on a permanent basis.

Migration Antecedents and Flows

Migration itself can be seen as the act or process by which people move from one location to another. A *migration system* implies a processual dimension, and is understood to be a network of interconnected countries linked by the interactions of actors in functioning networks within the system (Kritz, Lim and Zlotnick 1992). Migration can thus be understood also as the multiplicity of social relations that link migrants and non-migrants at the different ends of migration movements, a perspective which allows us to grasp the wider situational context of the relational systems (de Bernart 1997).

At the level of personal links, chain migration refers to a situation in which the migration of individuals is encouraged, facilitated and supported by others who have previously migrated to the same destination. The previous link in the chain can be a close family member, relative, friend or acquaintance. The concept is not restricted to facilitation by kin for family reunion. Rumbaut (1991, 189) has stated that many millions of immigrants and their children in the US today are 'embedded in often intricate webs of family ties, both here and abroad. Such ties form extraordinary transnational linkages and networks that can, by reducing the costs and risks of migration, expand and serve as a conduit to additional and thus potentially self-perpetuating migration.'

The catalysts of migration are complex. In the case of flows from so-called 'developing' countries, the propensity of citizens to emigrate is influenced by a combination of economic, demographic, political and ecological conditions, as well as by emigration policy in the country of origin and the policies of receiving countries. Many of the flows of a few decades ago were shaped by former colonial links together with the lure of the employment market in large centres of growth. The conditions in different countries continue to influence the actual flows by volume and type (for example, permanent, labour, forced, illegal) (Appleyard 1999, 5). At the individual level, migration decisions often depend upon the gravity of circumstances, specific community/family/individual variables, and on the availability of support through interpersonal links which would help to make migration a viable option (Appleyard 1999). Except in states with restrictive immigration policies, family reunification and chain migration tend to accompany migratory flows as crucial mechanisms for restoring social and kinship ties dislocated by emigration.

Zolberg, Suhkre and Aguayo (1989) emphasize the impact on migration by structural factors, events and forces which are part of broad historical processes. Migration is not a static phenomenon, but one that evolves from socio-historical events, societal conditions and dynamics in countries of origin and settlement. A parallel perspective is offered by Torpey (2000, 125) who points out that states' policies and nation-building processes have a basic connection with migration decisions and flows. Some countries facilitate and even covertly precipitate emigration as a safety valve for class conflict and the tensions generated by economic underdevelopment. Many groups are forced to leave their homes by violent processes of nation-state-building. Societal or cross-border conflicts displace large numbers of persons. Targeted repression or persecution, in many cases instigated through the institutional machinery of the state, force individuals and their families to leave as their safety is threatened.

Two Models for Migration Flows

The 'push/pull' model appeals through its simplicity. According to this model, individuals' decisions to leave are influenced by 'push' factors (such as political and economic insecurity – persecution or deprivation) in the country of origin. Simultaneously with push factors, 'pull' factors in the destination country offer perceived options or solutions, such as economic benefits, family reunion or political asylum, that also help to shape migration decisions (Richmond 1994). By taking into account a greater breadth of variables in these two basic categories, and the interrelationships between these, it is possible to arrive at more systemic or ecological understandings of migration processes. Studying the relationships between factors can help us to grasp the processes involved in migration decisions. In the settlement environment, the 'push' and 'pull' factors do not necessarily recede but might have implications on the chosen style of adaptation. Economic hardship in the country of origin, for example, is one of the forces fuelling the flow of remittances in that direction.

In a second model, Stahl and Bradford (1999) offer three categories into which the range of social, economic, demographic and political factors which impact on migration can be organized. These are *fundamental forces, facilitating factors* and *channeling factors*.[2] These factors, either independently or in conjunction, generate emigration pressures. These categories of factors are briefly described below, since some of the aspects have been discussed in the preceding section.

---

2   Stahl and Bradford's (1999) model elaborates on fundamental forces as the: macroeconomic – earnings differentials, capacity to finance migration, design and administration of development plans, relative deprivation and environmental degradation; demographic forces – younger population with greater propensity to migrate, fast population growth rate and age skew towards younger cohorts, and extent and rate of urbanization; political forces – political instability, possible political repression, concerns for personal security; facilitating and channelling factors – historical ties, migration networks, lowered cost of transportation, 'middlemen' mediating passage, intangible benefits such as maintenance of ties.

Fundamental forces   These refer to macroeconomic, demographic and political forces. One macroeconomic factor is the earnings differential between sending and receiving countries. The performance in national development processes is also important – whether positive benefits and opportunities are created for households and citizens, and whether the society is able, or is perceived as being able, to meet the basic and higher level needs of its citizens in areas such as safety, future well-being, life chances and cultural support. With regard to material well-being, migration can be a strategy for family income generation and diversifying economic risks. Migration is also related to long range planning for the well-being of the second generation (Stahl and Bradford 1999). My studies of migrant communities supports the perspective that an *opportunities differential* could be a significant macroeconomic force influencing second generation-related migration decisions.

The relevance of social and national development for the field of migration can be understood using the now well-established frame of human development. Human development is an area in which Nobel Laureate Amartya Sen has done pioneering work. The human development concept is different from that of the more structure-focused national and social development frames. Human development brings a people-centred approach to development and focuses on the choices which are open to people. It is defined as the process of enlarging choice in individuals' lives. The most critical choices are to be able to live a long and healthy life, to be educated and to have access to resources necessary for a decent standard of living. The broad line of reasoning is that the ultimate goal of economic development is social development. The advantage of wealth is not an increase of happiness as such, but an increase in the range of human choice (Lewis 1955).

Demographic forces   Demographic forces in sending countries include a fast population growth rate that will skew the age distribution numerically toward the younger cohorts and those of prime labour market age. Among younger cohorts the propensity to migrate can be strong. In general young people have proportionately fewer family ties of direct responsibility, such as those of marriage and children. They are attracted by the opportunity for wider experience, including employment experience, and can look forward to a longer payoff period over which to offset any future unevenness in earnings capacity.

In the range of *political forces*, political instability is an important determinant of emigration pressures. Administration cannot function effectively in the frame of short-term political survival, with consequent neglect of long-term national economic and social objectives which affects the stability and quality of life of citizens. Political instability daunts foreign investors. This is one factor relating to the poor performance of many economies, and ensuing emigration pressures in the country.

Political instability does not necessarily give rise to political repression. However, it often does, causing emigration pressure to be increased by individuals' concern for personal security and for that of their families. In periods of political instability, leaders stir up religious and/or ethnic differences that reinforce divisions and instability. Forced migration is directly related to political instability. It develops in extreme conditions with individuals facing persecution and fearing for their lives and those of their families. Flight is a survival strategy of the last resort.

Facilitating and channeling factors Progress in telecommunications, as mentioned above, leads to wider availability of information and greater familiarity with conditions and opportunities in other countries. The cost of travel might be more affordable, especially when facilitated by existing personal networks that fulfil a bridging function. Networks and contacts generate a wide range of intangible and tangible benefits ranging from the practical (accommodation, information and support in the job search) to cultural and social support mechanisms.

The operation of diverse forms of middleman activities, such as those of recruiting agencies, also constitute facilitating factors. When the opportunity costs of migration are perceived as manageable, migration becomes a viable strategy for individuals. Middleman-facilitated migration includes people-smuggling activity and people-trafficking activity. For the individuals concerned, this involves high and unpredictable risks with heavy human costs as a consequence of migration decisions that are invariably based on misleading information. According to Lyons, Manion and Carlsen (2006, 121), it has been suggested that there is more duress and threat in people-trafficking relative to a lesser degree of exploitation in people-smuggling. The authors point out that people might seek transportation from one country to another over considerable distances, for extortionate amounts of money and in dangerous conditions, yet the knowledge they might have about the living and working conditions at their destinations might be very scant.

Migration Flows

Prior to the 1960s, traditional destination countries were Canada, the United States, Australia, New Zealand, the UK and Argentina. Subsequently several countries of Western Europe, notably Germany, France, Belgium, Switzerland, Sweden and the Netherlands, have attracted significant numbers of immigrants. In the late 1970s, longtime countries of out-migration such as Italy, Spain and Portugal started receiving immigrants from the Middle East and Africa. After the 1974 escalation in oil prices, labour migration was sponsored extensively by capital-rich nations in the Gulf region. Migration has indeed become a global-level phenomenon with the increased number of both sending and receiving countries. Outflows now originate more and more in developing countries, when in the earlier part of the twentieth century, Europe was the major source of migrants (Massey 1999).

On the basis of 25 European Union (EU) country reports, Cyrus et al. (2005) suggest that states can be grouped into four categories: states that have experienced high levels of migration for several decades (for example, former colonial countries such as the Netherlands and the UK); states that have experienced immigration since the 1980s (for example, Ireland and Finland as well as Southern European former sending countries for recruited workers); states that have undergone a transition from emigration to immigration countries since the 1990s (for example, Malta and Cyprus); and states with a low level of current new immigration (the Baltic states, Slovenia and Slovakia, for example). The authors identified patterns in flows representing co-ethnic and returnee migration; colonial and post-colonial migration; pre-state formation settlement in newly founded states; immigration of asylum seekers and refugees; highly qualified immigration; new temporary workers; schemes migration and undocumented immigration.

The rapid increase in the number of persons seeking asylum in the EU area during the mid 1970s until the early 1990s comprised groups from countries affected by political intolerance, ethnic conflicts, and civil or international war. Latin America (Chile, Colombia, Ecuador), Africa (Ghana, Congo, Nigeria, Somalia), the wider Middle East (Palestine, Iraq, Iran, Algeria, Morocco) and Asia (Vietnam, Sri Lanka, Afghanistan) were the main regions of origin. In reaction to this, assessment criteria and regulations were tightened by several European countries by the mid 1990s. Some of the policy alterations allow for those asylum seekers who are legally identified as being from 'safe' countries to be returned to the country of origin (Cyrus et al. 2005). Lorenz (2006) comments that practices of selective exclusion, which had prevailed in the formation of nation-states, are now being reproduced rather uncritically at European level. He points out that the convergence of European immigration policies from the Schengen agreement to the Dublin convention, and their ratification in the Amsterdam Treaty of 1997, were moves to reinforce the perimeter fence around Europe while fostering greater mobility between EU countries. Lorenz (2006) further states that it is very significant that the Schengen criteria treat refugees and immigrants from outside the EU broadly in line with drug traffickers and terrorists for the purposes of controls and surveillance.

Rydgren (2004) points out that every country has its own profile of waves. In Sweden, this comprised a first period of predominantly labour immigration, of which almost 60 per cent originated from other Nordic countries including Finland. After 1973 and the oil crisis, the demand for labour immigration fell, but in the 1980s there was an increase in refugee immigration and non-European immigration. Fifty per cent of this increase came from outside Europe, especially from Iran and Iraq. Rydgren (2004) stated at the time of writing that individuals born abroad and living in Sweden formed 11.5 per cent of the total population.

Migration can be undertaken in the context of a decisive move. People can also reside for a specific period or even for decades in the destination country without having to, or feeling the need to, rule out options on where they would eventually settle. For those who move 'voluntarily', migration periods might be more open-ended with flexible periods of residence. The term 'circular migration' has been used to portray the situation in which migrants are able to move back and forth, on a more or less regular basis, between the country of origin and that of settlement or employment (Thomas-Hope 1992). Transnationalism, a currently popular construct with affinity to circular migration, reflects the volume, dynamism and complexity of the back and forth movements and transactions of modern-day migrants. Transnationalism implies the existence of a distinct social field or space, characterized by a dense web of transactions linking people in two or more home countries (Faist 2000a; Kivisto 2001). Modern communication makes it possible for migrants to maintain vibrant ties with their kin, communities and societies of origin.

Migration as a continuing trend   In sum, migration is a continuing trend evolving out of the complex interplay of many national and international forces in the socio-economic, political, demographic as well as human and social development processes. Major factors such as trade liberalization have created economic vulnerability in developing countries and corresponding pressures on citizens. Migratory flows are reflective of the level of interconnection and interdependence in global relations, and partly of greater asymmetry within the global system manifest in trade relations (Stiglitz 2002). The flows also arise as consequences of socio-political and geopolitical tragedy and its high cost in human terms, of environmental catastrophe or of weaknesses in national development processes. Migration is a process closely tied to the underlying dynamic in social life, aimed at survival and safety; the imperative of finding and establishing a livelihood; the synergies in social and economic relations and visions; and also much progressive initiative. The response to migration can be a range of more restrictive and controlling legal and policy instruments, but as Papademetriou (2003) points out, this would be to misread the complexities of the migration system and to deny receiving societies an essential ingredient for their own economic success and social enrichment.

Refugees and Immigrants

Differentiating 'voluntary' from 'forced' migrants is one of the ways employed for categorizing groups for administrative purposes. The distinction is based on individuals' reasons for departure from their country of origin, and their circumstances of arrival and admission in the destination country. For policy-makers, it is a device that initially helps to distinguish between the large forcibly displaced population groups of recent times, and the more traditional labour migrant groups which are already familiar in many receiving countries.

The backgrounds of forced migrants or refugees are generally situations where a significant force – political, economic, or social in nature – is exerted on people to leave their habitual place of residence, generally in circumstances of extreme duress and stress. Migration has been involuntary, and not a strategy shaped by social or economic goals. Regardless of different underlying personal, political or societal catalysts, for refugees, flight has been a common denominator for their survival. This has invariably resulted in departure for a comparatively unknown destination and under conditions of travel and entry that frequently offer little if any security to those migrating (Cox and Pawar 2006). Eventually, even in settlement, the often lengthy disruption of ties to the home country from which they fled makes it necessary to include the dimension of exile in any analysis of refugees' relations to their homeland.

The case of the Vietnamese boat people and other Indo-Chinese refugees brought international attention in the mid 1970s to the plight of waves of refugees fleeing for their lives from conditions of persecution and repression in their home countries. The war between Iraq and Iran, the Gulf uprising, the civil wars in Somalia and Afghanistan, and the unresolved plight of Palestinians and Kurds are other examples of conflict situations in more recent times that give rise to mass displacement and large numbers of refugees.

Stressful and traumatic effects of displacement are based not only on harrowing circumstances of flight, but often also on the preflight experience of societal upheaval, repression and institutional breakdown. Individuals may be the targets of political persecution, and the security of their kin endangered. The prolonged crisis situations of civil wars, such as that in Somalia, for example, perpetuate conditions of distress for its population. In worst case scenarios, these contingencies are the life conditions of whole generations. For those who manage to flee, the possibility of return is very often non-existent. The personal costs of civil wars are widespread among civilians.

When we understand it from the perspective of practical tasks and processes, settlement is substantially similar for immigrants and refugees. However, the aftermath of displacement events are not neatly cleared to pave the way for the pursuit of new plans and projects in the receiving country. Refugees have invariably had to leave close kin behind, often in situations of danger or distress. Most have suffered loss either through deaths of relatives or as a result of violent uprooting (Lyons, Manion and Carlsen 2006). For some groups, fleeing from the country of origin was an eventuality brought about by a sudden rise in conflict or rapid escalation of local life-threatening events. Few were able to undertake much, if any, preparation for flight to an uncertain destination. For refugees in general, the settlement experience is initially quite different from that of regular immigrants. The outstanding situations of distress of close kin and friends in the country of origin or in other locations of first asylum affect the settlement process; for example, long and anxious periods of waiting for family reunification often make the process of personal adjustment and adaptation more difficult.

Some refugees accept that the option of return might never be realized, since there might be no solution in sight to conditions in the home country. Additionally, as the second generation becomes rooted in the new society, the alternative of return becomes less practical. The loss of the original bonds to the homeland must be dealt with in the short and long term. The skill of refugees in managing this loss and transition will affect the integration process. Some individuals hold on to the 'myth of return'. We should note here that the recent advances in telecommunications are very significant in reducing or alleviating, in some way, the sense of separation and uncertainty which invariably features in the post-flight situations of forced migrants and their families.

As an important part of settlement, newcomers seek out networks and social circles. Voluntary migrants are generally seen as having greater ease of access to social support since they would have had prior opportunity to weigh their options, make advantageous decisions and establish contact as necessary. In chain- and family-facilitated migration, individuals are coming into previously identified networks of social support. For refugees, the need to create new networks can be markedly facilitated when communities of countrymen and women already exist in the country of settlement. Such contact is especially important when the language of the new country is different.

Conversely, the unplanned nature of forced migration means that individuals (and their family members, in such cases when they are able to leave together) are propelled into situations regarding which they have had little or no previous information. When ethnocultural communities are already present and developed in settlement countries, their members are very responsive to the needs of newcomers. A significant role is often played by such collectivities in the orientation of the newly arrived, even when this takes place in informal contexts. Communities and their subgroups can function as effective support systems, providing valuable information and social capital resources, and their contribution is often a major one, even alongside more formal systems.

Settlement and Integration as a Policy, Programme and Practice Agenda for Social Work

Cross-cultural, multicultural, ethnic-sensitive, anti-oppressive and diversity approaches capture core dimensions of practice with minorities. The generalist frame comprising macro, meso and micro levels is useful in a multidimensional conceptualization of the field. Generic practice approaches have the potential to address many of the concerns in integration work, even though the settlement approach to working with immigrant and refugee clients has distinct characteristics. Settlement and integration constitute an area of specialization which is in symbiosis with the full range of generic skills. For practitioners, it is an opportunity to widen the base of practice. Nash, Wong and Trlin (2006) state that research into social work experience with immigrants, refugees and asylum seekers in New Zealand supports the view that a new field of practice is emerging. Increased migration across frontiers means that social workers are brought into contact with clients from all over the world, as the latter strive to settle into their new communities.

'Social work with immigrants and refugees' is a long phrase, which is used alternatively with the terms 'settlement practice', 'settlement work' or 'settlement social work' to refer largely to areas of practice connected with the more immediate and practical tasks of settling into the new society. 'Integration practice' refers to activities and perspectives relating to long-term integration and its processes. These concepts are, of course, not mutually exclusive, but are used as tools to sharpen focus in the text. Additionally, different terms – 'agency', 'organisation' or sometimes 'institution' – are used in different social contexts to refer to the organizational aspect of social services.

This section highlights selected aspects of work with immigrants and refugees in order to give a preview of some of the parameters of practice in this field. Social work is a singular vehicle for carrying out critical human service interventions for the well-being and welfare of this client constituency of 'newcomers' or 'newer citizens'. Focus on particular approaches and areas of expertise is warranted in order to address settlement needs effectively and to facilitate the integration process.

In practice settings in general, more purposeful clarification of the responsibility and practice mandate of social work in settlement would help to avert the tendency for the services targeting immigrant client constituencies to be seen, from the administrative point of view, as simply an extension of existing services. Moreover, from the point of view of intersectoral networking and collaboration, clearer and more explicit delineation of the settlement portfolio would facilitate more collaborative work with colleagues. For example, the settlement practitioner is frequently called upon to function as an agency-based link between immigration authorities and immigrant clients or families. In the role of a broker of information, practitioners are able to use their institutional base to negotiate for information that is critical and valuable for immigrant clients. This information is related to immigration formalities, conditionalities and regulations, as well as to family reunification processes. Such information would often only be obtained by settling persons in a reactive sequence, a situation which puts them in a vulnerable position in relation to state authorities. Practitioners can facilitate the flow of such information which is otherwise difficult for clients to access directly. They are in a position to utilize communication channels internal to the network of official institutions.

The settlement transition of immigrants and refugees is a process of becoming re-established in the new social environment. In addition to a crossing between cultures and socio-geographical locations, it entails venturing into a whole new field of action. Settlement thus presents distinct tasks for immigrants. A straight allocation of some of the existing human service resources is not suitable as a service response which aims to be sensitive to the nature of settlement and, in particular, of integration challenges. The importance of individuals' human agency, for example, and the significance of accessing employment, are significant dimensions of participation in the new home society. Settlement social work calls for us to operationalize holistic approaches to incorporate the sites of settlement activity into the arena of professional practice.

The importance of information can never be emphasized enough. Information and insight into the new community and society are powerful tools for enabling individuals to develop short- and long-term life strategies with competence. The concrete demands of settlement require immigrants to amass salient information on the new society and the way it actually functions. The span of information generation and provision for settling groups includes the myriad aspects of societal, institutional and cultural life. The knowledge base which would benefit settling individuals and groups is not restricted to official sources. An understanding and ability to discern the actual codes, practices and expectations that guide human relations is probably best gleaned from wide and meaningful interaction with other groups. In addition to information on the range of available services, settling groups need some knowledge of rights, duties and the other implications of their formal status in the citizenry. For immigrants, settlement consists of making informed choices and directing energies in ways productive to themselves. The positioning of social work in settlement gives the profession a tactical advantage for generating, accessing and mediating critical information to newer citizens.

In the course of identifying and assessing problem situations, knowledge of the culture and social history of groups can help us to sharpen our ability to recognize and appreciate otherwise 'invisible' impacting factors. Identification of client strengths that occur in unique combinations and sometimes in cultural 'guise', and the mobilization of these, constitute essential steps for planning and implementing responses that will be appropriate, adequate and effective. The constellation of social resources in an extended family, for instance, is a significant asset in settlement. Work approaches and interventions in family-centred and community-centred modes, with some settlement populations, can often be significantly facilitated by innate solidarity-based forms of commitment and support that are attributed to culture and socio-cultural background.

In settlement practice, the use of self, authenticity and professional integrity, all function as important signposts for settling persons who seek to build new relations based on trust. As in other areas of practice, the worker's skill in relationship-building facilitates reciprocal and collaborative working relationships with clients. In practice with immigrants, these elements can be decisive factors in overcoming cultural distance and otherwise opening up a way for engaging effectively with the client and client constituency.

Applying and transposing professional ethics to situations of cultural diversity can spark fresh insights and associations, leading to broader and richer frames of analysis for problem-definition and assessment. Problematization of issues in settlement situations benefits from the use of a social justice perspective, as well as cultural competence and other perspectives. The social justice perspective leads to consideration of structural and institutional aspects of settlement and reduces the risk of taking the route of cultural relativism.

The dilemmas and problems related to cultural difference have dominated the immigration discourse, and invaded areas of practice in ways that are not always beneficial. 'Cultural relativism', or the interpretation and appraisal of phenomena almost exclusively through the lens of culture, can distort service responses particularly in those contexts where the culture of incoming groups has been hitherto unfamiliar to the majority population. On the other hand, the core social work value of respect and individualization is particularly salient for working to counteract reductionist approaches. Working at the juncture of cultures in the settlement field, social workers are, in a sense, cultural mediators as well as service brokers. Workers would need to build their knowledge bases of other cultures and, in particular, of their own majority or dominant culture in order to be able to broker valid and helpful perspectives and interpretations.

The style and pace of immigrants' adaptation to the new home society varies. Although adaptation is thought to be the duty of newer citizen groups, the acculturation process is essentially a two-way undertaking on the part of settling groups and the receiving society. Immigrants gradually become an integral part of the wider community and societal system. Their linkages with majority groups take diverse forms, many of which tend to go unrecognized by the public eye. Similarly, most adaptation processes are incremental and invisible. The process needs to be scrutinized on a longitudinal basis and through a wide societal lens. The settlement and integration arena is as wide as the receiving society itself, making the field one of the most fascinating in the social work portfolio.

The Policy Agenda

While many of the mechanisms for inclusion and exclusion are embedded in social and economic structures, which are not amenable to rapid change, the process of incorporation and integration can nonetheless be decisively ameliorated or exacerbated by states' policies or indeed their lack of policies (see Van Hear 1994). The immigration and integration policy framework, and the way in which it is implemented in practice, will influence the context and dynamics of settlement, and have a large part to play in determining the quality of integration processes and their outcomes.[3] In this arena, policy advocacy and policy practice[4] come to the forefront as one of the important methodologies in practice with immigrants. Participation in policy-making, and in its implementation process, involves comprehensive engagement with the service provision mandate and with its stakeholders at all levels.

Equity and social justice approaches aim to have the status of settling persons formally endorsed in different ways to strengthen their position in the surrounding society. Without formally articulated mechanisms to underwrite parity of status of settling individuals and groups, arrangements become subject to individual interpretation. Policy mechanisms work as proactive measures to prevent settling groups from falling into devalued status, or being ascribed a devalued position

---

3   Breton (1992) refers to integration as a process and at the same time as an outcome.

4   Policy practice is defined by Jansson (2003) as efforts to change policies in legislative, agency and community settings, whether by establishing new policies, improving existing ones, or defeating the policy initiatives of other people.

in an ad hoc fashion. Such formal mechanisms would ideally be woven into the settlement policy from the outset in order to reduce risks of marginalization and social exclusion among new groups at an early stage. The policy perspective and overview on settlement conditions reaches further than social service entitlements and the formal legal status in the country. Policy areas relating to the different spheres of participatory activity all belong directly or indirectly within the purview of settlement policies.

Castles and Miller (1993) observe that regardless of what policies are adopted, be they benign neglect or explicitly multicultural policies, certain preconditions must be met if marginalization and isolation of minorities are to be avoided. The state needs to take measures to ensure that there is no long-term link between ethnic origin and socio-economic disadvantage. This requires legal measures to combat discrimination, social policies to alleviate existing disadvantage and educational measures to ensure equal opportunities and to provide the channel for upward mobility. Should polarization arise between groups, it is the state which carries the authority and the responsibility for eliminating racism, combating racial violence and above all for dealing with organized racist groups.

Proactive and innovative policies can serve to utilize more effectively the talents, energies and other ranges of skills which immigrants bring into the resettlement situation. Many of these lie dormant for years or decades in situations where, for example, there is severe underemployment of skilled or qualified immigrants. Policies of an emancipatory nature address oppressive mechanisms such as discrimination and closure which hinder settlement and integration. Many types of proactive policies can serve to ensure from the outset that immigrants do not fall into devalued roles, but can take their place in the productive life of the society and enjoy equal respect alongside other citizens. Policies and programmes for universal language and labour market training provide examples of this.

Programme Implementation and Service Provision

The span of settlement service provisioning reaches from planning and development to implementation and post-implementation stages. Monitoring and evaluation are important sequences of planning. They generate important stocks of quality control data for building accountability systems into a field that is still evolving.

A key issue that moderates the position of immigrants with respect to the existing service system is whether or not they are entitled to the same range of services and rights as other citizens. Immigrants and their families come into a position of full entitlement and access when they formally acquire citizenship, or become 'naturalized'. Permanent residence is a status which is usually nearly equivalent to that of citizenship, with some caveats in the area of political participation. For example, those who are not naturalized generally do not have the right to vote in national elections. In practice, persons who are residing permanently in a settlement country are, with few areas of exception, accorded social citizenship rights on a par with others. In this text, I include this group under the term 'newer citizens'.

The existence of non-identified, or non-acknowledged, barriers and restrictions that inhibit newer citizens from benefiting and participating in all spheres of activities is a different issue. Existing services were developed incrementally over time to meet the needs and problem situations of the main population groups at that time. Newer groups are likely to be unable to meet formal criteria in certain areas, which in turn can affect negatively the level of entitlement or access.

The question of the appropriateness of services arises in settlement practice. The field of immigrant settlement and integration is constantly in development. Not only is it one of the newer areas in social work, but the client constituencies' cultural and societal backgrounds are diverse. The diversity profile in client groups causes us to revisit the mission and philosophies of programmes, from which point novel and innovative approaches and strategies can be shaped without losing sight of goals. In many cases, the issue is not necessarily one of having to create new services. Instead it might be a process of shaping the modes and conditions of delivery to be more relevant to the needs of new groups. Settlement services do not replace mainstream offerings, but operate alongside these in catering to the more specialized situations of newly settling groups.

The boundary between settlement tasks and settlement problem situations can sometimes become blurred. Routine problem-solving processes take place against the backdrop of immigrants' encounter and engagement with the new social and structural context of settlement. Settlement tasks refer to the multiple demands which settling persons and their families face when they engage purposefully with the new society in order to become re-established. A settlement problem situation is one in which people are encountering difficulties of a nature that calls for supportive measures or other types of interventions. The pressures of acculturation accompanying settlement can take their toll on the coping capacities of families and groups.

Effective settlement services cater to intermediate settlement needs but also focus upon long-term integration processes. The capacity of the profession to deliver appropriate interventions and supportive measures is greatly expanded when the approach is cross-sectoral. Regardless of practitioners' base of operations in the welfare mix (be it in state, private or civil society sectors), collaboration and linkage are key mechanisms in engaging with the scope of potential resources for settlement practice.

It is also particularly important to include ethnocultural community organizations as stakeholders in service provision. Even in countries with more highly organized and specialized social services, social work finds that it must rely on involvement with civil society and its organizations in order to fulfil its mandate. Many ethnic community organizations see themselves as serving a bridging function for their immigrant and minority client constituencies. Located outside of the informal circles of family and friends, they are concerned with aspects of settlement and integration on behalf of the wider group. Organizations can have highly pragmatic functions, for example, assistance with paperwork, interpreting and so on. They often undertake family counselling and support, and bring to the process the advantage of being grounded in the culture of settling persons (Valtonen 1999). Close collaboration with community organizations can make it possible to conceptualize and assess with accuracy difficult settlement problem situations and to fashion effective and appropriate interventions. Organizations can help in myriad ways to prevent the marginalization of members of the settling communities. Immigration can be a catalyst which makes it necessary for us to re-work the welfare mix to include more actors.

Closing Comments

In this chapter, the wider panorama of migration flows, catalysts and dynamics have been examined. The aim has been to deepen understanding of global events and trends, and at the same time to furnish a backdrop for national immigration scenarios. A brief overview of the social work portfolio in immigrant settlement and integration has been presented. The discussion is meant to open a window onto the field and the range of phenomena that constitute, on the one hand, possibilities for practice, and on the other, situations which call for social work response.

Chapter 2

Social Work Approaches to Practice with Immigrants and Refugees

This chapter examines the human rights and citizenship rights approaches for analysis and practice, after which the focus moves along to social work theories, concepts and models and their relevance to practice with immigrant and refugee populations.

The human rights approach establishes a supranational frame for practice with immigrants and, in particular, with refugees. As an idea, human rights is one of the most powerful in contemporary discourse (Ife 2001). Universal human rights constitutes a supranational instrument that articulates the basic protections and standards of treatment to which all persons, on the very basis of their humanity, are entitled. When individuals must escape life-threatening situations of repression and persecution in their own countries, they can claim protection on the basis of the violation of their basic human rights. Refugee protection is extended by the international regime,[1] which functions through the organized operations of its participating states and international organizations. The international protection that is extended includes arrangements for refugees' resettlement in safe countries. Social work with refugee clients and groups is one phase of the process of international protection. While settlement challenges become uppermost in a tangible way in the new home society, the configuration of events leading up to settlement and conditions that continue in the country of origin will have implications for the way refugee individuals, families and communities set about the tasks of settlement. The movement of refugees and asylum seekers reflect the patterns of international and civil political upheaval and conflict across the globe.[2]

---

1   The international refugee regime refers to the international organizations, cooperating states and supranational legal instruments which in concert frame the responses to refugee situations and flows. Immediate responses include different forms of aid and protection in the neighbouring regions, while long-term mechanisms refer, for example, to placement in third countries of settlement. Adelman (1995, 60) states that 'the evolution of the international refugee regime was marked by three major historical events, namely World War I, World War II and the processes of decolonizations and nation building in the Third World countries'. Organized response to the refugee problem dates back to the immediate post-World War I period when nearly 9.5 million refugees were produced as a result of the war.

2   See Jones (2001) on the plight of children and young people seeking asylum.

The citizenship rights model was created for its own time and contingencies in post-World War II Britain. The societal thrust of the idea, its basic principles and the simplicity of the model have made it a generic policy tool that is often used in policy science and policy-making as a reference frame when conceptualizing the scope and emphases of initiatives and measures to promote citizen welfare. Citizenship rights set out the types of relations which the state upholds with its citizens, 'fleshing out' the substantive dimensions of the relationship. In settlement work with newer citizens, these ideas can convey the range and types of connections and obligations that bind the state to its citizens, including its newer citizens.

The ethnic-sensitive and cultural competence approaches are well established in professional practice. It has become accepted in the newer models of immigrant incorporation that individuals have the right to maintain valued aspects of their own culture. Social work applies the principle of respect for the client and client constituency's values and culture-based characteristics, which can be seen at the same time as a positive resource for settlement and social life in general.

Critical social work, with its strands of structural and radical approaches, calls for settlement workers to direct their perspective to the social environment of settlement and the social structures and institutions in which are lodged root causes of many ongoing social problems. Critical social work would direct the change initiatives in social work and settlement practice to address barriers and other mechanisms in the environment in order to create the social conditions in which settling groups can exercise social citizenship fully. Anti-oppressive social work brings out for attention in the public space overt as well as covert mechanisms that put groups at a disadvantage. This approach is useful when analysing the features of resistance in social systems which, when carried on even into second generation cohorts, have socially excluding consequences.

The Human Rights and Citizenship Rights Approaches to Practice

The Declaration of Human Rights consists of four crucial notions: the basic right to human dignity; civil and political rights; economic, social and cultural rights; and solidarity rights (Wronka 1992). Human rights are meant to be an articulation of universal humane values and standards across societies and polities. In addition to the Universal Declaration of Human Rights, rights have been endorsed in a number of other human rights declarations, treaties and conventions.[3] Rights provide parameters of the perceived good for human beings at global and at national or citizen level. They are thus an important standard in the context of migration. Settlement and integration practice is embedded in the ethos of these

---

3   A few examples include the International Covenant on Economic, Social and Cultural Rights, the International Covenant on Civil and Political Rights, the United Nations Declaration on the Elimination of All Forms of Racist Discrimination, the Convention related to the Status of Refugees and the Protocol related to the Status of Refugees.

fundamental rights and freedoms. The value base adopted by social work is consistent with universal human rights (see Cox and Pawar 2006, 30–32; Lyons, Manion and Carlsen 2006, 50–60).

Human Rights

Human rights embody standards of conduct for relations between legitimate authority and individuals. Their function is to limit excesses or abuses of state power. As Brysk (2005) states, the human rights tradition represents a necessary and continuing struggle to limit repression instigated by states. By shielding individuals and collectivities from abuses, they constitute a way of intervening in situations of human vulnerability and danger.

Human rights were established after the excesses of World War II as a supranational instrument for limiting state power. They carry implications of a binding nature for individual states, collectivities, institutions and individuals within the state. It is incumbent upon states, their institutions and the members of the polity to strive to secure their universal and effective recognition and observance. The framework of the 12 international human rights instruments and UN monitoring mechanisms for compliance with these instruments confer upon states the legal obligations to protect, promote and implement human rights (Brysk 2005; Kothari 1999).

Regional and national frameworks of legislation and monitoring mechanisms constitute the regional and the state-level instruments for providing for citizens more extensive protection from abuses or infringements. The European Convention on Human Rights and Fundamental Freedoms and the European Court of Human Rights, the American Convention on Human Rights and the African Charter on Human and People's Rights are examples of regional level instruments.

Refugee protection is a human rights issue. The violations of human rights occurring and perpetrated during periods of repression, internal conflicts and wars give rise to forced migration and refugee situations. Conditions of persecution and danger to life force people to seek safety in other locations, or refuge in other countries. The circumstances of displacement vary in different political and geopolitical contexts. Human rights abuses, displacement and uprooting give rise to flight and asylum seeking as the sole alternative for survival. The restoration of social order and security in the country of origin is invariably a gradual and very complex process, which makes the possibility of return for most refugees a remote one.

Operating at supranational level, the international regime and its organizations, such as the United Nations High Commissioner for Refugees (UNHCR), organize activities to guarantee security to persons fleeing persecution and repression in their own countries. Refugees can be resettled in neighbouring countries of the region when this is possible and feasible. Alternatively, they are resettled in so-called Third Countries which, under the auspices of the UNHCR, undertake to receive refugees and make provisions for their settlement. In the country of reception and settlement, the refugee is under the protection of the national legislation and practice in that country.

In his work on the link between human rights and refugee protection, Kjaerum (2002) emphasizes the contribution made to refugee protection advocacy by international human rights bodies such as Amnesty International. He considers that such regular monitoring mechanisms for publicizing and tackling human rights abuses are a positive trend, especially in countries where the national instruments and guarantees have not been articulated in legislation and practice. Non-governmental organizations (NGOs) and advocacy groups often also carry responsibility for attending to the infringements that have occurred before the individual has received rights of residence and settlement in a receiving country (Kelson and DeLaet 1999).

States vary to some degree in the manner in which they categorize status for those individuals who arrive in the context of involuntary or forced migration and are allowed to reside. The categorization of humanitarian migrants reflects consideration of the following factors or a combination of them:

- Particular circumstances of flight, such as persecution, immediate danger to life and other factors which fit into the established criteria of 'refugee' under the Geneva Convention
- Flight from general and more widespread conditions of danger, for example, the zones of turmoil and pervasive conflict in civil war.[4] Such individuals, and generally large groups of them, are in 'refugee-like' situations, and in need of protection
- The existence and evidence of clear 'humanitarian reasons'. For example, the individual's application for asylum has been years in the processing phase, and there is evidence of some binding tie or ties to the society from which asylum is being sought
- Arrival in the context of family reunification programmes, as in the case of the dependants or close kin of refugees. The right to family reunification has been extended by some states also to those who have arrived in refugee-like situations.

Human rights and social work are inextricably linked. Refugee protection and settlement is one clear example of the link between human rights and social work. The wide significance of human rights as an approach for the profession is pointed out by Ife (2001) and Skegg (2005), who recommend using human rights as central analytic and practice frames for the profession. Ife (2001) argues that human rights can provide social workers with a moral basis for their practice, both at the level of day-to-day work with clients, and also in other areas such as policy advocacy and

---

4   See Dannreuther (2007).

activism. He sees human rights as having the capacity to link varying social work roles into a unified and holistic view of practice.

As pointed out by social work scholars and teachers, social work values and guiding principles are consonant with basic human rights. Sheafor, Horejsi and Horejsi (2000) state that the belief that every individual has certain basic rights is central to social work. Social justice rests on the belief that every human being is of intrinsic value, which in itself need not be earned or proven. Individuals all have a right to be treated with fairness and respect, to be protected from abuse and exploitation, and to be granted the opportunity of having a family, a basic education, meaningful work, and access to essential health care and social services (Sheafor, Horejsi and Horejsi 2000).

Kothari (1999) brings out aspects of the wider instrumental use of human rights by citizens. For communities and individuals struggling for the means to meet basic needs and to be represented at a political level, human rights instruments can provide a standard at which to aim, while for civil society groups, they represent a set of rights to be claimed. Kothari (1999) points out that human rights instruments are underpinned by the basic principles of non-discrimination, equality, self-determination, and the right to political participation. It follows that a forthright and comprehensive approach to human rights would involve critical thinking on government responsibility and would provide benchmarks for interventions and affirmative tasks in all sectors of society.

Citizenship Rights

Settlement and integration can be understood as the implementation of social citizenship for immigrant and refugee groups who are newer citizen groups in the society. As a system of policy and principles for effecting equality and welfare in the citizenry, it is also highly pertinent to the conditions of settling groups. In social citizenship, social work finds a mode to address the challenges of the integration portfolio. Many societies of settlement, moreover, situate and conceptualize the pursuit of equality and citizen well-being in a frame of social citizenship. On the other hand, this system of policy has to be put in place and implemented directly or indirectly by the state. As an undertaking and commitment with wide implications, social citizenship needs to be supported and legitimized by a base of solidarity in the citizenry. Looking at how it might be possible for social work to proceed in its effort to link the concerns of immigrants into the national agenda, Lorenz (1998, 263) states that 'social work methods are geared towards creating the conditions for citizenship as a means of establishing mutually negotiated rights and obligations as the "non-essentialist" basis for solidarity'. On the one hand, adapting a social citizenship approach would be a more viable course than that of conceptualizing and promoting immigrant interests through ethnification processes and projects, or working through a nation-state solidarity perspective and thrust. On the other hand, the nature of citizenship overall, according to Lorenz (2006), is defined by the everyday practice of citizenship between citizens and state officials, clients and professionals, and claimants and service providers. Lorenz (2006, 78) proposes that it is at this point that the political dimension of social work comes to bear much more than in campaigning and being explicitly politically active. He argues that the exclusion of minorities is not an outcome of migration processes, but of processes of social construction and definition which can cause individuals to find themselves on the wrong side of a divide without ever having changed location.

Citizenship, from a lay perspective, is a formal and binary variable that distinguishes between the categories of aliens and naturalized immigrants (see Kabeer 2004). Distinctions are made, for example, between models of ethnic citizenship that give preference to ancestry and hence to the nationality of parents and grandparents, and models of civic citizenship which employ the place of birth criterion that confers citizenship to children born in their territory without regard to the nationality of their parents (Vogel and Triandafyllidou 2005). Many countries feature a mixture of both models, for example, the US, Canada, Israel and Germany. France is an example of a country that uses the civic citizenship model.

Citizenship has subsequently come to embody substantial dimensions referring to rights and duties as aspects of membership within the specific political community to which the citizen belongs (Baubock 1991; Brubaker 1989; Hammar 1990; Kabeer 2004). Rights and duties thus derive from status and membership in the nation. The evolution of these 'thicker' concepts of 'social citizenship' and 'citizenship rights' is closely associated with their prominent proponent, T.H. Marshall. According to Marshall (1950, 14), citizenship is 'a status bestowed on those who are full members of a community. All who possess the status are equal with respect to the rights and duties with which the status is endowed.' Baubock (1991, 28) elaborates on the concept, defining citizenship as a 'set of rights, exercised by the individuals who hold the rights, equal for all citizens, and universally distributed within a political community, as well as a corresponding set of institutions guaranteeing these rights'. Citizenship thus implies institutional arrangements in a political system, for underpinning a particular political status held by individuals.

Citizenship was shaped as a tool for redressing the inequalities of social class and based on the principle of equality (see Reisman 2005). In the social citizenship relation between the state and the citizen, the state functions as *a guarantor of rights*. The purpose was to address social inequality by having the state formally recognize specific areas of rights to which citizens are entitled and to which they can lay *claims*. From a policy perspective, therefore, citizenship rights are a blueprint or a system of guidelines for creating and guaranteeing conditions that promote greater social equality and well-being in the society.

The idea of citizenship rights underpinned much of social policy building in Britain in the post-war period, when the process was closely linked to the debate over welfare state capitalism (Bulmer and Rees 1996). Marshall's (1963, 74) model set out a typology of civil, political and social rights, the development of which he ascribed to the eighteenth, nineteenth and twentieth centuries respectively.

Civil rights comprise those rights that are necessary for individual freedom – liberty of person, freedom of speech, thought and faith, the right to own property and to conclude valid contracts, and the right to justice. The institutions which are closely associated with the establishment of these rights are the civil and criminal courts of justice.

Political rights, according to Marshall (1963, 74), refer to the right to participate in an exercise of political power, either as a member of a body invested with political authority or as an elector of such a body. These rights refer, in the main, to seeking and holding political office and to voting. Parliament and local elective bodies are institutions closely connected with the implementation and exercise of these rights. After the franchise was extended and opportunities for political participation opened up, Marshall's concept of political citizenship was expanded by scholars to include freedom of association and speech.

Freedom of speech refers to the right to express opinions and ideas without hindrance, and especially without fear of punishment. Liberals hold that the free interchange of ideas, when not violating the rights of others or leading to predictable or avoidable harm, is basic to democracy and resistance to tyranny, as well as important for progress and improvement in the society. Freedom of speech cannot be an absolute principle. Laws have been enacted to regulate incitement, sedition, defamation, slander and libel, blasphemy, the expression of racial hatred, and conspiracy (McLean 1996). For some refugee groups, the restoration of their right to freedom of speech is one of the immediately experienced positive features in settlement.

Social rights were set out in very broad terms, as ranging from economic welfare and security to the right to share fully in the social heritage and to be able to live in accordance with the standards prevailing in the society. The institutions seen as most closely connected with social rights are the educational system and social services.

This concept is ambitiously pitched but less precisely articulated, and social policy-makers and scholars have had to work within its constraints. As Reisman (2005) observes, social rights are under-explained in Marshall's model, which means that the interpretation of the breadth and content of social rights is devolved to policy-makers and legislators. Social rights are, moreover, very much grounded in context. They are resource-constrained, and their profile ultimately takes shape subject to consensus at decision-making level (see Reisman 2005). Foweraker and Landman (1997, 14) argue that while civil and political rights are universal and amenable to formal expression in the rule of law, 'social rights' are fiscally constricted and require distributional decisions, and therefore they are best described not as equal and universal rights but as 'conditional opportunities'.

Citizenship rights or social citizenship rights are embodied at national level in states' constitutions, laws and policies. States, however, vary as to how the principles of citizenship rights are articulated in policy. There is also great variation in how policies, once made, are actually implemented in practice. Some are simply left at the formal level. Regardless of variations in different contexts, the declaration and formalization of such rights in legislation and policy constitute guarantees which the state extends to its citizens, with the implication that they will be implemented at different levels of practice. Social citizenship implies a relationship of responsibility between the state and its citizens, who individually are bearers of rights. The nature and extent of the guarantees of social citizenship depend on the moral choices that are made when shaping legislation. Another decisive factor is the allocation arrangements for the requisite structural and institutional infrastructure and the resources necessary for implementation. When rights are not implemented, we understand them as not having proceeded beyond the stage of *nominal* rights.

Originally focused on social class inequalities, the citizenship rights frame can be used as a reference against which other patterns or types of inequality can be charted and analysed. Nyamu-Musembi (2004) suggests that citizenship should be investigated from the perspective of how the exercise of rights in everyday experience is affected by factors such as gender, ethnicity, caste and kinship structure. Individuals might be restricted from exercising rights fully because of gender or ethnic background. They might be on the periphery of the labour market, for example, or outside of educational institutions, especially at higher levels. The discussion of rights necessarily includes consideration of the impediments that obstruct individuals from exercising rights in different spheres of social activity. Thus the existence of marginality, vulnerability and disadvantage is not compatible with the idea of full and equal membership in the society. Rights are potentially instruments of empowerment for citizens. If individuals are not able to exercise them in practice, their membership is correspondingly diminished.

Political, civil and social rights are not exclusive domains, but are closely interlinked. For example, civil rights to seek legal redress are weak if a citizen does not have the resources to pay for legal services. Individuals might access employment but not be upwardly mobile because of artificial barriers that indirectly screen out minority group members (Woo 2000). Being debarred in a de facto sense from participating as a full and equal member of society can have far-reaching ramifications for an individual's life chances and for eventual positioning in society.

Young (1990) has observed that rights refer to 'doing' more than they relate to 'having', and to social relationships that enable or constrain action. Against the matrix of citizenship rights it is possible to identify those areas and levels of activity in society where newer citizens can participate fully. The particular areas in which blockages exist are targets for different types of interventions aimed at opening up access to all groups in the citizenry. Formal equality of rights can be present alongside great inequality in actual conditions, demonstrating the difference between formal rights and real choices. Discussion of opportunity and choice should be balanced by examination of the ways in which participatory choices are constrained by social factors and patterns. The lack of a base of requisite social resources can signify that individuals are not able to benefit from legal or formal rights (see Yuval-Davis 1997).

While citizenship rights guarantee a certain level and quality of living for the citizenry, some groups who reside within the borders of the country do not enjoy access to rights. Those who hold entitlements are demarcated sharply from those who do not. Persons with asylum seeking status, for example, do not hold entitlements but can be granted some level of minimal benefits. Brubaker (1992) notes that citizenship is not only a vehicle for participation and integration, but can at the same time constitute an instrument of social closure and exclusion. The dynamics of social closure are inherent in the instituted process of citizenship as they are also in the systems of nationhood (see Jacobs 1998). Yet citizenship is not static as a concept or policy system. The debate is a continuing one over the principles by which the rights of citizenship should be extended. A central issue is over whether those who desire rights or who reside within the borders of the country should be considered as full members, or should this be reserved only for those who belong on the basis of having been born in the country or of having fulfilled lengthy residence requirements.

Scrutiny of the integration processes in different societies suggests, on one hand, that the more developed the systems of rights and entitlements, the more tightly the lines of eligibility can be defined between the eligible and the ineligible. The state's immigration and integration policies, which are themselves products of political processes, are decisive factors in defining citizenship and social citizenship boundaries.

Social Citizenship and Settlement Practice

Settlement practice has a singular interest in citizenship and social rights. From a rights-based perspective, we see immigrants and refugees alongside all other citizens – as members of the nation and citizenry – as *bearers of rights*. Correspondingly, we see governments as responsible or having the mandate to protect and promote the well-being of all citizens by recognizing and honouring these rights. In the case of immigrants and majority society alike, citizenship rights concern issues that are broader than that of rights to particular material benefits, even though these constitute a key area of entitlements. Rights pertain to access to all spheres of society and areas of societal participation. These include access to social services and welfare, but also to education, employment and other areas of civic and associational activity which are not articulated emphatically.

Civil rights are concerned with the implementation of just arrangements and with the principles of equality. Political rights enable members of the society to participate as subjects in decision-making on matters directly concerning their own conditions. Citizenship rights on the whole reinforce the idea that parity should characterize the participatory process of groups in the society. For instance, the ethnic community organizations in Canada have identified three major principles that underpin the integration thrust. These are access, equity and representation. Access refers to the openness of society and its institutions to all, including non-majority groups and individuals. Equity calls for fair practices in public administration, in hiring and in other critical spheres of activity where gate-keeping mechanisms can lead to inequality and discriminatory patterns of action. Representation is achieved when immigrants are participating widely in the full range of roles and responsibilities in the society, and are able to pursue and attain, on a par with others, different social and occupational positions and levels in society (Fleras and Elliott 1996).

Conditions of disadvantage that develop over time, such as the segmented labour market (clustering of immigrants in low-paid and low-skilled sectors), closing off higher levels of employment through the operation of glass ceilings and other forms of artificial barriers, tell of the inability of individuals to exercise citizenship rights fully, a situation leading to their consequent non-representation or low representation in valued positions and spaces.

The time factor and linear explanation of the settlement process is inadequate for explaining persisting patterns of inequality in educational and employment sectors. Using, for example, income differential as one of the facets of inequality, continuing patterns would be associated with *lifetime income inequality*, to use Esping-Andersen's (2005) term. While equity principles are central to integration, immigrants are seldom in a position to pursue justice through the complex procedures for redress in situations of inequitable practices. Referring to the case of Asian Americans, Woo (2000, 211) remarks that: 'Litigation in general has been a last resort to workplace barriers.' She states that, like any other group, Asian Americans are likely to demonstrate a range of coping strategies or individual responses to glass ceilings, for instance. A typical response to blocked mobility has been 'overachievement' or further investments in education (Sue and Okazaki 1990). Other personal strategies include the individual's efforts to develop an image, set of behaviours, or 'corporate manners' consistent with the organizational culture (Wu 1997, 195–228). Reactions have also included lateral transfers to other companies or decisions to pursue self-employment (Woo 2000). In practice these situations speak to inequitable conditions.

Settlement countries with a high level of economic development have often expanded social service and welfare systems. It becomes more common for needs to be addressed from a social rights-based principle, or at least from an equality of access approach, even when policies do not articulate 'rights' as such. While progress in the area of social rights is important, the ability of immigrants to exercise and avail themselves of rights in the civil and political spheres is critically important for working towards equitable conditions in areas such as the labour market, about which social rights are vague. The parameters of settlement and integration practice extend into all the areas of citizenship rights. Since settlement is an encompassing challenge involving wide engagement and interface in many societal spheres, developing practice approaches to promote participation in economic, social, cultural and civic/political life would work toward a better fit between the settlement portfolio and the actual parameters of settlement challenges.

The citizenship rights approach brings to the settlement field a robust policy dimension to balance the humanitarian and morally based arguments which surround refugee settlement issues. Valuable as the latter are, they can invite the conflation of equity with issues of charity and humanitarianism. Additionally, regardless of the degree to which basic citizenship rights are articulated in national policy, it is possible to use the model as a matrix for scrutinizing the range, coverage and role of particular mechanisms in addressing well-being/welfare among citizens. The frame of social citizenship is comprehensive and suitable for conceptualizing and charting the scope of settlement service mechanisms in the civil, political and social rights areas. It also provides a reference point for determining the scope of state responsibility.

Social citizenship can also serve as a structure within which to analyse and develop central aspects of national policy, legislation and programmes. Rights can establish an accepted baseline which the state deems to be its level of responsibility for citizen well-being. Existing gaps and inequalities could be identified for requisite interventions and measures. Proactive measures would work toward strengthening the pre-conditions for equal citizenship.

Since the exercise of rights among immigrants might be hindered in varied ways, it is imperative for immigrants to build the social resources which might be lacking to them, such as those of information, social capital and qualifications. Yeoh, Willis and Abdul Khader Fakri (1999, 210) observe that the 'range of administrative policies and bureaucratic procedures' in which citizenship rights are embedded are structures which differentiate easily 'between those "within" and those "without"'.[5] Immigrants are the actors on whose shoulders also falls the task of redefining and shaping the terms of their own citizenship. Thus social citizenship is not only about a status, but about involvement and participation, a *process* of involvement and bringing about change (Yuval-Davis 1997). Citizenship must be an active condition of struggling to make rights real (Phillips, A. 1991).

It should be recognized that the pursuit of rights is part of the portfolio of human service institutions and agencies where, for example, social workers (who are part of the administrative structure) would have access to opportunities for promoting rights through administrative channels. This provides an alternative to confrontational and often contentious processes in courts, which often lead to unsatisfactory outcomes.

In general, rights have tended to be much more clearly specified than duties. It is possible that the citizenship rights discourse resonates to some degree with the human rights discourse, in which the aspect of inherent rights is clearly of central weight. Moreover, the administration of equality, as a pillar of citizenship rights, would not benefit from strong connections to the conditionalities of corresponding duties, as the workfare issue has demonstrated. Nonetheless, the thoughtful

---

5   See also Weiss (2006).

commodification of the social contribution of immigrants to the society could be a counterforce to the negative debate. The idea of duties being conceptualized as the province of both individuals and social collectivities is yet to be explored.

Ethnic-sensitive and Culturally Competent Approaches

The concept and term 'ethnic-sensitive social work practice' was originally introduced by Devore and Schlesinger (1981). Ethnic-sensitive and culturally competent social work has brought to the field the realization that a specialized body of knowledge and skills is necessary to work with people from ethnic, cultural and racial backgrounds that differ from their own (Rogers 1995). This area of practice with clients of different cultural backgrounds is referred to as ethnic-sensitive, culturally competent or cross-cultural social work. Each can be attributed a slightly different emphasis as indicated by the descriptor. These approaches converge on core emphases around the understanding and valorization of the different cultural backgrounds of clients as the basis of effective, high quality and respectful interventions.

It is essential for practitioners to be self-aware and to understand the client's culture, values, belief systems, traditions and world view (Lum 1999). Lum (1992) suggests that, in contact and relationship building, the practitioner should distinguish between the etic and emic goals of the client. Etic goals are derived from the assumption that all human beings are alike in some important respects and have certain priorities and values in common. Emic goals can be understood as those that derive from the client's own cultural background. We can readily appreciate that insight into emic goals would make for greater authenticity in interventions, as well as reinforcing the principles of self-determination and respect.

Green (1982; 1995) proposes ethnic competence as including:

- Awareness of one's own cultural limitations
- Openness to cultural difference
- A client-oriented, systematic learning style with the worker as learner
- Appropriate utilization of cultural resources
- Acknowledgement of the cultural integrity of other people's culture and acceptance of a multitude of life ways.

Cultural competence is reflected in programmes and work environments by respect for the beliefs, world views, behaviours and customs of different client groups and colleagues of other ethnocultural backgrounds. In so doing, it incorporates these values at the level of policy, administration and practice. Cultural competence is thus located within the context of the multiple levels of social work practice and service provision (Tsang and George 1998).

Culturally competent practice is congruent with a variety of communities and ways of life (Weaver 2000; Greene 2002). Thus the capacity for valuing differences contrasts with an ethnocentric approach (using one's own culture as the standard or measurement of others), or being culturally encapsulated. Practitioners using this approach would give value to the diversity of strengths in settling groups and be able to engage these client-based resources. While culturally competent practice shapes responses to particular features of cultures, anti-racist approaches primarily address oppression related to race. At present, anti-oppressive practice is a term more commonly used in the UK to include anti-racism as well as other forms of discrimination, based, for example, on age, sexual orientation or disability.

O'Melia and Miley (2002) emphasize the importance of contextual social work practice and of taking environments into account in empowering clients. They state that, for culturally competent practice, settlement practitioners would need to know more about the social environments and contexts of their clients' migration experiences. Taking this idea further into the operationalization stage, Fong (2001, 6) states that cultural competence also entails knowledge of the indigenous interventions of the client system and being able to use these in planning and implementing services. Fong's (2001) interpretation introduces a substantial dimension to ethnic-sensitive approaches, suggesting that knowledge possessed by settling communities would be valuable to the development of settlement social work approaches. This question has also been studied by Leonard (1997) who argues that the profession–client relationship should take a dialogical rather than an authoritarian form, and that social workers and consumers should work together in the construction of alternative forms of knowledge. Leonard (1994) states that the disciplinary power of the profession could constitute a factor of resistance to this perceived hierarchy shift, while Parker, Fook and Pease (1999) suggest that using client-centred approaches to construct alternative forms of knowledge would potentially challenge the traditional expertise base with its 'absolute truth claims'.

Davies (1991) considers being able to work with the subtle nuances of inter- and intra-cultural relations as one skill set in working effectively with a multicultural clientele. Indeed skills in intercultural relations are good currency not only in micro and meso level work but are also vital in the societal or national level arena of ethnic relations, including majority/minority relations. This skill set is part of the expertise in human relations and relationship building which is one of the distinguishing features of social work.

Rogers (1995) has noted that the emphasis on ethnically sensitive and cross-cultural approaches in the Canadian setting did not include a position on topics of racism, sexism, classism or homophobia, nor was an anti-discriminatory or anti-oppressive stance taken. The cross-cultural strategies contributed to a serious examination of the barriers, obstacles and subsequent strategies for working effectively across difference, but did not purport to challenge the structural and systemic nature of oppression. In the same vein, Gamble and Weil (1995) express concern that culturally appropriate services should reflect a resilience-based orientation, requiring practitioners to open up client opportunities and seek to ensure that a client has an equitable distribution of community and societal resources. These observations can help to draw an analytic distinction between culturally competent approaches and more structural methodologies in practice.

Preventive Approaches

The thrust of 'prevention' in social work has been defined in broad terms covering three angles: preventing problems from occurring; preventing these from becoming worse or escalating; and preventing such situations from recurring. This broad perspective is not entirely functional as it makes for overlap with other approaches and, in a sense, dilutes the concept. Prevention in the first sense – engaging in actions that would reduce the incidence of problems and adverse situations – would be a more distinct starting point. The challenges in implementing prevention programmes have been related to the difficulties of identifying appropriate target populations without labelling or singling out particular individuals for services, in designing effective intervention programmes, and in evaluating programme effectiveness (Schinke 1997).

The early identification of problems that are related to transition difficulties, acculturation and settlement issues is critical. Due to circumstances in the communities such as language barriers, the reluctance of many individuals to seek out formal services, and also the initial lack of strong social support networks, the input of workers of immigrant background with access to communities could be critical. Having persons from the settling groups working on the staff of the main settlement service system would invigorate the linkage into families and communities and foster timely recognition of potential problem areas. A strong outreach function of settlement practice would also serve to bridge the distance between communities and the formal services.

At the macro-level, tardiness in creating and implementing non-discriminatory mechanisms in legislation and in institutional practice means that much effort needs to be expended in reactive measures. A proactive approach to integration would include policy frames and mechanisms which, from the outset, are geared to promoting positive outcomes of access, for example, to areas in higher education. Preventative work can thus be implemented through direct programmes as well as through social policies. They can often be targeted at wider populations, and are closely tied to the pursuit of change. Preventative approaches can be integrated across the different areas of practice.

Critical Social Work

Critical social work is situated within the critical social science paradigm and is informed by the body of critical social theory or critical theory. The conflict perspective on society is a distinct feature of this branch of social theory, built on the idea that social problems arise out of the conflictual relations between social groups (Mullaly 1997; 2002). Critical theory is driven by its interest in systems of oppression and in those who are oppressed. The goal of critical social theory is to move society to a state of liberation and freedom from domination by addressing and removing existing exploitation, inequality and oppression (Kellner 1989).

A main concern of critical theory is with issues of unfreedom and freedom in social relations. Such situations are reflected in power discrepancies and differential control of resource and privilege that sustain oppressive and unjust systems of social relations (Gil 1998a; 1998b; Mullaly 1997; 2002). The persistent quality of oppression takes place through the internalization of dominant–subordinate relations. This phenomenon is also related to Tilly's (1998) concept of durable inequality that is sustained through processes of emulation and adaptation.

Critical social theory encompasses the critique of traditional or mainstream social theory, and of existing social and political institutions and practices. Another facet of social theory is the imperative that critique should lead on to the conceptualization of viable alternatives, and to the implementation of change strategies. Thus the link between social theory and political practice is its defining characteristic. Critical theory has a practical aim of bringing about change for a more just society (Leonard 1990). The practical mission of critical social theory is the translation of its developed understandings of domination, exploitation and oppression into a political (anti-oppressive) practice of social transformation to free society from these phenomena (Mullaly 1997). Post-colonial theory, liberation theology and Freire's (1970) pedagogy of the oppressed constitute different strands in a group of critical social theories.

Critical theory thus differs from conventional social science, as it carries analytic understandings forward into action modes, the critical preliminaries of which are consciousness-raising and ownership by the actual groups themselves of the initiatives and actions to address the targeted unsatisfactory structural arrangements. Critical social work practice approaches include Marxist social work, feminist social work, radical social work, structural social work, anti-racist social work, anti-oppressive social work and anti-discriminatory social work (Healy 2005).

The critical social science paradigm is well suited as an overarching frame to facilitate the scrutiny of prevailing approaches to settlement in both policy and human service areas. Critical social theory offers a frame for analysing conditions of systemic-level and institutional-level exclusionary patterns which affect integration processes negatively. It extends a clear call for the revisiting of the field to identify goal displacement processes that take place as the profession becomes established within the powerful institutional structures of the public sector.[6] The appraisal and monitoring of existing social citizenship arrangements that might be sustaining unequal outcomes for immigrant groups (in contradiction to their original intent) are also important.

---

6   See Lorenz (2006, 78); Weiss (2006, 135).

Analysis directed to structure-based causes underpinning the persistence of disadvantage and inequality is very salient in the settlement field. In highly organized settlement societies, the newest citizens meet arrangements and established practices that have been largely shaped through gradual and incremental social processes. Settlement practitioners seek understanding of the root causes of oppression and the location of these within the social and institutional fabric in order to intervene with change strategies. Such initiatives need to go deeper than the level of distributive justice in order to achieve sustainable 'improvement' in client situations, by forging positive actions to bring about actual conditions for the exercise of full citizenship.

Different strands of critical social work were focused upon different cleavage lines of oppression and power differential, ranging from the class-focused perspective of radical social work to the institution-based oppression focus in anti-oppressive practice. It is possible to trace the critical traditions of social work from early radical critique using Marxist analysis, through feminist and structural developments, to the perspective based on critical theory and postmodern perspectives (Fook 2003; Pease and Fook 1999).

Radical Social Work

Grounded in class-based analyses of social injustices, radical social work approaches held that service users' problems were directly linked to social structures, and did not arise out of clients' personal histories, inherent attributes or shortcomings (Healy 2005). Inequality and oppression came to be recognized as having structural antecedents, and as lodged in prevailing societal institutions, policies and values (Gil 1998a). This period marked a turning point as social workers started to adopt more active roles in pressure groups, giving up the long-held principle that professional practice should be politically neutral, and that ethical practice was based on the principle of the separation of politics and practice (Gil 1998a). It was accepted that social work practice has its roots in politics and the consequences of politics, regardless of the intentions and consciousness of practitioners. If social workers were to assume a position of neutrality, this in itself would constitute a political act in support of the status quo (Gil 1998a).

Radical practice advocates for social change argued that the capacity for changing and transforming the social order is possessed by people themselves. In radical social work, an emphasis on power-sharing with clients comes to the fore. Importance is given to alliances that can be formed from the outset between workers and clients in the pursuit of more equitable relations and a redistribution of power to include those who lack power. Radical practice calls for developing critical consciousness toward practice, and a re-appraisal of conventional social work approaches which aim to help people adjust to and cope with the status quo. It implies re-orientation of practice principles, as well as theoretical and philosophical perspectives (Gil 1998a).

In the 1970s, structural social work extended the radical social work focus of injustice from class-based to all forms of oppression. It brought out the fact that different forms of oppression are mutually reinforcing and overlapping. This perspective is similar to the concept of structural disadvantage.

Anti-racism became identified with black perspectives and for designating the term 'black' as an inclusive category for persons of colour who are affected by racism. The analytical adequacy of the term 'black' to subsume diverse experiences of discrimination across minority and non-white groups in Britain was heavily critiqued and challenged. Stanfield and Dennis (1993) observe that reified categories such as black and white served to reproduce traditional racial stereotypes rather than facilitate adequate data collection. Macey and Moxon (1996) state that social work literature on anti-racism tended to oversimplify the extent and nature of the myriad influences needing to be addressed, including high levels of poverty, inequality, competition and widespread, violent racism. From another perspective, Williams (1999) points to the significance of gains made through the efforts of anti-racist activists, using the argument that it has now become possible to problematize the anti-racist struggle, to understand the constraints of institutional change, to confirm strategies for mobilization, and to acknowledge the great personal costs to many 'black' people that this voyage has entailed.

Anti-racism is acknowledged as having made an impact on the quality of service for service users. It has brought a particular aspect of discrimination into the public arena, and presented a challenge to the established institutions. Anti-racist practice has been drawn into, or at least strongly connected with, anti-oppressive practice that has a wider and more inclusive focus on oppressions.

Anti-oppressive Social Work

Anti-oppressive practice is defined by Dominelli (1994, 3) as:

> A form of social work practice which addresses social divisions and structural inequalities in the work that is done with people whether they be users ('clients') or workers. [Anti-oppressive practice] AOP aims to provide more appropriate and sensitive services by responding to people's needs regardless of their social status. AOP embodies a person centred philosophy; an egalitarian value system concerned with reducing the deleterious effects of structural inequalities upon people's lives; a methodology focusing on both process and outcome; and a way of structuring relationships between individuals that aims to empower users by reducing the negative effects of social hierarchies on their interaction and the work they do together.

Practitioners who adopt an anti-oppressive approach consciously seek to be aware of and to avoid reinforcing inequality in worker–client relationships arising out of the power differential based on the practitioners' power position and close affiliation to institutional power. Workers' awareness of the social divisions and structural inequalities that affect the lives of clients helps them to avoid becoming themselves agents of oppression and reproducing oppressive relationship patterns (Young 1990). Such awareness also contributes to the quality and efficacy of the working relationship.

In order to arrive at an understanding of how oppression is practised, Foucault (1977) states that it is necessary for us to go beyond thinking of oppression as the conscious and intentional acts of one group against another, or the exercise of tyranny by a ruling group. Oppression is found in areas of social life such as education, public administration, health and social services delivery. Inequality is often systemic and complex, while people who perpetrate it may have no idea that by following certain time-honoured ways of doing things, they are actually sustaining unjust practices (Young 1990). Thompson (1997) states that inequality, discrimination and oppression are largely sustained by ideology, the power of ideas. If we are not aware of the subtle workings of ideology, we are likely to find ourselves practising in ways that unwittingly reinforce existing power relations and thereby maintain the status quo with its inherent inequalities.

Critical social work sends a strong message to settlement practice to investigate the structural and institutional environment in order to identify critical factors which give rise to, or are associated with, some of the difficulties and constraints that inhibit citizens, including newer citizens, from taking part in full and satisfying roles in different spheres of social life. Critical social work approaches turn the focus onto institutional structures and systems of which we are a part, and furnish the tools for critical appraisal of oppressive procedures and practices which might unwittingly have worked their way into the system. The negative consequences of oppressive processes are the weakening of the citizenship relation; increase in power asymmetry between institutional bodies and the citizen; and loss of efficacy and quality in service. From the settlement perspective, the approach calls for a critical strategy of *institutional reflectivity* – reflective appraisal of existing structures and practices in the interest of promoting substantial citizenship for immigrant and refugee client constituencies.

Closing Comments

Settlement practice involves working with groups who cannot take human rights and citizenship rights for granted. For settlement practitioners who are, in a sense, pioneering a new field of work, human rights and citizenship rights serve as generic frameworks. They are also instruments for social justice and for building bridges between peoples and societies. The practice approaches, which have been discussed here, give increased emphasis to structural factors and their role in facilitating integration. This is not to detract from the salience of direct work methods. The emphasis can be understood as a thrust to ensure that analysis and intervention are directed also to the societal bases of integration barriers.

Chapter 3
Immigrants and Refugees in Society: The Field of Action, Relations, Roles and Status

Immigrants' Relations to Societal Institutions: The State, the Market and Civil Society

Social work approaches have a generic focus on the social functioning of individuals and groups. This focus is operationalized in strategy that seeks to strengthen and enhance the individual's person-in-environment links. Strong relationships or ties with the social environment evolve from the participation, involvement and engagement of individuals in meaningful and productive activity. Relationships derive also from various forms of interaction including discourse. The ecological approach emphasizes understanding the nature of people's ongoing transactions with the surrounding society and the goodness of fit between people and their environments that should emerge from such interchanges.

Society itself is understood as a system of intermeshing relationships. The concept of social inclusion/exclusion, which is in common usage in migration and settlement discourse, has at its core the idea of relationships between individuals and groups with the main institutions of society. Social exclusion refers to breakdown in relations to the mainstream of social life.

In this chapter, the focus moves from macro-level relationships to focus on the level of group and individual links with institutions. The scrutiny of relations is then extended out to transnational and diasporic links. The first part of this chapter examines individuals' engagement with the three overarching institutional systems of society – the state, the market and civil society. Although this frame is not exhaustive, it accommodates the main spheres of participatory activity and action of citizens in the public space. Civil society is sometimes understood as including the family and primary social networks, in which case the concept also spans private spheres of social life. Should our understanding of integration and mainstream linkages be focused narrowly on social relations with the majority or on formal institutional links, we run the risk of losing sight of large areas of activity and effort involved in the ongoing pursuit of settlement goals.

The relationship to the state is partially covered in Chapter 2 in the section on social citizenship and citizenship rights. This chapter focuses on the area of social rights and on the welfare state as the main vehicle for implementing these rights. Since political, civil and social rights are inter-related and inter-dependent, the welfare state can be seen from one perspective as a state-level instrument for promoting rights in general. In the case of newer groups, the area of civil rights is not frequently elaborated in societies of settlement, and indeed often elided in integration issues. This is due to the central emphasis on social rights provisions and possibly an assumption that social rights will suffice on their own to bring about the equality of social citizenship.

The relationship to the market in the role of member of the labour force has high significance for immigrants. Among the many reasons underpinning the priority placed on employment is the preference for having a social role as an active member of the labour force rather than as a claimant on the welfare state. From this perspective, although social rights and social service provisioning form a critical component of life quality, individuals need to strengthen their roles and relations in other societal spheres, not least the workplace.

Civil society is, like the other spheres, a locus of citizen inclusion. It is also a field of action in which immigrants can participate alongside others in many collective projects that focus on improving the quality and substance of social citizenship. A holistic picture of immigrants' fields of action is sensitive to process and capacity-building activity, as well as to outcome. Such an approach gives recognition to vital activity such as gathering information, acquiring language skill, training and retraining, as well as networking, all of which underpin and expedite settlement into a new society. The relations and roles of migrants within the state and the market tend to command more attention, possibly because these areas are more formally structured than the arena of civil society. Yet civil society embraces the family, community and networks which are critical arenas of settlement activity. It is also a prime vehicle for the shaping of ethnic relations.

Status and Role in Relationships

Status is a reference point which indicates an individual's *positioning* in the society. Social status tells of an individual's ranking with respect to some socially important characteristics. As a concept in the context of settlement and integration, status also provides valuable information on where the individual or community is located in the public sphere, which is a critical arena of participation from the perspective of long-range integration. It is a reflection of the individual's progress in establishing roles and relations with the surrounding society. Furthermore it says something about the level at which an individual fits into the authority or power structure.

Role refers to the functional aspects of status or position, and is a concept used for specifying attitudes, behaviours and, most of all, responsibilities that come to be expected of people in particular positions. The concept of role constitutes one dimension of participation, since individuals interact with the social system through the roles they carry out within it. Relationships evolve from roles and from the types of participatory processes in which individuals engage. Integration can be understood as connection, location and place within the society-wide system of social relations. Washington and Paylor (1998) state that social work activity is situated at the interface between the individual and society, and indeed between the citizen and the state, thus between the processes which promote solidarity in society and those which result in marginalization.

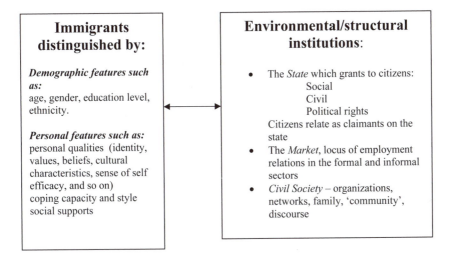

Immigrants distinguished by:	**Environmental/structural institutions:**

Demographic features such as:
age, gender, education level, ethnicity.
 	
Personal features such as:
personal qualities (identity, values, beliefs, cultural characteristics, sense of self efficacy, and so on)
coping capacity and style
social supports
	• The *State* which grants to citizens:
	  Social
	  Civil
	  Political rights
	Citizens relate as claimants on the state
	• The *Market*, locus of employment relations in the formal and informal sectors
	• *Civil Society* – organizations, networks, family, 'community', discourse

Figure 3.1 Immigrant engagement with societal institutions

Within the state, market, civil society matrix, the relations with the state and the market involve official actors and explicitly articulated procedures. Admittedly, significant spheres of informal actions and transactions co-exist in these institutions, but they are, at base, formally structured. In the field of settlement, the relations of immigrants with the twin poles of the state and the market tend to attract greater attention among government statisticians, policy-makers and planners, service providers and other officials. From the social work perspective, however, the professional arena straddles all three areas, which are subsumed under our comprehensive social functioning concept. A holistic assessment of a problem issue or client system situation would take into account impacting factors in the total environment.

If the aspects of participation in civil society which research findings have shown to have particular salience for settlement and integration are highlighted, this makes for a more accurate representation of the activity, roles and responsibilities which engage immigrants from early settlement and, in a sense, make settlement a more socially grounded experience.

Relations to the State

The setting of an individual's category of admission as designated by the authorities of the receiving state reflects the purpose and projected length of sojourn in the country. This designated class or official status comprises the main legal relation of the state to the individual, and at the same time determines the entitlements of the immigrant, and degree of access to services, benefits, employment and other opportunities which are otherwise accessible to the majority of citizens. Each country has honed its own immigration policies and procedures, which reflect the national and political position on immigration. The emphasis in this book is on the situation of persons settling on a permanent basis.

Policies guide the level and organization of service responses that are extended by the state to newcomers. Some of the traditional immigrant-receiving countries, such as Canada, have had a policy of organizing and articulating in an explicit fashion the criteria for selection and admission, as well as the grades of access to services permitted to different categories of immigrants. Based on a strong element of labour immigration, Canada's policy gives weight to employability of immigrants, within a stated multicultural policy of integration (Lindström 1995).

In designing and implementing specific policies and service responses for immigrants, states have invariably made use of their already established infrastructure of social services and welfare. This has been the trend in many European countries. For those states with less developed social service systems, the ready adaptation of existing infrastructure and established service components for a new client cohort is not an alternative. Thus the type of services extended to settling persons is moderated by the legal residence or immigration status granted to the individual, as well as the general level of provisioning in the society. Asylum seekers fall into a separate category and in many countries are granted some areas of access and a minimum level of benefits during the period that their applications for asylum are being processed.

On attaining formal status as full members of society, immigrants in principle are entitled to exercise the same citizenship rights, claims and obligations on a par with the rest of the citizenry. The ability to exercise rights fully constitutes one form of empowerment for settling persons, especially if this is facilitated by effective mechanisms to ensure that they enjoy access to the range of social, political and civil spheres. However, there is considerable variation in how rights are formally articulated and the extent to which they are actually implemented and exercised.

According to Esping-Andersen (1990), states can be differentiated by:

- The extent to which social rights are recognized – for example, through the availability of near universal social programmes and services
- The nature of stratification in the society
- The manner in which the responsibility for citizen well-being and welfare falls on state, market or civil society systems.

Welfare Systems in Settlement

For the settlement field in social work, the state's implementation of social rights is of central importance, since it will largely frame the service provision area. Esping-Andersen's (1990) classification of capitalist welfare states into regime types is useful for understanding how citizens' relations to the state are differentially structured in countries of settlement. His model features the social democratic, corporatist and liberal welfare regime models. These are obviously not pure types, and arrangements in different areas of human services and welfare do not always fall neatly into the country's main profile. We should note that if we took into account a wider spectrum of societies with diverse arrangements for social welfare, this model would not be directly applicable. The context, socio-political history, phases and modes of economic development would in turn affect the way in which social welfare in different societies is organized or neglected.

Those states which assume central responsibility for the welfare of citizens through a well-developed public sector have been classified as belonging to the so-called 'social democratic' model of welfare. Social rights in this model are extensive, with private welfare provision playing a marginal role. The social democratic model is strongly associated with the feature of universalism, placing emphasis on comprehensive social security and a generous level of welfare coverage that aims to be inclusive of all citizens. Income transfers and social services constitute equity-promoting mechanisms that moderate income inequality and extend a safety net to prevent the incidence of poverty.[1] This model is based on egalitarian principles, and is meant to emphasize equality of citizenship over the preservation of status differences (Myles 1998). Thus, redistribution mechanisms and a generous level of basic security are prioritized. This model has been systematically developed in the Scandinavian countries since the late 1970s. The interface of settling groups with state-sponsored services is markedly high in this setting, and their access to the range of social services is generally on a par with others. Moreover, services meet basic needs at a generous level.

The degree to which services mesh with the particular needs in immigrant settlement and long-term integration is not always a question of service quality measured by majority standards. Integration challenges and tasks often require a different approach. Service design and delivery modes need to be revisited by those who fashion and implement policy in order to ensure that mechanisms for addressing the central settlement concerns and risk areas are built into service and welfare responses. Universalism also needs to respond to particular need.

Mature social welfare systems are distinguished by 'decommodification', which de-couples the individual's labour market relation from the right to basic social security and welfare. In other words, the employment relation does not constitute a criterion for accessing basic social security and welfare. All citizens have the right of access to the welfare state. Decommodification has been developed into

---

1   See Swank (2000).

policies, especially in the Scandinavian countries. Decommodification is not, however, a total process. Central forms of social insurance relating to pensions, unemployment and sickness benefits can still be tied to the individual's employment history – number of years and level of income – which in turn have an effect on the level of entitlement.

The social democratic model, as exemplified in Sweden, for example, is a model originally founded on the principle of full employment, which is, however, subject to cycles in the national economy. This dual basis upon which benefits may be claimed has important consequences for migrant labour, as pointed out by Freeman (1986). In practice, immigrants can turn out to be a very vulnerable group in this particular area of welfare because the length of their period in the labour market is shorter, due not only to age on arrival but also to difficulties in obtaining employment. Income levels can also be related to the level at which glass ceilings operate, a phenomenon which itself is part of the wider social mobility problematic. Universal flat rate benefits are generally much lower than earnings-related entitlements. From this aspect, participation in the labour market can give access to an altogether different tier in the welfare state. While the highest levels of income and gender equality have been achieved in developed social service and welfare systems in societies with advanced market-oriented democracies, welfare state arrangements would still need to be considered from the aspect of their linkage with the labour market, and not as totally independent and universal mechanisms of equality for individuals.

In the corporatist model, the entitlements and level of entitlements are closely tied to the individual's employment status. This model favours employment-linked social insurance with family provisions ahead of universal programmes. This system can be seen as a type of market-based social security. Most European Union countries exemplify the corporatist model, including France and Germany. In the liberal model, the state has a lesser role in welfare provision, and the social rights of citizens vis-à-vis the state, are more tenuous or 'thin'. There is reluctance in general to replace market relations with social rights and the thrust is for welfare to be sought from the market. In the liberal model, there is bias towards means-tested assistance, as in the UK. One critique of the liberal model is that it does not profess egalitarian ideals, even though its aim might be to reduce inequalities to some degree by providing social protection up to a minimum level (Briskin and Eliasson 1999).

Corporatist and liberal models of mature welfare systems feature greater variation in the modes of welfare generation, since this responsibility is discharged also by the market, and by organizational and informal actors. For settling groups, this could signify riskier access to services. On the other hand, it could also open up a greater range of choice in seeking out services, as well as a different and more comprehensive style of institutional engagement. Settlement service provision that is state centralized, as in the social democratic model, derives great stability from its location in the mainstream structure. Public sector-based agencies are supported by taxes and need not rely on fund-raising. Even though agencies' budgets in the public sector vary with the current priority areas and the levels of the national budget, their funding is nevertheless more stable than that of their counterparts in the private or third sector. McInniss-Dittrich (1994) points out a drawback in that the size and complexity of the bureaucratic structure of public agencies is often a very frustrating problem for clients who are in need of services. Public agencies are often subject to rigid sets of rules and hierarchical structures that preclude a flexible approach to individual problem situations. Settlement service arrangements will thus vary in different contexts since they themselves are embedded in broader national welfare systems.

Welfare state boundaries are often problematic, as is indicated in Chapter 1. Kelson and DeLaet (1999, 196) state that: 'Unfortunately, the reality of immigrant life in most receiving nations is still characterized by discrimination and less than equal access to social services.' Freeman (1986) points out that national welfare states are compelled by their logic to be closed systems that seek to insulate themselves from external pressures through restricting rights and benefits to their own members. Free movement of labour across national borders exposes the tension between closed welfare states and open economies and the likelihood that, ultimately, national welfare states will not be able to co-exist with the free movement of labour. Freeman (1986) implies that the welfare state model will have to undergo change in order to be viable in conditions of international labour mobility. Globalization processes and marketization trends to create pressure for change. The institutional response to such pressures will be different in different societies, depending on context.[2] The Nordic countries are, however, one example of universal programmes retaining their popularity and sustaining support for the welfare state.[3]

Geddes (2003, 152–3) comments that migration is a fascinating boundary issue precisely because of the pressures that have existed particularly since the 1990s to tighten the demarcation lines around the 'community of legitimate receivers of welfare state benefits'. This author makes an interesting point that, while welfare states in Europe function as important symbols of membership, entitlement, identity and belonging, from another angle, they have also used internal measures to regulate migration. By providing or denying access to welfare support, some forms of migration can be welcomed and others deterred. Subject to a system of reception and accommodation in detention centres, asylum seekers, for example, have found themselves strongly exposed to this more coercive and disciplinary side of European welfare states. Geddes (2003) observes further that welfare states are powerful institutional forces which embody ideas and practices relating to the classic boundary issues that occupy migration scholars and policy-makers.

---

2   See Esping-Andersen (1996).
3   See, for example, Ervasti and Kangas (1995).

Relations to the Market

Immigrants' engagement with the market is identified closely, although not exclusively, with their participation in the labour force and their employment role. The employment role exerts strong influence on many other spheres of activity, on the level of consumption and, not least, on social status. As well as having central socio-economic implications for individuals and their families, employment is regarded as a key indicator of the vitality of ties, roles and status in the society. Moreover, from a societal perspective, citizens' employment relations create sound ties to public life and reinforce social cohesion in society.

The gateway to employment is usually seen to lie in education. The state is the body which normally provides channels for newer citizens to acquire education and training. This is part of its overall investment in settlement and, at the same time, in the supply side of the labour market. Labour force training and retraining programmes are 'positive action' measures to raise employment levels and to facilitate the 'insertion' of individuals into employment.

State training programmes are directed at increasing immigrants' employability, or those competencies and qualifications which would make them more 'marketable' and stronger candidates in the employment market. Such preliminary human capital-building programmes constitute very important mechanisms for equipping immigrants to cross the labour market threshold into employment. Apart from utilitarian concerns, such policies and measures can also have as their point of departure an egalitarian ideal which sees education and training as contributing to equality of opportunity in the society and as ensuring that its outcomes are not determined by criteria other than innate inability (Hill 1996, 223). Access to resources for acquiring human capital and marketable skills is an equity-promoting mechanism for settling groups.

On the *demand* side of the labour market, policies and mechanisms to foster the inclusion of newer citizens into the formal labour market have high significance for immigrant integration, since there are otherwise factors which can militate against successful outcomes of 'positive action'. The level of human capital might be quite high in an immigrant community, but this might co-exist with high levels of unemployment. This settlement situation can be brought about by several circumstances. Human capital might not be taken fully into account if selection criteria are arbitrarily set. One example of this is the situation in which the 'suitability' of applicants refers to their education and technical qualifications, while 'acceptability' refers to other informal and subjectively judged characteristics on which recruiters form judgments as to whether or not someone will fit into the organization (Jenkins 1994). Immigrants, and especially those from cultures perceived as less familiar, face the hurdle of such 'acceptability' criteria. In the interest of fair hiring and as actual commitment to this practice, some employers have developed hiring policies. Decisive influence can also be exercised over hiring practices by individuals who are inside institutions in human resource management and administration positions. In the human and settlement service area itself, the promotion of 'ethnic equality' in workplace hiring and career paths is still largely overlooked.

Comprehensive welfare structures and well-developed components of social rights, including educational components, do not reach into the area of equal access to employment. In a study on racism in the workplace in 16 EU countries, Wrench (1996) points out that the abolition of legal restrictions and the greater extension of citizenship rights do not necessarily bring about fairness in the labour market. Although most post-war migrants have citizenship and civil rights and face no legal barriers to employment opportunity, there are still serious problems of discrimination and exclusion. In sum, dependence on the ability of strong welfare arrangements to remove inequalities and integrate people ignores the effect of important dynamics on the ground in the labour market.

For immigrants, the dysfunctional effects of long-term unemployment are multiple. Sen (1997) has stated that the nature of the deprivation among unemployed persons is such that their ability to exercise freedom of decision is curtailed even in areas such as social activities and in the life of the community. Settlement processes are affected by their tenuous position in society. In unemployment, immigrants, as newer citizens, are exposed to the risk of remaining in a socially vulnerable or powerless position, since an important source of power derives from an individual's position in the labour market. Prolonged unemployment and its consequences raise the risks of social exclusion of newer groups, even though they are included in the welfare state. Employment is high in symbolic value especially in societies of the west which have made full employment a national goal and, in many ways, a national responsibility. An individual's employment is seen as a prime and well-regarded mode of fulfilling citizenship 'duties' to the society.

In the context of settlement social work, the most dysfunctional aspect of unemployment is that settling individuals are left out of formally productive circles, or debarred, as it were, from performing a socially valued function in the new home society. Employment is associated very closely with social citizenship and full membership of society. Immigrants' inclusion into the welfare state, alongside exclusion from the labour market, makes for a variant of social citizenship that rests on a foundation of social rights but not social justice in an important sphere. This situation presents a stubborn contradiction in integration dynamics. A sign that integration is being attained would be evidence of newer citizens also being entrusted with valued roles in the society. Inequality in the distribution of valued and value-producing opportunities is a fundamental risk to citizenship. From a policy perspective, in addition to giving insight into the positioning of immigrants in society, the levels and features of immigrant employment/unemployment function as a sensitive indicator of the society's level of priority on harder integration questions.

Marshall (1963) regards the development of social citizenship as the gradual ushering in of a measure of social justice and protection from the risks in market relations. For him, the citizenship rights that accrue to members of a political community would integrate previously un-integrated segments of the population and serve to mitigate some of the inequalities of class. The pattern of social inequality would thus be altered.

As generic concepts, social rights embody basic principles of equality and justice. These are, however, implemented through social policies once shaped for specific populations and social conditions. Policy instruments would need to respond to, and reflect in their thrust, contemporary configurations of vulnerability and risk. Patterns of immigrant vulnerability could be approached through a combination of policy and practice instruments shaped in all three areas of social citizenship rights which would address, in a concerted strategy, the issue of equality and inequality in society.

Relations to Civil Society

Civil society can be understood as a sphere of engagement and the locus of multiple layers of relations which bind the individual to other actors in the social environment. Civil society ties tend to feature a strong interactional dimension regardless of their focus. Less narrowly formulated than the relations with the state or the market, relations in civil society can be equally binding as ties to institutions. Rueschemeyer, Stephens and Stephens (1992, 29) propose an understanding of civil society as 'the totality of social institutions and associations, both formal and informal, that are not strictly production oriented nor governmental or familial in character'. It is a sphere, as Fennema (2004, 429) states, that is not under coercion of the state, nor is it within the sphere of the family or the market economy: 'it excludes those spheres where human relations are driven either by biological necessities (the family), by economic necessity (the market) or by force (the state). ... it is the sphere where the citizen reigns and not the administrator, nor the bourgeois or the pater – or mater – familias.'

The formal and informal modes of action and interaction constitute fertile ground for grass-roots engagement, making civil society an arena of inclusive rather than exclusive participation. Relations and transactions can be of a social, cultural or political/civic nature and are often underpinned by a base of solidarity, common interest or agenda. For practitioners in immigrant settlement work, the establishment of clients' links with civil society is clearly an important step towards being socially included.

The civil society construct proves to be very useful for aggregating the varied forms of participatory activity which lead to greater empowerment of immigrants in the public sphere, and to increased control over their own resettlement conditions. While some types of civil society activity are not necessarily formalized, they may be very significant for integration in the long term. Participation in interest-based organizations, for instance, can facilitate the development of social affiliations and resources that are critical to the eventual exercise of full citizenship. Through involvement and commitment in the civil society, immigrants can incrementally build their capacity, resources, network bases and strategies to influence policies in direct, indirect and collaborative ways. In this channel, they can become involved in exercising agency, and can link into the wider circles of activity.

For social work, civil society is critical as a vehicle for valorizing solidarity among citizens. Solidarity is the force that will underpin integration. On a policy dimension it forms the legitimacy base for institutional welfare and social service systems. Civil society activity relates directly to the project of reconstructing and renewing the social fabric. Through its processes of engagement, common understandings are honed in the citizenry and lay the preconditions for social change. The activity in civil society has potential not only for making sense of diversity, but for legitimizing it as a way of living. It gives the opportunity for interaction in various modes of collective activity and can foster different levels of understanding. The social processes in civil society play their own part in shaping ethnic relations.

Four spheres or understandings of civil society capture different dimensions of actions, interactions and relationships. These are the social solidarity base in civil society, the public sphere of rational/critical discourse that can inform public policy, the political arena and the community organization field.[4] In the following sections, these areas are discussed in relation to their relevance for resettlement and integration processes.

The Social Solidarity Base in Civil Society

Civil society recognizes social solidarity as an attribute of societies. Alexander (1997, 118) speaks of:

> the 'we-ness' of a national community taken in the strongest possible sense, the feeling of connectedness to 'every member' of that community that transcends particular commitments, narrow loyalties and sectarian interests. Only this kind of solidarity can provide a thread of identity uniting people dispersed by religion, class or race.

Shils (1997) points to a society-wide collective self-consciousness which, co-existing alongside the various sectional collective self-consciousnesses, imposes limits on the demand for the realization of the divergent ideals and interests and, on occasion, can supersede them. Civil society is thus understood as anchored in the inclusive collective self-consciousness which can moderate opposing, divisive and contradictory forces in human relations in the citizenry.

Solidarity around common and agreed goals engenders shared responsibility. As such it differs from 'social cohesion', which does not entail this dimension of responsibility and commitment. This understanding of solidarity can be aligned to Johnson and Johnson's (2000) idea of 'promotive interaction' in civil society with people working in shared interests, by assisting, helping and encouraging

---

4   These categories derived from Alexander (1997).

each other's efforts to achieve. Promotive interaction contrasts with 'oppositional interaction' (individuals attempting to obstruct and frustrate each other's goal achievement), and no interaction (individuals ignoring – neither facilitating nor frustrating – each other's goal achievement) (Johnson and Johnson 2000).

Participation in the civil sphere is productive of mainstream linkages when resettling persons are established in solidarity networks and institutions, which are, at the same time, contiguous and overlapping with the formal societal structure. Civil society can thus be a source of wider so-called 'weak ties' which, while different from strong, close ties, can channel valuable information and contacts. Immigrants and their communities, through affiliation with more established collectivities, are better placed to 'voice' concerns, advocate and carry issues forward. This is particularly important when 'newer' citizens have as yet little direct formal power of their own.

It is possible and sometimes useful to differentiate between solidarity in the two senses proposed by Spicker (1991). Solidarity in networks of mutual support refers to when people come to share, through affiliation or through reciprocal obligations, both duties to help others and expectations of support. Solidarity in collective social action is based on 'fraternity' rather than 'mutualism'. People act together because they accept a common social identity as a collective grouping. They might be moved by social preferences, such as those revolving around a 'common good' or 'the public good'(see Spicker 1993, 12). These are not discrete categories in practice, but the distinction gives us insight into the dynamics of solidarity.

The Public Sphere

The public sphere is an arena of debate – a social institution where citizens articulate, exchange, critique and develop ideas. It is a major form of participation and representation in the channels of 'voice' across the society. The media has become a leading forum of public discourse, but it is far from being the only one. The public sphere is the forum where issues are brought out from the private sphere to be debated and critiqued in the public and political space. This process can sometimes lead to wider recognition and ownership of ideas. The public discourse facilitates the stages through which information is processed collectively and shaped into significant systems of insight and ideas that in turn legitimize public policy-making. Public discourse is a collective activity, in which differences can be articulated, ideas contested and, through multiple paths to understanding and recognition, distilled into workable patterns which elicit levels of public legitimacy for social change.

Immigrants' role in the public discourse can remain latent for long periods due to lack of language skill, lack of familiarity with the current of discourse, or other preoccupations. Settlement work facilitates the voice of clients and immigrant clients, who are a central group of stakeholders in the immigration discourse. The lack of opportunities for immigrants to participate in decisions that affect their lives is a persistent and disturbing policy and practice issue.

Majority–minority relations invariably come to be impacted by information and information skew in the media. The stereotyping which can arise from biased information is very damaging to ethnic relations and jeopardizes, or at least slows down, the integration process as a whole. There is potential for strengthening the part that immigrants play in public level discourse as one way of redressing the imbalance of 'voice' on the public platform. Professional participation in the public discourse is an area of the social work and the settlement portfolio which has not yet come into its own as a tool for promoting equal citizenship for settling constituencies.

Activity in the Political Arena

When settling individuals take part in electoral activity, or run for candidacy, they are seeking to affect outcomes from the 'bottom up'. In many countries, the right to vote in municipal elections is granted after a specified period of residence. Participation in the political life of the receiving society depends to a great extent on the rate at which individuals become familiar with the socio-political arena. The political 'centre' for some settling persons might remain in the country of origin for a considerable period. Since there is also a time lag before a numerical base is built, the level of political influence and leverage of the immigrant population in many receiving countries is not realized in the early period of settlement. A critical mass of immigrants augments the immigrant vote, which can carry decisive weight in many matters relating to their citizenship conditionalities. In general we can assume that political rights are more frequently seen as a vehicle for citizenship among those immigrants who have been settled over a longer period, and are more aware of nationally current issues and implications.

The political arena is directly related to issues of 'power'. Small groups in the electorate generally do not carry the same weight as larger groups. This disadvantage can be overcome to some extent if groups are ready to seek out coalitions and affiliations. Engagement in the political arena brings the individual close to the competitive transactions in the public power distribution and redistribution processes.

Fennema and Tillie (2002) maintain that civil society serves as a counterweight to institutional arrangements and needs to remain relatively free to challenge the state in order to prohibit or restrain the bureaucratic apparatus of state action from becoming too dominant. Cox and Pawar (2006) point out also that because civil society is seen as constituting the linkages between people-in-community and the economic and political systems of the state, as such it enables people to participate in society in strength, by working together within a range of voluntary associations, thereby ensuring that political and economic systems are accountable.

Jacobs and Tillie (2004), writing in a European context, point out that undue emphasis on immigrants' voting behaviour, political party and associational membership might well result in a failure to notice their participation in more demanding and stable forms of civic activities that take place in different formal and informal settings with different degrees of organization. These authors warn against the risk of overlooking a large part of immigrant activism, and thus underestimating its potential for a civic revival of societies.

Community Organizations

Participation through voluntary associations is usually considered one of the key features of civil society. According to Odmalm (2004), this constitutes an important form of citizen participation in public life, since organizations function as a supplement to the institutional arrangements of representative democracy, and thus sustain the democratic culture by introducing new values and issues into the public sphere. In addition, participation in voluntary associations can potentially generate a number of socially valued skills such as habits of co-operation, solidarity and public spiritedness which in turn suggest the creation of a more tightly knit community (Putnam, Leonardi and Nanette 1993).

In settlement, organizational activity is perhaps the most easily recognizable basis of civil society linkages. It often emerges out of the spontaneous formation of civil solidarity subsets, or subgroups. Organizations thrive as communities grow to a viable size, and as bases of interest and commonality grow. One key prerequisite is a core of persons with the will, capacity and commitment to take on the tasks of organizing collective activity.

Many immigrant organizations have some type of integration objective, such as to facilitate the settlement process, to function as a link between members and mainstream society, or to promote the interests of their communities as well as of the wider immigrant community. In order to pursue these goals effectively, the instrumental nature of activity has to be uppermost.

Instrumentally focused activity, such as interest group activity, requires a degree of consensus and legitimized representation on chosen issues. This can make it a demanding mode of participatory activity because of the heterogeneous nature, and extant lines of cleavage in many settling communities. There is an ever-present danger that political, cultural and other forms of diversity inherent in settling communities would constitute a risk to an effective organizational agenda (Wahlbeck 1998). A strong issue-focused approach and a cross-community style of organization could be a viable alternative to ethnic community organizations. This would be well in keeping with the 'solidarity' principle in civil society and the value it places on the 'common good'.

Organizational activity in a community can start with a focus on retaining forms of the original culture and on the organization of social activities and festivals. If there are common socio-economic interests, this can give rise to *ethnic interest organizations*. In turn, shared conceptions of, and commitment to, the common good are the pillars of *ethnic political associations* (Fennema 2004). Participation in various types of ethnic and other associations marks an increase in the group's own capacity and competence in organizational efficacy, for example, in the areas of planning, collaboration, networking and lobbying.

Outcomes of Civil Society Dynamics

Social Capital

Engagement in all the above areas of civil society activity can be seen as productive of social capital. Social capital refers to the mobilization of people through connections, social networks and group membership.[5] It resides in the web of connections along which flow valuable information and support. Social capital is an asset which is 'convertible',[6] materializing into valuable forms of assistance, for example, into employment references, or insider information on cultural norms and expectations.

Agency and Actor Roles

Civil societies can be described as 'dense'[7] when reference is made to a richness of opportunity for transactions and action. Newer citizens have scope for functioning as 'actors' and 'agents' in ways that might not be possible in their relations to the more structured institutions of the market and the state. Immigrants can link into the formal and informal institutional networks through a range of participatory modes, the outcome of which can be a rise in capacity and resources for settlement.

Thus immigrants' involvement in the civil society sphere can result in various types of affiliation, access to information networks, links into interest groups and opportunities for action, including collective action. Such activity invariably will have positive repercussions in other participatory spheres, which in turn can draw newer citizens into the institutional fabric of resettlement society.

Gradual attainment of meaningful roles and positions in the community and society attests to progress in the integration process. The public discourse, political arena and community action forms are the established arena of contentious politics, and emancipatory struggles against hierarchies and inequalities. Immigrants' linkages with civil society make possible their participation as change agents in bringing about the very conditions that are critical for the integration process.

---

5   See Peillon (1998).

6   Of special significance in this context is the notion of 'fungibility', or convertibility of the different forms of capital. Fungibility refers to the property of being exchangeable or replaceable, in whole or in part, for another form of capital. It is possible to convert a particular form into another, although the extent and ease of convertibility is likely to be quite different in different contexts (Bourdieu 1986; Calhoun, LiPuma and Postone 1993).

7   See Rosanvallon (1988).

Relations to the Transnational Community

The contemporary concept of transnationalism has aroused great interest as a tool that can help us to understand how immigrants, refugees and their communities maintain ties with the homeland and original circles. Such ties have been found to retain their salience over time and distance. Transnationalism phenomena are not new. Immigrants and immigrant communities have generally endeavoured to maintain links with their homelands, and to overcome the geographical divide (see, for example, Kivisto 2001; Faist 2000a). Transnationalism is used as an analytic tool for exploring the nature and processes of these networks which represent another dimension of migration. Advances in technology and changing immigration laws play an important part in consolidating economic, social or cultural relationships over distance and enabling migrant populations to live their lives out across two or more national borders (Law 2002).

Transnationalism has been defined by Basch, Glick Schiller and Szanton Blanc (1994) as the processes by which immigrants forge and sustain simultaneous multi-stranded social relations that link together their societies of origin and settlement. Immigrants thus build social fields that cross geographic, cultural and political borders. Transnational communities are defined as those which are spread across borders, have an enduring presence abroad, and take part in some kind of exchange between or among component groups that are spatially separated. Transnational activities can be defined as those that take place on a recurrent basis across national borders and require a regular and significant commitment of time by participants (see Portes 1999). Van Hear (1998) states that the level and nature of transactions with the place of origin have given researchers the scope for generating theoretical frames. In the following, the work of Portes (1999) and Faist (2000a; 2000b) is briefly presented.

The work of Portes, Guarnizo and Landholt (1999) is grounded in empirical study. Their elaboration of transnationalism includes a working typology of economic, political and socio-cultural transnationalism, based on (1) the economic initiatives and activities of transnational entrepreneurs who mobilize and utilize their contacts across borders, (2) the political activities of party officials, government functionaries, or community leaders whose aim is to strengthen a base of influence and political power in the sending or the receiving country, and (3) the socio-cultural transactions which are oriented towards reinforcing individuals' national identity abroad or which can facilitate collective enjoyment of, access to and development of cultural goods and events. The third category can be seen as referring to the interpersonal transactions, in their myriad forms, which derive from networks of closer ties, such as those of kin and friends. These three categories in the model of Portes, Guarnizo and Landholt (1999) adhere, as it were, to the main modes of linkage in social life.

In Faist's (2000a; 2000b) work, three types of transnational social *spaces* are identified. The first form of transnational social space comprises transnational reciprocity in small groups, usually kinship-based. Remittances are one example, often functioning as a form of informal risk insurance for members of the collective, especially where kin are in vulnerable circumstances. The second form of transnational social space is characterized by exchange in circuits. Economic entrepreneurship activities constitute one aspect of the cross-border movements of goods, people and information – the resource in transnational business networks that Yeung (1998, 65) terms 'economics of synergy'. The third transnational social space is characterized by solidarity within transnational communities.

Those who move and those who stay are connected over time and across space by dense and strong social and symbolic ties. This social space frame, according to Faist (2000a; 2000b) encompasses the social life, the larger opportunity structures, subjective images, values and meanings that the specific and limited place represents to migrants.

The circumstances of forced migration in the case of refugees also have critical significance. Vertovec (2003) points out that the groups who have been resettled in Europe and other major receiving countries fled their countries of origin because of political persecution or widespread repression, and escalated levels of violence in civil or other warfare. While the conditions in the country of origin might change in time, human rights and security questions often preclude the consideration of return as a realistic and viable option. However, refugees do not give up their homeland ties in settlement, and transnational links assume special significance. Vertovec (2003) observes significantly that migration is a process that both depends on, and creates, social networks.

Diaspora

The concept of diaspora has affinity with transnationalism. Diaspora has been understood as one type of transnational community which is distinguished by dispersal among several, usually separated territories (Van Hear 1998). It is commonly held that one criterion of diaspora is forcible dispersal. Diasporas conscientiously strive to keep a memory of the past alive. They foster the will to transmit a heritage and to survive as a diaspora. In general, diaspora describes various well-established communities which have had an experience of displacement, such as the overseas Chinese, Armenians in exile and different strands of the African diaspora. Diaspora is also associated with the idea of a homeland, and indicates a nationalism in exile (Wahlbeck 1999; Chaliand 1989). Wahlbeck (2002) argues that political allegiances and relations in the society of origin have a special significance for refugees, and that their very strong political orientation towards the 'homeland' is different from the relations other migrants have towards their countries of origin. Sheffer (1995, 18) has noted that many migrants argue that not only family and friendship ties create a strong attachment to the homeland, but that they are also attached to the 'country'" and to the 'people' at large. Sheffer (1995) emphasizes that this is a crucial factor, since it should be attributed to the primordial rather than to the instrumental nature of ethnicity at large and of ethnic national diasporas in particular.

Dimensions of Transnationalism: The Vietnamese in Finland

Selected facets of transnational reciprocity which emerged from a study conducted by Valtonen (2002) in the Vietnamese community in Finland are presented here to provide a window into the 'lived' experience of transnationalism. The subjects had been settled in Finland for approximately ten years.

The norm of reciprocity was tangibly and intangibly evident in this target group. Remittances to kin were meant to meet critical living expenses of parents, to assist with schooling expenses of siblings, to pay medical expenses or to meet emergencies. These transactions are a manifestation of the norm of collective as well as direct responsibility and obligation regarding the well-being of kin. They might be conceptualized as welfare mechanisms that are part of the cultural and social fabric of the original community, and operate in a borderless field.

Intangible aspects of reciprocity are embedded in kinship support systems that can function across distance. Subjects mentioned that the maintenance of family relations and the strengthening of ties helped to reduce the loneliness of individuals living outside their country of origin. This sentiment was expressed in the following ways:

> Family ties are especially important to me. It is good that our networks make it possible to support our close relatives in many ways. We can also extend psychological support when necessary.

> Keeping up ties with kin helps people to retain their family relations and strengthen the ties, also to reduce the loneliness of Vietnamese living in Finland.

> Keeping up ties makes possible many things, but especially it gives one the psychological strength to carry on.

The subjects, for the most part, felt that the second generation would find their own place in the society better when they know, and are proud, of their own roots. It was thought that the ability to understand and compare competently the culture of origin with that of settlement is an advantage in the integration process. Ethnocultural identity and valorization of culture were seen to be greatly facilitated by the transnational family connections and transactions that were now possible.

Orientation to the Country of Origin

The majority of subjects shared a strong interest in the social and economic development of their home country, although the wish to return permanently was not articulated. Development would bring an improvement in the lives and life chances for the society of origin as a whole. It could help to reverse some of the conditions which had had such a decisive impact on their life choices in the past. Two subjects expressed the wish to participate in the development process in

Vietnam, if this were possible, by using the knowledge and skills gained in Finland to help build the human capital base in the homeland. This disposition to contribute to the development in the country of origin was found across different refugee groups (for example, Somalians, Iranians, Iraqis, Kurds) who participated in a national follow-up study on refugee integration in Finland in 1998–99 (Valtonen 1999).

The reported opinions also give an indication of the nature of ties to the settlement society. The data showed that the subjects experience their membership in the citizenry and their relation to the settlement society very strongly along the institutional dimension. The social rights that guarantee a level of basic income security, educational opportunity and other services are a cornerstone of inclusion, and taken as the society's level of regard for its citizens. These structures of citizenship are a liberating element in refugee settlement, in that they can provide for and protect individuals and their families, to the extent of empowering them to fashion distinct transnational solutions to the problem of dispersal.

Closing Comments

Transnational activity can extend the range of options for participation and offers an added dimension of life quality in the participatory spheres of action. Transnational spaces can function as a vehicle for enhancing the settlement process in significant ways, rather than as a discrete alternative to other modes of incorporation. Effective settlement is still grounded in the structural conditions of the receiving society.

As an option for migrants to retain vibrant ties with the homeland, transnationalism might even be understood as an evolving pattern of settlement. Transnationalism seems to offer individuals and communities the opportunity to shape coherent options for managing separation and distance, in addition to affording tangible instrumental advantages to those who belong to its various types of networks. According to Yeoh, Willis and Abdul Khader Fakri (1999, 207–8) it also has every potential to reconfigure the way we think of key concepts underpinning contemporary social life, from notions which serve to 'ground' social life such as 'identity', 'family', 'community', 'place' and 'nation', to those which 'transgress' and 'unmoor', including 'migration' and 'mobility'.

Soysal (1994) has put forward the idea of 'post-national citizenship'. In this arrangement, rights claims would be based on a universal code of human rights rather than on national membership. States and civic, religious and political institutions would play a central role in creating and reinforcing lasting transnational involvements. Observing that transnational families bring specific international dimensions to settlement practice, Healy (2004) points to the fact that this would warrant cross-national collaboration between social workers. Lyons (1999) speaks of the importance of viewing and understanding individual societies and the global environment in order to develop practices which are responsive to identified and emerging needs. This also includes the building of comparative perspectives or cross-national activity, which also can contribute to international policy change.

Chapter 4

Frames for Understanding Settlement and Integration Processes

This chapter will present a selection of some of the main theoretical and conceptual frames relating to settlement. The themes will deal with current integration approaches and explore different trajectories of ideas, such as that of the new 'assimilation' discourse. The building of frames for understanding, interpretation and explanation is a dynamic process in the field of migration and settlement. There is considerable ongoing discourse informing the development of models and concepts so that the theoretical arena is far from static. The breadth and variance in the features of settlement processes, settlement policies and settlement services, as well as the diversity across settling communities, all generate rich patterns. The field is studied from many disciplinary perspectives, such as anthropology, demography, cultural studies, sociology, social work, psychology, social psychology, law, geography and economics.

Conceptual frames outline interconnected ideas to facilitate our understanding of the social world. Theory emerges when frames prove to be robust through testing in various methodologies, or when they are found to hold explanatory power in usage. Theories and frames have utility, providing a structure for analysing complex human problems and situations, and for organizing information into a meaningful or coherent whole. Theory facilitates communication among those working or having an interest or a stake in the field, from settling individuals and communities to professionals and researchers. In professional practice, such frames help to shape decision-making and action by functioning as guidelines for analysing and developing practice responses (Sheafor, Horejsi and Horejsi 2000; Healy 2005).

Knowledge of a range of settlement and integration approaches and models provides the tools for analysing the design and content of one's own national model or any particular model. Models that are adopted in societies are not, and indeed cannot be, implemented as pure types, but feature within the main distinctive profile, a pragmatically built combination of methods for organizing activities in the different spheres of settlement. All models are seen as incorporating facets of assimilation, as, for example, in labour market relations, or in educational institutions.

Acculturation and Culture

Acculturation is a pivotal process which refers to the newcomers' adaptation to the culture of the new society. Individuals adjust to or adopt behaviour patterns or practices, values, rules and symbols of the new environment. People can become acculturated along some dimensions while choosing not to become acculturated along others. By cultural retention, we mean that individuals or groups do not give up valued aspects of their original culture. They retain selected intrinsic aspects, the giving up of which would be tantamount to losing their distinctiveness as a group. These generally relate to institutions such as the family; language; forms of social association and affiliation; behaviours; customs and traditions (Gans 1999). Cultural retention is not necessarily a reaction to an experienced threat from a different culture. In retaining aspects of culture, individuals can keep primary bonds alive, while for others, culture retention can be a guarantee of continuity (Gans 1999). Contemporary understandings and interpretations of integration increasingly acknowledge the role and function of culture in individuals' lives.

Orville Taylor (2002) writes that while there are several interpretations of 'culture', most writers agree that there is a relationship between the cultural patterns of groups of people and their survival strategies. Culture can be described as the totality of the non-biological activities of a people. From an anthropological perspective, Harris (1974) observes that culture is directly related to concrete material conditions of existence. It is a set of attitudinal and behavioural tools as well as a map for adapting to one's environment. Culture is thus essentially 'adaptive' (Harris 1974, 65). These definitions emphasize the instrumental dimension (see Roer-Strier and Rosenthal (2001) on the model of the 'adaptive adult' in Chapter 7).

We can hold culture to comprise the values, beliefs and practices which are shared by members of collectivities. Culture furthermore can be understood as constituting a world view or an orientation to the world, which can be depicted as ways of being and doing (Anthias 2002). Culture is understood as the stock of knowledge and life experience that is passed along between generations. These understandings portray culture as a collectivity's blueprint for living, comprising shared and socially transmitted assumptions about the nature of the physical and social world, and ways of coping and engaging with it. D'Andrade (1984) views culture as providing meaning systems which structure cognitive reality for an entire society.

Culture has grown to be a dominant topic in migration discourse. Pierik (2004), however, warns of the pitfalls of essentializing cultural groups in the process of conceptualizing difference. Scholars run the risk of falling prey to culturalistic fallacy should they take cultural groups for granted as distinct entities, internally homogenous, externally bounded, and seen as basic constituents of social life. Culturalistic fallacy is committed, according to Bidney (1953, 51) when culture is defined as an independent ontological entity governed by its own laws of development and 'conceived through itself alone'.

Pierik (2004, 524) distinguishes three aspects of the culturalistic fallacy. First, the *reification* of culture: to regard something abstract as something material or concrete.[1] Second, the *compartmentalization* of culture: the tendency to view cultures as discrete entities with sharp borders. Third, the *essentializing* of culture: the tendency to see culture as an autonomous and immutable entity, in which its individual members are regarded as only the passive bearers of culture. The essentialist view has receded in significance with the general acceptance that culture is a socially constructed concept. This warning against the risks of succumbing to culturalistic fallacy has general relevance in the context of the very frequent use of culture as a universal marker for indicating difference and distinctiveness.

Acculturation is generally assumed to be an immigrant-centred activity, with the main emphasis on immigrants' process of adaptation to the majority culture. It is often held to be an antecedent for other styles of settlement, such as integration or assimilation. Gans (1999) argues to the contrary that acculturation processes can take place regardless of whether an immigrant is becoming assimilated or integrated. The rationale, from a structural perspective, is that settling persons are indeed free to engage in acculturation on their own, while those processes defined as integration and assimilation hinge, in large part, on policy and practice adjustments initiated on the part of the receiving society to open up structural access to areas of participation. Without this, settlement is problematic even when individuals and communities might be inclined to engage in acculturation. Gans (1999) is thus making a distinction between structural aspects of incorporation and individuals' process of cultural adaptation.

An understanding of acculturation is incomplete without taking into account the changes in the receiving society, which evolve as a result of interaction among groups and their co-existence over time. Acculturation is at base a two-way process. The majority society possibly takes a stance of resistance to changes brought about by in-migration. D'Andrade (1984) notes that in actuality immigration and settlement do impact on the meaning systems and cognitive reality of the receiving society, even though there might be reluctance to analyse these changes objectively. On the other hand, persons who are settling experience much greater pressure from many quarters, to acculturate or conform.

Berry's (1988) acculturation model is based on analysis of the encounter between minority groups and the larger society. It gives us a social psychology perspective on acculturation. This model uses selectively the two variables of identity maintenance and links to outgroups to portray the acculturation process, and features four outcomes: assimilation, separation, marginalization and integration. Assimilation takes place when relations to outgroups are so enveloping

---

1   This issue has been pointed out by Baumann (1996: 188), for example, who states that the problem with multiculturalism is that 'the dominant discourse equates ethnic categories with social groups under the name "community" and it identifies each community with a reified culture'.

that immigrants melt into surrounding society and do not retain their own identity. They merge into the majority society. Separation denotes a state in which a group has minimal relations to other groups and retains its own cultural identity. When a group loses or gives up its original identity, yet does not become part of the wider society, marginalization occurs. Marginalization signifies a break in linkages to one's own group without forming connections to other groups or the majority society in place of these. Integration is the term applied to the situation in which a group is able to maintain its identity and also relate to and participate effectively in the surrounding society.

Integration

The formal usage of the term integration in the European Union is currently quite common. Integration is understood as the situation in which settling persons can participate fully in the economic, social, cultural and political life of a society, while also being able to retain their own identity. The acceptance of the importance and value of immigrants' culture is reflected in the current understanding. Breton (1992) defined integration as 'the process whereby immigrants become part of the social, institutional and cultural fabric of a society'. The term integration has not been static. Previously it carried overtones of coercion on the part of the receiving institutions for immigrants to conform to majority society. However, as it is currently interpreted, the 'integration' concept proves to be very useful. It has an affinity to policy frames, and a comprehensive participatory thrust. The central idea of participation also emphasizes an active mode of settlement.

Integration, as it is defined above, can help us to grasp the scope of settlement processes. The more recent acceptance of identity retention by groups and individuals is a positive indication of the valorization of diversity by policy-makers in receiving societies which are becoming increasingly multiethnic. Integration can be understood in terms of immigrants' relations to the institutions of the state, the market and civil society, as described in Chapter 3. It is alternatively conceptualized as full membership in a society, and thereby associated with the social citizenship frame.

Integration is understood as entailing the creation of a shared political framework which embodies institutional mechanisms for ensuring that those who see themselves as belonging to distinctive groups or communities can nonetheless participate effectively in all aspects of the political, economic, social or cultural structures of the society in which they live (Hadden 2002).

Eisenstadt's (1954) earlier model of incorporation is near to the lived experience of settlement. It comprises four stages: first, the acquisition of language, norms, roles and customs; second, learning to perform a range of new roles and thereby to handle the numerous new situations that will occur in engaging with the new environment; third, development of a new identity and status-image, new values about oneself – a basic personal adjustment; and fourth, movement from participation in the institutions of the new ethnic group to participation in the institutions of the host society.

Eisentstadt's (1954) model has the quality of being grounded and insightful along behavioural dimensions. It retains its salience for integration. However, current understandings of settlement and integration do not encroach on the integrity of immigrants' original cultural identity and in this way have changed since Eisenstadt's (1954) model was shaped.

Gordon's (1964) early linear model differentiates between the initial processes of behavioural assimilation or acculturation – learning the cultural patterns of the new country, and later phases of structural assimilation, marked by immigrants' entry into the primary group life of the new land through intermarriage, joining clubs, acquiring their identity, an absence of prejudice or discrimination, a lack of power or value conflicts between natives and refugees. Subsequently, he places less emphasis on the linear aspect of the model, as it was increasingly recognized that assimilation processes could take place in different sequences.

Kallen's (1995) Model of Structural Integration

Kallen's (1995) structural integration model portrays different facets of the settlement and integration process. Integration is seen as taking place along cultural and structural dimensions. Structural integration refers to institutional participation, and actual assimilation processes into the formal institutional structures (most frequently the economic and political/civil arenas) of the receiving society, while cultural integration refers to cultural exchange or acculturation. This approach corresponds to the matrix of economic, social, cultural and political spheres presented in the definitions of integration. There is some similarity to Milton Gordon's (1964) earlier linear model of 'assimilation' which was shaped in the American context. A fuller elaboration of structural integration is given below, as it brings an analytically clear perspective on settlement that lends itself to social work systems and policy approaches.

Cultural Integration

Cultural integration refers to the process of learning cultural ways of an ethnic collectivity to which one does not belong. The corresponding concepts of 'enculturation' or 'socialization' refer to the process of learning the cultural patterns of the ethnic collectivity to which one does belong. Settling persons may eventually adopt new cultural attributes. Indeed the existence of a majority or dominant culture in the society will exert pressure for the main direction of change in the process of acculturation to be toward the norms, values and patterns of the majority (Kallen 1995, 154). In the process of acculturating to majority societal culture, individuals adjust to majority cultural mores and patterns, and also acquire some proficiency in engaging with these in order to participate effectively in society. The approach to cultural adaptation can thus be a pragmatic one.

Structural Integration

Structural integration occurs when relations between members of different ethnic collectivities result in the participation of these individuals in ethnocultural institutions other than those of the ethnic community in which they were raised. Structural integration is broken up into three sub-processes:

Secondary structural integration refers to formal participation in the secondary institutions of the society, such as the economic, political, legal and educational institutions. It is in this process where many of the more difficult challenges of integration are encountered, and where equity mechanisms are especially critical for settlement. Additionally, from the perspective of long-term integration, it is important to recognize that secondary structural integration that progresses laterally into different social spheres does not necessarily entail social mobility. Social mobility implies upward progression between the levels in a socially stratified system. Social mobility would result in representation of immigrants, or persons of immigrant background, at different levels and in different capacities in organizations, in proportion to their occurrence in the larger population.

Primary structural integration refers to participation by individuals and ethnic collectivities in the private institutions of other collectivities (for example, religious, social and recreational institutions; friendship and kinship networks; family and marital alliances).

Identificational integration is a function of both cultural and structural integration. It refers to the process whereby an ethnic group other than one's own eventually comes to provide one's primary source of expressive symbolic ties and roots, and also becomes one's primary reference group (Kallen 1995). Identification is discussed in Chapter 8 in connection with second generation issues.

In the above situation, individuals do not necessarily become integrated along all three dimensions. They might be well integrated into primary structures but less so into the secondary structures, and might yet exercise free choice regarding how they self-identify. Alternatively all three areas can be seen as inter-related, with individuals shaping for themselves the most functional option by selecting areas of emphasis along the three dimensions. Thus there can be marked variation in individual styles of adaptation and integration. However, using Kallen's (1995) frame, long-term integration would imply the secondary structural integration of settling individuals. Ideally it would also include opportunities for upward social mobility.

According to Kallen (1995), integration is more likely to be a two-way process in reality when ethnocultural collectivities are relatively balanced in expressive and/or instrumental strength. When integration takes place as a two-way process, the original ethnocultural collectivities can become fused to create a new, culturally homogeneous society. Alternatively, the retention and federation of the original ethnic collectivities result in an ethnically heterogeneous, multi-ethnocultural society, featuring 'cultural pluralism', 'mosaic' or multiculturalism', as in the Canadian model.

When collectivities are unequal, numerically and otherwise, the process of integration is likely to be weighted in favour of the stronger ethnic collectivity (the majority or dominant group). A hypothetical situation is that the smaller or 'weaker' group might be absorbed by the stronger one, resulting in an ethnically homogeneous society modelled upon the characteristics of the original stronger ethnic collectivity ('dominant conformity' or 'absorption'). 'Absorption' or 'dominant conformity' would seem to be a reasonable outcome of imbalance between majority and minority groups. In actuality integration processes in their complexity can diverge from set patterns of sequence or linear progression. The main exception is in the case of language, which constitutes 'a domain of adaptation most likely to proceed exactly as a linear function' (Rumbaut 1999, 191).

These patterns must be seen as being moderated by self-determination on the part of immigrants. Individuals can determine through choice the type of links they will establish and the type of cultural 'compromises' they will entertain. There is generally less covert and overt pressure to conform when the society itself is already to some degree multiethnic or multicultural. The presence of ethnic communities can deflect some of the pressures to conform in a society with an otherwise dominant culture.

Many personal and structural factors contribute to the overall style and outcome of settlement. The model of structural integration is helpful in capturing the breadth of processes involved in settlement. These processes are inter-related and indeed mutually reinforcing. The social work mandate extends into all these areas of settlement in which immigrants seek the space to assume meaningful roles through a range of participatory modes. The quality of public and social policy-making and skill, standards and competence in policy implementation are key factors in guiding national settlement projects. These topics are dealt with more fully in Chapter 9.

Assimilation

Concepts of assimilation have previously been basic to understandings of immigration experience in the United States, for example, and in many of the large immigrant receiving countries such as Britain, Canada and Australia. 'Assimilation' emerged during the era of immigration to America early in the last century and was based on studies conducted in Chicago where the immigrant first and second generations then constituted the great majority of residents (Alba and Nee 1999). Park and Burgess's 1921–24) classic formulation states that assimilation is a process of interpenetration and fusion in which persons and groups can acquire the memories, sentiments and attitudes of other persons and groups, and, in the process of sharing their experience and history, are incorporated with them in a common cultural life. The idea of assimilation underlay the melting pot theory (Ramakrishnan and Balgopal 1995).

In the post-World War II era, international migration displayed increased complexity. Flows originated in regions geographically and culturally distant from Europe. Forced migration from wars and repression brought about changes in the patterns of flows. It was gradually recognized that more recent immigrant groups were not being rapidly assimilated. They tended, moreover, not to relinquish their social and cultural patterns, and retained their political affiliations. In response to this, overt assimilation policies began to be replaced in the 1960s in Australia, Canada and Britain with policies of integration that sought to accommodate diversity (Castles 1995). Social scientists also found that assimilation had less salience as an organizing concept for studying settlement. Its 'ethnocentric and patronizing demands on minority peoples struggling to retain their cultural and ethnic integrity' became less acceptable (Alba and Nee 1999, 137).

Of late, the assimilation approach is being revisited and is the subject of lively contemporary discourse (Rumbaut 1999; Kivisto 2002). The 'new' assimilation theory ignores the normative overtones of the older Chicago version and proposes possible combinations of 'assimilative' outcomes along various dimensions of social life. Upward mobility, combined with a lack of 'identificational assimilation', comprises one of these. The link between upward social mobility and assimilation is broken or weakened (Brubaker 2001; Rumbaut 1999; Zhou 1997).

The structural aspects of assimilation have kept their salience. Socio-economic assimilation, for example, refers to achieving 'parity' with the native majority along indicators such as education, employment and income. One of these indicators is the rate at which immigrant earnings catch up with those of natives as both groups age in the United States (Borjas 1990). Castles (1995) proposes that integration policies are often simply a weaker form of assimilation. They may be based on the idea that adaptation is a gradual process in which group cohesion and interaction play an important part, but the final goal is, nonetheless, complete absorption into the dominant culture. Schnapper (1991) has pointed out that the assimilationist tradition implemented by state action is an end-state principle of the French model, but not a description of society. This author predicts that integration, which is defended by present-day republicans as an interactive rather than a one-way process, will eventually result in a two-way acculturation process.

Assimilation is seen as being out of touch with contemporary multicultural developments in settlement societies (Alba and Nee 1999). However, it probably will hold significance for settlement research if only because it captures important aspects of cognitive and emotive processes evoked by cultural encounter, with the potential for deep change at individual and community levels. It is being linked to differential outcomes, as demonstrated by the development of ideas around segmented assimilation – assimilating to the segment of society to which particular immigrant groups are exposed (Portes and Zhou 1993). It is also possible to understand assimilation within a structural frame of settlement comprising distinct areas (such as socio-economic). Assimilation is used as a sounding board in appraising the protean features of cultural change processes and it will continue to be a useful analytical tool.

Policy Models

Castles' (1995) typology of policy models is based on the strategies used in highly developed nations facing major changes in the ethnic composition of their populations. The models are termed differential exclusion, assimilation and pluralist. The differential exclusion model seeks to prevent permanent settlement, for example, when the admission of migrants is seen to be a temporary expedient, to meet labour demand. Immigrants might thus be incorporated into the labour market but denied access to other spheres such as welfare systems, citizenship and political participation. The differential exclusion is problematic to implement because it invariably leads to social tension and, at the same time, contradicts the democratic principle of including all members of civil society as participants in economic, social, cultural and political spheres of society.

Access can be denied through legal mechanisms such as sharp distinctions between the rights of citizens and non-citizens, or through informal practices of discrimination. Many receiving societies are not particularly characterized by exclusion through legal mechanisms. They are officially 'inclusive' of permanent settlers and residents. On the other hand, informal practices such as racism and discrimination can limit the scope of immigrants' participation, rights and citizenship. The differential exclusion model would correspond to restricted structural integration and, within the citizenship framework, a different relation to the state since the individual is not holding the status of a bearer of citizenship rights.

Castles' (1995) assimilationist model is more or less convergent with the dominant-conformity model (Kallen 1995) outlined above. Castles develops the policy dimension, pointing out that the role of the state in assimilation is to create conditions favourable to individual adaptation and the transferring of majority culture and values, through, for example, insistence on use of the dominant language by migrants and their attendance in mainstream schooling.

The pluralist model allows for immigrant populations, as ethnic communities, to remain distinguishable from the majority population over several generations with regard to language, culture, social behaviour and associations. Pluralism implies, nonetheless, the granting of equal rights to immigrants in all spheres of society, without the expectation that they would give up their diversity. They are expected, however, to conform to certain key values (Higham 1975; Van Hear 1994). Parekh (1997) has pointed to this aspect of society's expectation that immigrants will identify themselves with it and this is discussed further in Chapter 8.

Pluralism has two main variants. The 'laissez faire' approach is typical of the USA. The pluralistic character of the society is formally recognized and difference is tolerated. The role of the state is not extended to supporting the maintenance of ethnic cultures. The second variant is explicit multicultural policies, which entail the willingness of the majority group to accept cultural difference, and to effect necessary changes in institutional structures and social behaviours. Overall, policies of multiculturalism exist in Canada, Australia and Sweden, while multicultural policies exist in specific sectors, such as education, in several other countries. Multiculturalism is usually linked to state-interventionist approaches to social policy (Castles 1995). The pluralism type thus comprises a basically descriptive model, as well as the prescriptive model, 'multiculturalism', that has come to the fore in the policies of many immigrant-receiving societies, as well as in the immigration discourse (see Gould 1995).

Multiculturalism

Multiculturalism is an official approach to the organizing and managing of ethnocultural diversity. It is effected through policies, programmes and strategies that are shaped for this purpose as part of the state's recognition and accommodation of distinctive groups and communities within the broader policy framework. Multiculturalism policy is developed and implemented in many forms to reflect the settlement priorities and plans of the society. Goldberg (1994) states that multiculturalism is not a single doctrine, which is characterized by one political strategy. Far from representing an already achieved state of affairs, it describes a variety of political strategies and processes which are in progress in different societies. The outcomes will also be quite reflective of the contexts in which they are being shaped.

Multicultural approaches and principles have evolved in several advanced industrial societies, including the United States, Canada, Australia, Britain, Germany, France and Sweden. However, while these countries are multicultural in the descriptive sense, Canada, Australia and Sweden have adopted 'multiculturalism' as explicit government policy. In 1989, the National Agenda for a Multicultural Australia proclaimed the right of all Australians to enjoy equal life chances, participate fully in society, and 'develop and make use of their potential for Australia's economic and social development' (Office of Multicultural Affairs 1989, 9). Multicultural policies focus increasingly on combating racism and discrimination in addition to facilitating the preservation of language, culture and ethno-religious traditions, within a unified civil society (Kivisto 2002).

The multicultural model was first introduced in Canada (see the discussion in Chapter 9). McAll (1990, 4) states that the policy was founded on a 'politically charged vision' of the society. Organized immigration formed the basis of Canada's national strategy for building its demographic and economic base. Canada has consistently been among the countries with the highest levels of immigration. The declared goal of the multiculturalism policy was twofold: to help minority groups preserve and share their language and culture, and to remove the cultural barriers which they faced in society (Lindström 1995).

Subsequent critique of multiculturalism policy in Canada (and elsewhere) was that priority was given to cultural recognition and retention, diverting attention away from the harder issues of equality and opportunities for upward social mobility (see, for example, Bullivant 1981). A mistaken impression is one which holds multiculturalism as functioning solely to 'enrich' settlement cultures. Valued and desired as this is, multiculturalism is indeed a critical question of newer groups' access to full membership in the citizenry on a par with other citizens. Porter (1979, 132–3) warned that ethnic communities might become a permanent compensation for low status, or used as psychic shelters in the urban industrial world. More recently, social work literature frequently links the attainment of *social justice* with the goals of social diversity or multiculturalism, and also with challenges to the normative power structure and the oppression which it produces (Hyde 1998).

Modood (1997; 2003) underscores the importance of egalitarian multiculturalism. He uses the case of Muslims who form a significant minority in countries where the secularization of public life has meant that religion and religious matters have been relegated to the private sphere. Modood (1997; 2003; 2006) argues for a shift from an understanding of 'equality' in terms of individualism and cultural assimilation to a politics of recognition. He calls for the broadening of 'equality' to encompass public ethnicity, or ethnicity in the public sphere. This perception of equality would mean not having to apologize for one's origin, family or community, and would require due respect from others.

Comments on Multiculturalism

Multiculturalism seeks to move away from an ethnocentric alignment in policy and practice, and to reduce possible elements of cultural hegemony. This purposive stance has marked an important turning point in shaping ideas on the type and content of ethnic relations which the state prioritizes in its model of immigrant settlement and integration. Multiculturalism is different from the other models in that it requires state commitment to the enactment and implementation of its prescriptive policies. Formally stated policies need to be substantiated in programmes, institutional measures and practices. The dimension of relevant policy and policy implementation are integral to the model. The prescriptive aspect of multiculturalism policy in Canada, Australia and Sweden has facilitated the building of the organizational fabric for implementing the policy.

The idea in multiculturalism which captured the enthusiasm of its proponents was that of the formal extension of value and respect for the diversity of cultures in society and a clear visualization of the place of minorities in the national public space. The later critique of multiculturalism focused on its absorption with or diversion into cultural aspects of settlement to the detriment of responses to the harder questions of equality and access for immigrants which represent the substantive elements of membership. Multiculturalism, on one hand, can still be seen as strengthening the collective positioning of diverse groups, both politically and symbolically, which can facilitate the mounting of collective claims. This approach on its own, however, diffuses the responsibility for bringing about more equitable conditions and for removing barriers to settlement, as it shifts the onus onto citizen initiative and resources. The claims-making process cannot be the main vehicle to equal citizenship which, in the case of immigrants, calls for positive action and functioning affirmative mechanisms on the part of the state, to promote equity.

The efficacy of multiculturalism is measured by the level of representation of minority groups in all sectors of society and at all levels. This holds as well for the range of models for managing diversity in society. From the social work perspective, Reisch (2005) has pointed out that an urgent task facing the discipline is the development of a multicultural framework for critical practice to replace formulations that focus narrowly on racial and class-based lines of division.

The range of models for incorporation of immigrants has put weight differentially on specific aspects of settlement, which include:

- Policy and structural features for the management of immigration, as in Castles' (1995) typology; citizenship approaches with attendant issues of boundaries and barriers; principles of service organization including the locus of responsibility
- Outcomes based on observed characteristics of style of settlement, for example, volume and direction of social contacts; participation and representation in different spheres and at different levels such as in the labour market
- Behavioural, emotive, or cognitive aspects in the adaptation process
- Identity formation processes.

The evolution of settlement theory can be understood as a journey through the following stages:

- Assimilation or convergence seen as a logical path for newcomers
- In societies with clearly articulated structures of social, political and civil rights: concern over how immigrants fit into the system vis-à-vis other citizens and the state, questions over the terms of membership to be granted to them, decisions on the partial or full extension of citizenship rights
- Weight given to identity and cultural integrity as part of minority rights
- Equality, equity, social justice and human rights issues coming to the fore as central principles in integration
- The ongoing search for core principles to shape policies and processes for meeting the challenges of increasing diversity. Multiculturalism is recognized for its acceptance of diversity. The outstanding question concerns whether and in what ways the model can be applied as a more powerful instrument for bringing about equal citizenship.

Stakeholding Integration

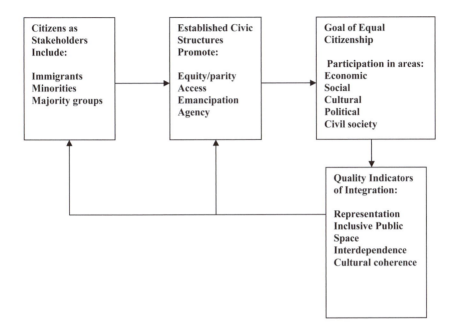

Figure 4.1 Stakeholder integration

The perspective of settling immigrants and refugees as stakeholders in the new home society and in the process of integration is proposed here. The conceptual frame is displayed in Figure 4.1 above. The role of *stakeholder* admits a different role for settling individuals and communities. It is more robust than roles perceived through the lens of service user, rights claimant, minority member or humanitarian migrant. Stakeholding is not compatible with ideas of exclusion, marginalization or any status of lesser value in society. The idea of stakeholding reinforces the positioning of immigrant constituencies as active members with commitment to engage and confirms the aspect of contribution by all parties. In one sense it aims to legitimize the input of settling individuals and groups into social processes. It also implies the property of synergy, which can be advantageously tapped into as a settlement resource.

Within the stakeholding dynamic, settling individuals seek to participate actively and productively in various societal spheres: this process is ideally facilitated by conditions which promote rather than deter progression in the different spheres of actions and transactions. These conditions are:

1. Equity or parity, referring to fair treatment. Fair treatment might entail positive action and affirmative tasks for the state in order to ensure the securing of rights (see the discussion of Nussbaum 2006, 286)
2. Access, or the openness of social institutions, as opposed to closure or exclusiveness
3. Emancipation, or the removal of barriers to participation and different forms of un-freedom which constrain the agency and goal-oriented settlement efforts of citizens
4. Agency, which embodies the principle of autonomy and self-determination in the context of meaningful activity.

Facilitating civic structures can be implemented proactively as opposed to being put in place as a reaction to the escalation of problem issues, which is damaging to ethnic relations. Papademetriou (2003) admits that migration poses challenges to societies, and these easily expose fault lines in structures. This is an important point as it resets the point of service response to a more fundamental stage. In the case of immigrant integration, timely appraisal of the policy and policy implementation structures is needed from the perspective of whether the scope and thrust of existing instruments address the integration agenda.

If the society creates the conditions for equal citizenship, it facilitates individuals' participation in different societal spheres. Settlement and integration processes are progressing effectively when there is evidence of specific indicators. I list these as representation, an inclusive public space, interdependence and cultural coherence.

Representation refers to the participation of immigrants widely across the different realms of activity and functioning in formal roles at all levels of responsibility. The labour market is the prime arena where this condition should be demonstrated. An *inclusive public space* is one in which diverse groups are recognized in the public sphere. Not only are diversity and distinctiveness accepted but these are compatible with the solidarity base in the citizenry. *Interdependence* signifies the establishment of relations of substance with the surrounding society. Individuals are participating in contributor as well as recipient capacities in connection with both formal and informal institutions. *Cultural coherence* is a condition in which diverse cultures have shaped a mode of common cultural value. This skirts the extremes of cultural reification and cultural hegemony to bring about inter-related cultural understandings which give worth and meaning to ethnic relations.

The indicators are a sign of empowerment of newer citizens, who in turn shape and invigorate civic processes in concert with the efforts of all stakeholding citizens. The conceptual frame is not tied to particular national policy models or programme contexts, but seeks to identify generic principles.

From the settlement practice view, target areas would give specific focus to the area of facilitating civic structures. Concrete tasks include appraisal of the integration environment, policies and programme effectiveness. Wide lateral and vertical networking and collaboration must build the support basis for change initiatives, which usually require a degree of consensus in order to be legitimized in the first place. Quality indicators can lead to the incorporation into practice of workable accountability principles if they become integral parts of the professional settlement portfolio.

Closing Comments

The frameworks which have been discussed here are evolving constructs. So far, social work has not taken a high profile in the building of theoretical frameworks in the immigration and integration field, even though practice approaches which have been developed, such as anti-racist and anti-oppressive practice, hold distinct salience for these issues. Rich empirical evidence which is part of the information base that grows in the course of settlement practice offers a clear opportunity for social work theory building in this particular field.

Culture has been featured centrally in this chapter, as in other works on integration. The task ahead is to fashion ways of shaping culture and cultures into widely uniting rather than divisive forces. One of the stages in this process is recognition of the value of different and unique cultures. Dunn (1998) mentions the dynamism of unassimilated cultural difference as a significant and largely untapped resource. An account of his studies of areas in the western Sydney suburbs is given in Chapter 9.

The model of stakeholder integration revolves around the idea of pragmatic solidarity in the citizenry, based on shared interests and perceptions of the common good. Alternatively, we can conceptualize this model as the formalizing of inter-group synergies.

Chapter 5

The Politics of Inclusion and Exclusion

This chapter presents, in the first section, the concepts of equality, equity and social justice which are central considerations in immigrant settlement and key principles for facilitating full membership in society. Social justice is discussed more fully in Chapter 10 under ethics. The next section examines different forms of existing equity instruments which function as legal and civic mechanisms facilitating integration. From the structural social work perspective, initiatives for promoting equal citizenship are integral to the settlement portfolio. Social work is a profession which occupies a strategic position for working with existing equity mechanisms on behalf of their immigrant client constituencies. The latter generally do not attain positions from which they would be able to effect needed change in systems (equivalent to those which operate for majority members) for considerable periods.

The following section presents a scrutiny of discriminatory barriers to participation and the impact of these on integration. Insight into the nature of these processes is important for formulating counter-strategies on the personal and societal levels. Prejudice and discrimination invariably form one dimension of the settlement experience, which is coped with in different ways. Since employment is a critical settlement area for immigrants, the dynamics of labour market discrimination are discussed, as well as recruitment discrimination in institutional settings. An explanation for the 'logic' of discrimination in organizational culture is presented in the final section.

Equality

Equality is a challenging and multifaceted concept with surprising versatility in interpretation. As a principle it is related to parity and egalitarianism. Even though approaches to equality often start from the narrow economic frame of income, Schaar (1997, 137) reminds us that: 'Equality is one of those political symbols ... into which men have poured the deepest urgings of their hearts. Every strongly held theory or conception of equality is at once a psychology, an ethic, a theory of social relations, and a vision of the good society.'

Equality with reference to equal worth proposes a moral principle that, as human beings, everyone should be accorded treatment on the basis of equal worth without regard to differences such as gender, race, ethnicity and class. Pojman and Westmoreland (1997, 1) state that even though non-egalitarians might argue that equality has little or no moral significance, it is nonetheless a basic tenet of almost all contemporary moral and political theories. In history the principle that each individual is of equal worth has been the basis for rights claims, prominent examples of which are the civil rights movements in the US and South Africa.

Drawing from Pojman and Westmoreland (1997, 2–6) on equality theory, theories can be seen to fall into formal or substantive types. Formal equality sets out a formula or policy with specific content. Substantive equality, on the other hand, identifies a concrete criterion or metric by which distribution policies are to be assessed. The formal or 'thin' version conveys primarily the principle of being entitled to equal treatment before the law without bias or prejudice. This legal or formal equality calls for all to be judged with consistency by the same laws. The actual laws are not stated, neither is there any indication as to what they ought to be. It is understandable why formal equality is rarely contested even by those who would otherwise oppose the principle of economic equality. Individuals can refer to themselves as egalitarians even when their adherence to the principle is restricted to the formal version.

The 'thick' or substantive version of equality is opposed to privilege and social hierarchy. Alternatively referred to as 'social equality', or 'equality of regard', it concerns the fundamental equality that should govern the relationships between human beings. It entails the identification of a metric in areas of morally indefensible inequality, on which basis all relevant parties should receive equal amounts. Pojman and Westmoreland (1997) state that in matters of redress, socialists and liberals tend to be interventionist, while conservatives and libertarians tend to limit the role of the state and leave the matter for the sphere of voluntary action.

Equality as Equal Worth and Distribution

The principle of equal worth, when it is applied to distribution, calls for individuals with similar needs to receive similar resources and for those with different needs to receive different resources. This distribution would be in line with their treatment as equals rather than as being administered equal treatment. This pattern of distribution can be said to reflect a fair division of resources, since it recognizes that, when individual and group differences are taken into account, a just set of outcomes is not always best achieved by treating everyone in the same way.

The concern over equality and social justice issues being overshadowed by the emphasis on culture was voiced in Canada in the 1980s when multicultural policies were found not to have made inroads into patterns of inequality and unequal relations in the society (Fleras and Elliott 1996). Multicultural approaches have been gaining credence in other societies of settlement, but there is awareness, at least in the academic discourse, that critical social justice and equality issues could be neglected by depending exclusively on this model of settlement which, in the past, has focused strongly on cultural aspects in institutional and social life. Countries in the EU have been shaping the idea of integration as participation and social citizenship, which is meant to bring consideration of equity aspects to multicultural arrangements.

Social Justice

Social justice has been very broadly defined by Barker (1995, 94) as conditions in which 'all members of society have the same basic rights, protections, opportunities, obligations, and social benefits'. Looking at the converse aspect, the NASW Code of Ethics (1996, 5) states that social injustices refer to such conditions as poverty, unemployment and discrimination. Social justice can be understood in the light of philosophical theories and world views. Van Soest (1992) sets out a frame of three contemporary views spanning the legal, commutative and distributive forms of justice. Legal justice is concerned with what a person owes to society and generally involves a debate over retribution versus restitution. Commutative justice is concerned with what people owe to each other and is related to issues of interpersonal equity. Distributive justice is concerned with what society owes to individuals.

Distributive justice, or justice as fair shares, constitutes a specific aspect of social justice. Reisch (2002) proposed six ways of understanding distributive justice, using the lens of equality:

- Equal rights (to intangibles such as freedom) and equal opportunity to obtain social goods, such as property
- Equal distribution to those of equal merit
- Equal distribution to those of equal productivity
- Unequal distribution based upon an individual's needs or requirements
- Unequal distribution based upon an individual's status or position
- Unequal distribution based upon different 'contractual' agreements.

Dominelli (1988) has noted that even progressive social work and social welfare writers have tended to equate social justice with a redistribution of goods and services. She argues that while some oppressed groups might be in need of and demand this form of justice, such an approach is limited from the perspective of social justice, since it does nothing to alter the processes and practices that allow for society's resources to be shared unjustly from the outset. Dominelli (1988) thus stresses the need to look to structural factors as sources of the root causes of inequality.

Equity

Equity is a term used in conjunction with equality. In the social work literature, it occurs less frequently than social justice, but in settlement it is a term that is central to issues of access to important spheres of participation, such as the labour market and education. Equity denotes even-handed treatment, requiring that relevantly similar cases be treated in similar ways. For example, individuals who perform the same job for the same employer with similar results would expect to receive the same remuneration. The same principle applies in the hiring processes. Controversy can arise in delineating relevant similarity, and in the handling of precedents and the way in which they should feature in the determination of equitable practices.

Equity in older usage stood for the application of the dictates of conscience or the principles of natural justice in the settlement of controversies. Equity represents thus, on the one hand, a system of jurisprudence or a body of doctrines and rules developed to supplement and remedy the limitations of the common law. On the other, it refers to the need to modify the consequences of a strict application of the law to avoid unfair or unconscionable outcomes (McLean 1996). Equity in both of the above meanings carries heavy significance for settlement and integration issues.

From the perspective of distribution, equity refers to fairness in the distribution of social goods such as social services and benefits. The principle of equity also applies to distribution of opportunities, such as work and education, which have weighty implications for immigrants' life quality and life chances in the new society. Perspectives on equity are thus not restricted to questions of service and benefit distribution if settlement practice is to be effective. Settlement practice is justified in connecting with the structures and institutions in the interest of equal citizenship and in working with the current structure of legislation, policies and practices to achieve applications which would promote equity. As McLean (1996, 162) has pointed out, strict applications of the law can lead to unfair and unconscionable outcomes. Statistical and other indicators of sustained areas of disadvantage among immigrants are an indication of inequitable processes and suggest the evasion of equity.

Positive Action Modes for Fostering Equality and Equity Practices

Positive Action

Positive action is part of the wider body of anti-discriminatory policy and action initiatives which have been shaped and put into practice in different societies to correct discriminatory practices and to move forward from previous discriminatory patterns. They are meant to address the inequality of access, hiring and representation in different sectors and levels of the labour market, and in the labour market in general. Some of the policies were originally generated in response to the situation of traditional population groups experiencing discrimination, such as African Americans in the United States. Positive action has been incorporated into policy approaches in order to address the situations of the diverse groups facing discrimination. Measures have been targeted at the situation of women, old and new minorities, first nations, the physically disabled, and other designated groups. For our purpose, the focus is on discrimination issues faced by new immigrants and refugees, and the equal opportunity and affirmative action/employment equity-type approaches are examined below.

Equal Opportunity

Compared to thicker versions of positive action, equality of opportunity tends to find approval readily as a concept, since its implications seem to be lighter. It holds that individuals should have equal rights and opportunities to develop their own talents and virtues and that there should be equal reward for equal performances. Equal opportunity assumes that each person will compete with others for scarce goods on an equal footing while abiding by the same rules of the game. It does not take outcome into account.

Equal opportunity has resonance with the generic concept of equality. Pojman and Westmoreland (1997, 7) distinguish two notions of equal opportunity. Weak or formal equal opportunity is 'meritocratic' and holds that offices should be open to talent. It leaves the matter of initial starting points untouched, skirting those advantages which people might derive from natural or family resources. Strong or substantive equal opportunity holds that individuals ought to have equal life chances to progress to the same levels through self-fulfilment. Those who have had less fortune early in life should be allowed the chance to attain the level of those who have had advantages. Thus weak equal opportunity leaves the substantive outcomes open-ended. Strong equal opportunity and the question of whether policies and guarantees should be imbued with a moral or a social content remain central to contemporary controversies (Przeworski 1995).

Affirmative Action and Employment Equity

Affirmative action policies are based on compensatory principles and aim at facilitating the success of groups in obtaining coveted positions in proportion to their representation in the population. Affirmative action and employment equity are concepts pioneered in America some 30 years ago. Employment equity is based on the principle that all persons, regardless of membership in designated groups (for example, based on racial or ethnocultural origin), should be recruited, hired, promoted, trained and rewarded like any other persons. Thus recruitment should be on the basis of job-related skills, assuming that individuals are qualified and that positions are available, without barriers that discriminate against them because of membership in certain devalued groups (Fleras and Elliott 1996).

Affirmative action is a set of strategies for promoting the inclusion of any group that has had a history of exclusion. It was directed at ameliorating the systemic discrimination and labour market disadvantages experienced by various groups. The policy aims to overcome the effects of past discrimination by enabling persons or groups who were discriminated against to compete on level terms with the advantaged group. It attempts to enforce equal opportunity by monitoring the outcomes of the hiring and promotion processes of businesses (Hodges-Aeberhard

1999; Jain 1992; Pratkanis and Turner 1996). For example, it is described by the Affirmative Action Directorate of the Canadian Employment and Immigration Commission (CEIC) (1982) as a comprehensive planning process adopted by an employer to: identify and remove discrimination in employment policies and practices; remedy effects of past discrimination through special measures; and ensure appropriate representation of target groups throughout the organization. Special measures with aims similar to affirmative action are also termed employment equity, workplace diversity, maximalization or inclusion. Controversy has arisen when this form of labour market intervention has been used in the two specific areas of discrimination relating to race and sex (Hodges-Aeberhard 1999). However, gender equality has made significant strides in Scandinavian countries, for instance.

Pratkanis and Turner (1996) state that a reason given by opponents for dismantling affirmative action is that it leads to the perception that recipients are unqualified for their positions. Employment equity initiatives are not, however, designed to confer preferential treatment for designated minorities. The objective is to expand the number of qualified candidates by eliminating bias that can reward certain sectors at the expense of other groups. Fleras and Elliott (1996) explain that employment equity is not in the business of hiring or promoting unqualified personnel, neither does it set out to dilute competition by restricting the pool of qualified applicants. Rather the removal of discriminatory barriers is intended to expand the number of qualified applicants in competition for employment.

The thrust of employment equity is to make the competition more equal by opening it up to those formerly excluded unfairly from participation, with merit being the hiring principle for all employment decisions. Under employment equity, minorities are considered on the basis of merit or credentials, in contrast with scenarios in which people are hired because they fit the right type. Fleras and Elliott (1996) point out that, under employment equity, only the best candidates need to be hired. Targeted minorities should get the posts only when candidates are of comparable quality in a minority-depleted occupation or institution.

At the workplace level, an employment equity programme entails several steps that include: the preparation of the workforce in the organization; drawing up a management statement of commitment to the concept; as well as communication and educational strategy to help workers and management understand the concept; the identification of any discriminatory structures and barriers within the workplace itself; and the development of goals and timetables for hiring and promoting previously under-represented groups. The last step includes conducting a workforce analysis to compare representation of groups within the establishment with their availability in the larger population. The 'targets' are generally women, visible minorities, native peoples and people with disabilities (Das Gupta 1996, 98).

Hodges-Aeberhard (1999) addresses the question of why affirmative action cases might be struck down in court settings, pointing to the need for greater gender and race sensitivity on the bench. This author sees also the possibility that the proponents of affirmative action, the practitioners arguing cases and the courts themselves are likely to be unaware of the legal concepts that could come to their aid in deciding such matters. Available information is not widely applied because it is not widely disseminated.

Hodges-Aeberhard (1999, 271) suggests that the time is ripe for anti-discrimination measures at macro level. An international labour standard on affirmative action could remove many of the ambiguities in policy and practice by, for example:

- Defining the concept, highlighting the temporary nature of such measures
- Clarifying unconditionally that affirmative action is not 'reverse' discrimination
- Outlining the limits of its aims
- Giving examples of methods proportional to those aims
- Providing guidance on the relative claims of individual and group damage
- Clarifying the balance to be reached in respecting/diminishing other groups' rights
- Taking a stand on the egregious nature of the discrimination to be overcome.

Hawthorne (1997) has observed that, despite the evolution of anti-discrimination and equal opportunity legislation in Australia during the 1970s and 1980s, the onus for change and adaptation has remained primarily with immigrant job seekers. Immigrants are expected to pursue success by making an active attempt to adapt their existing skills, acquire new or additional skills, seek out job opportunities, and generally improve their knowledge of the Australian labour market. Employers have been mostly absolved from blame or shared responsibility in this process.

In the Netherlands, a minority groups policy was developed by the Dutch government in response to the arrival of large numbers of immigrants from Surinam, and with the gradual realization that Turkish and Moroccan guest workers who were recruited in the 1960s were staying in the country permanently (Glastra, Schedler and Kats 1998). With a sharp increase in unemployment among immigrants in the 1980s, an agreement was voluntarily signed in 1990 regarding the allocation of 60,000 extra jobs for ethnic minority groups over a five-year period. Ethnic interest organizations and government advisory bodies had advocated that employment equity measures be complemented by a policy of contract compliance, but there was not enough support to pass such wide-ranging legislation in parliament. The Law on the Encouragement of Proportional Labour Participation by Ethnic Minorities (Equity Law) came into effect in 1994 for a period of five years. The law obliged employers with more than 35 employees in the private and public sectors to move towards a greater representation of ethnic minority groups in their organizations. Employers were required to keep data on the ethnic composition of their workforce and to develop action plans to improve employment equity, in co-operation with workers' councils. Ethnic representation statistics are reported to chambers of commerce on an annual basis, where they can be checked by ethnic interest groups and made available to the public (Glastra, Schedler and Kats 1998, 168).

Barriers to Inclusion

Definitions

In this section, barriers to integration, such as ethnocentrism, prejudice and discrimination, are defined and discussed. The principles and mechanisms of equality, equity and affirmative action which were examined in the previous section are wider concepts and frames for strategies. Discriminatory practices, behaviours, attitudes and beliefs are part of the dynamics of human relationships and have impact on settlement and integration. Prejudice, stereotypes and ethnocentrism constitute attitudes and beliefs about individuals and groups, while discrimination is a behaviour as discussed at greater length in relevant literature.

Prejudice

Prejudice is a prejudgment or attitude about a person or group without verification or examination of the merits of the judgment. Prejudgments can exist about minorities regardless of lack of evidence or evidence to the contrary (Hutchinson 2005; Vander Zanden 1983). Young-Bruehl (1996) stresses the importance of taking into account the differences among different species of prejudices, even though various prejudices have common features. Common features are listed by Young-Bruehl (1996) who states that, psychologically, prejudices all involve some kind of projection of the victimizer's feelings onto the victimized. They all display a dimension of 'us versus them' identification and narcissism. They generally operate as social mechanisms of defence, and they all require social learning or transmission.

Young-Bruehl (1996, 5) states that prejudices are heightened by conditions of uncertainty, rapid change, migrations, and both downward and upward mobility, while being fed by their own histories, accumulated stereotypes and cultural images. Even though differences among the types of prejudices have been neglected (for instance, such as those between racism and anti-Semitism), understanding of the differences is crucial to any education work that attempts to alleviate prejudice effectively. Appreciating the differences allows the diagnoses – differential diagnoses – without which there can be no solutions. It is also evident that prejudices often overlap.

A valuable insight is offered by Young-Bruehl (1996, 3) into processes associated with publicized instances of prejudice. In such cases, prejudice might be manifested in slurs, acts of discrimination, or attack, which phase is itself followed by prejudices that are not necessarily the same ones. These would be manifested in rationalizations, self-serving descriptions, denials and commentaries which often are designed to discredit the victims' truthfulness or belittle their pain. Young-Bruehl (1996) unpacks the prejudice phenomenon, explicating its processes and identifying its different strains and aetiologies. This work generates useful information for purposes of analysing prejudice and for shaping measures to address it from many angles as well as in the different media.

Ethnocentrism

Sumner (1907) first developed the concept of ethnocentrism, which posits that in intergroup situations, the individual's own group would be the central standard, and all other groups would be scaled and rated with reference to it. The ingroup was generally evaluated in a more positive light than the outgroup whenever the individual needed to make a distinction or comparison between groups. Berry (1996) has suggested that ethnocentrism in multiethnic societies of today can become diffused into a more general antipathy towards outgroups.

Young-Bruehl (1996, 184–5) defines ethnocentrism as group prejudices that are 'shared in more or less the same form by members of an existing group, particularly a tradition-directed, relatively homogeneous group'. Ethnocentrism involves 'the practice of putting ones own *ethnos* or group ... at the center of the world, or the culture, as well as at the center of one's attention, and it encompasses negative judgments toward one out-group, or toward a few, or many, or all out-groups'. Ethnocentrisms come with differences of degree and scope that will vary over time and changing circumstances for any given *ethnos*.

Stereotypes

A stereotype is a highly stylized and simplified image of the characteristics of a social category. Stereotyping, on the other hand, is a process where someone attributes to another person characteristics which are seen to be shared by all or most of his or her fellow group members (Brown 1995). Young-Bruehl (1996, 191) refers to stereotypes as 'molds or patterns of evaluation set down upon the world regularly, invariably, monotonously'. Lippmann (1922) wrote that a stereotype is the guarantee of our self-respect and the projection upon the world of our sense of our own value, our own position and our own rights. He further described stereotypes as the fortress of tradition behind which individuals could continue to feel safe in their occupied position.

Mullaly (2002, 84) defines a stereotype as 'a biased, oversimplified, universal, and inflexible conception of a social group', and notes that, although stereotypes may be positive, most stereotypes are harmful and destructive. Thompson (1997; 1998) maintains that stereotypes have a number of characteristics: they defy logic or evidence, and tend to be resistant to challenge and change. They are often unduly negative and thus potentially oppressive. Moreover, they become ingrained, with the result that we can remain unaware of their effect on our perceptions and actions.

Reality is generally too complex to be perceived and comprehended without the use of social categorizations. While these are necessary, they can lead to stereotype formation. People tend to become over-reliant on such categorizations, and eventually can use them indiscriminately. Decision-making at critical gatekeeping points can be based on stereotypical thinking and rationale, leading to discriminatory outcomes, and cumulatively to social closure.

Racism

Racism can be understood as a strategy which involves safeguarding, or shortcutting to, some desired tangible or intangible good, which is pursued or achieved by transferring social and personal costs directly onto the 'other' individual or group. As such, it is unjust action. Other types of discrimination share these features. The effect is also disempowering when the vulnerability of the targeted group is passively reinforced on a social level. Racism involves a unilateral process of devaluing the 'other'. It is particularly damaging because it is an elusive phenomenon and accountability for its negative ramifications is weak. Tacit acceptance of unjust practice in the wider or institutional settings actually serves to diffuse accountability. Berry (1996) states that racism is generally directed against people who are relatively powerless in society and not in a position to avoid or to retaliate against racism. Racism is therefore likely to be long-lasting and particularly harmful to its victims.

Henry et al. (2000) define racism as a system in which one group of people exercises power over another group on the basis of skin colour. It is an implicit or explicit set of beliefs, erroneous assumptions and actions based on an ideology of the inherent superiority of one racial group over another. It is evident in organizational or institutional structures and programmes as well as in individual thought or behaviour patterns. Racial discrimination is defined by Henry et al. (2000, 409) as: 'Any distinction, exclusion, restriction, or preference based on race that has the purpose of nullifying or impairing the recognition, enjoyment, or exercise, on an equal footing, of human rights and fundamental freedoms in the political, economic, social, cultural, or any other field of public life.'

From another perspective, racism is learned and shared by members of a society. Racism is learned as part of the enculturation process – the process of learning one's culture (Kottak 2000). While individuals have free will and culture does not determine behaviour, it does condition people to think and behave in certain ways. Enculturation can foster the transmission of racist perspectives from one generation to the next. Since racism is learned behaviour, it can be unlearned, and should be amenable to interventive measures (Hutchinson 2005).

Racism can be characterized as unsolicited and unwarranted violence – whether it be physical or mental, covert or overt, since were they allowed to, members of non-dominant groups would choose not to experience the social and psychological manifestations of racism (Dobbins and Skillings 2000). In the same vein as Berry (1996) above, these authors state that invariably there is also a large power imbalance between the dominant group and the outgroup, and that the obvious functional advantages associated with this (for those who hold power) means that the system will tend to be self-perpetuating. Dobbins and Skillings (2000) state further that there are profound repercussions at the individual level for both the targets of racism and the recipients of privilege in such a brutal system, since, as a violent form of social distancing, racism depersonalizes and dehumanizes. Racism thus holds the potential to be deeply damaging to those in the target group. At the same time, it depletes the human qualities of groups and individuals who hold racist views.

Quillian (1995, 591) offers four conceptual approaches that are informed by the work of Blumer (1958), Blalock (1967) and Lieberson (1980):

- Racial prejudice is conceptualized as the result of a feeling by the dominant group that their prerogatives are threatened by the subordinate group, which adopts prejudice as a response to perceived threat
- The size of the subordinate group relative to the dominant group is seen as a major demographic cause of perceived threat
- Outgroups are more threatening when the economic situation of a host country is precarious
- Specific individual level characteristics predict which individuals are most at risk for developing prejudicial attitudes when their group prerogatives are threatened. The more the dominant group is threatened, then the stronger the association between some specific characters and prejudice (Quillian 1995, 591).

Xenophobia

Xenophobia means, literally, fear of strangers (from the Greek 'xenos' for strange and 'phobia', a fear or aversion). If racism and xenophobia are to be distinguished, racism can be seen as relying on ideas of inferiority, where xenophobia relies on ideas of fundamental differences between cultures (Cashmore 1996). Stating that xenophobia is an attitude that is thought to be inherent in human nature, Stocke (1999) proposes that it constitutes the ideological underpinning of cultural fundamentalism, accounting for people's alleged tendency to value their own culture to the exclusion of any other. Contemporary cultural fundamentalism is based on two assumptions: that different cultures are incompatible, and that, because humans are inherently ethnocentric, relations between cultures are antagonistic by nature.

Discrimination

Discrimination is the behavioural and action expression of the attitudinal qualities
of prejudice, ethnocentrism, racism and xenophobia. Discrimination can also be
a function of pure self-interest, and is understood as the practices and actions that
make unjust use of differences or diversity. Strains of discrimination include those
based on racial, ethnocentric, xenophobic and other types of negative prejudices.
These actions promulgate or sustain inequality in human relations in a society.

An understanding of the distinction between individual racism and systemic
racism is important for understanding the forces that impact on settlement and
integration in multiethnic societies. According to Henry et al. (2000), individual
racism is a form of racial discrimination that stems from conscious, personal
prejudice. Systemic racism or discrimination consists of policies and practices
which are entrenched in established institutions. This results in the exclusion or
advancement of specific groups of people. It manifests itself in two ways: (1)
institutional racism, or racial discrimination that derives from individuals carrying
out the dictates of others who are prejudiced or of a prejudiced society; and (2)
structural racism, that is, inequalities rooted in the system-wide operation of a
society that excludes substantial numbers of members of particular groups from
significant participation in major social institutions.

On Shaping Anti-discrimination Interventions

Since discrimination derives basic features from context, it is difficult to delineate
prescriptive approaches to it. However, it is possible to discuss some of the more
general principles which might be helpful in shaping interventions.

Positive action would need to be broad-based both strategically and conceptually.
Large-scale social actions serve to heighten awareness about problems in equity
and equality, and set the stage for laws and policies that provide an institutional
context for change (Dobbins and Skillings 2000). Gibelman (2000) argues for
anti-discrimination to be defined in terms of the larger public good or that which
is in the interest of all segments of society, rather than as competition between
individual or group interests. The author elaborates further that 'the problem needs
to be reframed in a way that better addresses the educational, social and economic
conditions which continue to challenge the concepts of a society that espouses
equality and equity for all' (Gibelman 2000, 164). The universality of the gender
equality movement, for example, is a potential precursor for large-scale anti-
discrimination efforts.

Anti-discrimination effort should establish a high profile in the civil society
arena where much negotiation around forces of equity and racism takes place. The
effectiveness of anti-discriminatory action would call for broad-based strategies,
support and appeal in order to engage that particular range of actors which would
be pivotal in carrying issues forward to transformative stage. Vigorous civil society
debate would pull discrimination issues out of the private realm into the public

sphere, where it could emerge from its de facto status into a social problem with social costs, thereby becoming amenable to concrete actions and accountability mechanisms.

The use of the findings of scientific research can be critical. Young-Bruehl (1996, 90–92) presents the case of Kenneth Clark's effective use of research findings in bringing about a shift in ideas and policy. Clark's (1953; 1955; 1965) empirical studies of desegregated schools in the USA provided evidence for countering the then prevailing belief that the social change sequence in anti-discrimination measures, for example, required attitudinal changes before structural and institutional changes could or should be undertaken. The use of scientific evidence in this case lent effective support for the idea that situationally determined behavioural changes can precede attitudinal changes, and for the position that initiatives for positive action should not be disallowed on the grounds that attitudinal change had not yet taken place. This is an extremely important point and at the crux of much policy-making where the idea still prevails that attitudinal changes are a necessary step before policy and organizational changes for combatting discrimination can be made and put in place (see Young-Bruehl 1996).

Gibelman (2000, 165) writes that 'social workers need to be able to actively apply social planning knowledge and policy development skills to identify new solutions. It is time for the profession to lend its expertise to the collection and analysis of empirical data on the outcomes of the past, present and future approaches to end discrimination.'

Societal-level Phenomena

Marginalization

Marginalization and exclusion refer to individuals' and groups' positioning in society. As the term suggests, marginalization refers to the ways in which certain groups of people are placed at the margins of society, and thus are not part of the mainstream. This situation can be understood as developing when people cannot participate fully in social, political and economic activities. To be marginalized is to occupy a precarious and peripheral status that is detached from many of the main institutions.

Social Exclusion

The term 'social exclusion' was adopted by the European Commission to describe the inequalities and barriers to full participation in otherwise affluent societies. Sociologists adopted the terminology, drawing a distinction between social exclusion and poverty. Social exclusion means not sharing the same opportunities as the majority. This may be due to social isolation, as in the case of elderly or disabled people, or through discrimination based on nationality, language, 'race' or religion. The denial of human rights to any category of persons is also a form of social exclusion (Richmond 1994, 40).

Robert Castel (1996) distinguishes three zones of organization and social cohesion: the zone of integration, the zone of vulnerability characterized by precariousness of employment and fragility of relational supports, and a third zone, that of exclusion or extreme marginality. The zone of vulnerability produces extreme situations at its borders and is the strategic region. Vulnerability designates the crumbling of social ties before they break.

The concept of social exclusion has featured in French discourse to refer to poverty and inequality. In 1990 the European Observatory on National Policies to Combat Social Exclusion was established by the Commission of the European Community. The principal focus of the Observatory's work has been on the effectiveness of different national, regional and local policies. While social exclusion was defined by the Observatory in relation to the social rights of citizenship, the aim was also to study multiple, persisting and cumulative disadvantage, as well as processes of generalized and persisting disadvantage, which undermine people's social and occupational participation. A central issue has been whether persons suffering disadvantages in obtaining education, training, employment, housing and financial resources have substantially lower chances than the rest of the population of gaining access to the major social institutions.

Silver (1994, 536) observes that, while the concept of exclusion remains 'vague … multidimensional and elastic', the term is now being used to denote the changing nature of social disadvantage in western societies. Silver (1994) introduces three paradigms of social exclusion which account, from three different perspectives, for economic disadvantages such as poverty and long-term unemployment. These are the 'solidarity', 'specialization' and 'monopoly' paradigms which are based on the philosophies of republicanism, liberalism and social democracy respectively. In the *solidarity* paradigm, exclusion occurs when the social bond between the individual and the society, known as social solidarity, breaks down. This is based on the Durkheimian tradition that focuses on social bonds, organic solidarity and social order.

The *specialization* paradigm conceptualizes the social order and the economic and political spheres as networks of voluntary exchanges between autonomous individuals with their own interests and motivations. Specialization processes or social differentiation in the market and in social groups arise as a consequence of the differences among individuals. Group boundaries might impede the freedom of individuals to participate in social exchanges, resulting in exclusion. Thus in this paradigm, exclusion is a form of 'discrimination' that is a consequence of specialization or social differentiation. In the *monopoly* paradigm, exclusion is an outcome of the interplay of class, status and political power, and serves the interests of the included. The monopoly creates a bond of common interest between insiders who might be otherwise unequal. The result is social 'closure' when institutions and cultural distinctions not only create boundaries that keep others out against their will, but are also used to perpetuate inequality. Silver (1994) says that these boundaries of exclusion may be drawn within or between nation-states, localities, firms or social groups. Exclusion, in the monopoly model, can be combated through citizenship and the extension of equal membership and full participation in the community to outsiders. The Swedish model has been classified as belonging to the monopoly paradigm.

According to Gore (1995), the concept of social exclusion is of value and relevance for policy analysis in the following ways. First, it describes the current state of affairs, going beyond economic and social aspects of poverty to embrace political aspects such as political rights and citizenship which outline a relationship between the individual and the state. Second, the concept facilitates analytical understanding of the inter-relationships between poverty, employment and social integration. Third, social exclusion, when it is understood as a normative concept, raises questions about social justice.

Employment and Integration

Employment is recognized as a crucial area of settlement. Indeed immigrants' social inclusion in the new home society is often linked first of all to their integration in the labour market, and then, to a lesser degree, on other forms of social, economic and political inclusion. Disproportionate and persistent high levels of immigrant unemployment, their non-representation across different occupational sectors and their absence in higher level positions are an indication of closure, discrimination and low 'glass ceilings'.

In the economic sphere, while high immigrant unemployment constitutes the under-utilization of human capital, for the affected individuals themselves, unemployment means being on the outside of formal value-producing circles. They are placed at a disadvantage in being denied 'scarce' resources such as employment in social allocation processes (see Bovenkerk, Miles and Verbunt 1990). The individual has to expend a great deal of effort in extended job search and to deal with the lack of employment, especially if this is of long duration and without a more positive prospect in view.

Sen (1997) has portrayed the situation with the aim not only of improving understanding of the nature and effects of unemployment, but also of facilitating the fashioning of appropriate policy responses. His work scrutinizes unemployment from many angles. This information is useful for settlement practitioners who work in communities and who carry out settlement work that is directly or indirectly affected by the spectrum of employment and unemployment experiences. Sen's (1997) analysis of the phenomenon is wide ranging and insightful, helping us to draw many salient parallels with situations of settlement and integration.

Sen (1997, 156) first of all draws attention to the fact that, on the national level, unemployment cuts down the national output and increases the share of the output that has to be devoted to income transfers. For the individual, unemployment signifies a basic loss of freedom and a risk of social exclusion. When locked into a state of unemployment, and even when materially supported by social insurance, the individual is not able to exercise freedom of choice. This loss of freedom is seen by many unemployed people as a crucial deprivation, making unemployment a major causal factor predisposing people to social exclusion. The exclusion applies not only to economic opportunities, but also to social activities, such as participation in the life of the community, which may be quite problematic for jobless people.

Sen (1997) points out that a serious loss in the long term is that of skill. Individuals can become de-skilled when out of work and practice, without the opportunity of keeping up with their occupation. Prolonged joblessness can be damaging for morale. This is also associated with motivational decline and resignation, which can be detrimental to the search for future employment. Sen (1997) observes further that the loss of human relationships caused by unemployment may weaken harmony and coherence within the family, consequences which are related to some extent to the decline of self-confidence, in addition to the drop in economic means. In some cases, a crisis of identity can be involved in this type of disruption.

When jobs are scarce, Sen (1997) reminds us that the groups most affected are often minorities, which worsens the prospects for easy integration of legal immigrants into the regular life of mainstream society. Unemployment thus feeds the politics of intolerance and racism. With regard to civic life, Sen (1997) observes an effect on social values and responsibility. There is evidence that large-scale unemployment has a tendency to weaken some social values. People in continued unemployment can develop cynicism about the fairness of social arrangements and also a perception of dependence on others. Sen (1997) concludes that social cohesion faces many difficulties in a society that features a majority of people with comfortable jobs and a minority of unemployed people in a peripheral situation.

In the public sphere, employment is the basis of a robust role in the society, which allows for social positioning that is difficult to achieve otherwise (Valtonen 1998). On the scale of the group or community, social positioning generally denotes greater power and voice in public life, alongside other groups in society. Immigrants intend to participate in value-producing activity and to contribute on a par with other citizens. Being debarred from this activity and role cannot be compensated for by generous social security measures. The situation of disproportionately high immigrant unemployment is an indication that social justice is elusive for newer citizens. This situation can be interpreted from a social work perspective. Despite generally progressive views on social rights within social work, such a situation is a stark reminder of a much earlier era when the profession was battling to bring social justice principles to the forefront, ahead of charity as the fundamental value.

Drawing closer to personal and interpersonal spaces, employment is a prime source of self-actualization, self-development and continuing education and training opportunities. Moreover, the workplace can also be the locus of a significant amount of social activity and networking for individuals. In other words, individuals can locate opportunities to meet the basic needs for achievement, affiliation and power through employment (see McClelland 1955).

What are the background factors impacting on labour market inclusion and exclusion? There is considerable variation in different receiving contexts. Macro-level economic conditions, such as recession, affect the 'climate' of the labour market, as well as restructuring of work and employment. There are different configurations of facilitating and inhibiting factors that affect hiring, labour mobility and promotion. However, it is possible to identify some of the central mechanisms which immigrants encounter in their job search and in the course of their employment activity.

The 'glass ceiling' phenomenon has been examined in relation to the situation of women and minorities. Glass ceilings have generally been studied in the higher levels of management and professional life. However, in the case of immigrants, this ceiling could in actuality operate at a much lower level, affecting upward social mobility at an earlier point. Woo (2000, 15) explains that, although race and ethnicity are very much a part of our consciousness, the majority of glass ceiling barriers involve 'subtle biases, sometimes imperceptible or ineffable, quietly or unconsciously reproduced. Some are embedded into the routines or practices of institutions, other reflected in attitudinal orientations, which over time chisel racially contoured outcomes into the workplace experience, even when there is no discriminatory intent.'

Employment equity legislation, policies and measures have been established in a large number of receiving countries. Nonetheless there is wide variation in the range and efficacy of mechanisms for complaint and redress. In Canada, for example, such mechanisms are officially implemented through various well-known channels such as the ombudsman system and through human rights organizations. Immigrants who experience discrimination, especially in those situations where the complaint process is burdensome and not known to be effective, do not willingly lodge official complaints. The results are not predictable, in addition to which they run the risk of reprisals which is not in the interest of their long-term settlement. Discrimination in general seldom reaches the stage of official complaint since, in addition to being burdensome or impossible to prove, many individuals cannot afford its social costs.

Signalling theory suggests that employers do not have proper or adequate information about job applicants' human capital and will seek informational shortcuts, or signals, that indicate academic skill levels and work habits. Miller and Rosenbaum's (1997) study of youth labour market problems examines employer behaviour in hiring through interviews in 51 firms in Chicago and its western suburbs. Their findings suggest that employers may not only need to receive information but to receive it in the context of a social infrastructure that reassures them of its trustworthiness and relevance. If we extrapolate these findings to the situation of immigrant applicants, it is evident that they would hardly be in a position to benefit from such strategic circuits of information, and would be at a de facto disadvantage in such processes.

Long-term unemployment in the case of immigrant professionals is possibly a fundamental problem of the *non-commodification* of their labour. Unless equivalency procedures are undertaken competently and rigorously, with their results recognized as currency on the labour market, more highly educated immigrants will in practice be excluded from employment. Weak representation of immigrants in the professions and at higher occupational levels, disproportionate to their availability, is an indication of problems of access or non-commodification of their labour. When severe occupational downgrading is the condition of becoming employed, we can speak of chronic immigrant underemployment or immigrant professional underemployment. Matinheikki-Kokko, Koivumaki and Kuortti (2003) studied how career counselling affects the employment prospects of highly educated immigrants. On the basis of the participants' experiences, along with the labour market services that were provided, counselling succeeded in supporting the professional identity of the individuals and their propensity to continue education, labour market training or practical training. However, it could do little to help the participants to find a permanent place in the labour market, which the authors concluded would call for structural changes in working life.

The Logic of Discrimination

The causes, processes and consequences of discrimination are recurring themes in integration literature, which tells of the gravity of its implications for the integration process. It also tells of the 'resilience' of the phenomenon. Discrimination, as Woo (2000) observes, can be endemic in practices in the institutional settings. This section examines some of the dynamics that can lead to discriminatory practice in the institutional context, arguing that such subsets of the formal structure comprise basic elements of the systemic phenomenon. In other words, we seek to understand the dynamics of systemic discrimination in the institutional or organizational setting.

Stereotypical and negatively discriminating categorizations of immigrant (or other categories) as the 'other' can take root, even unwittingly, in organizational settings and in time covertly bias the rationale for hiring and promotion policies and decisions. Attitudes of prejudice are generally not shared by all members of the collectivity, but can come to be tolerated, sometimes even seen as a 'necessity', in the interest of cohesion and working consensus. Attitudes of discrimination can be found in leadership, but not necessarily so since modern organizations seek a flatter power structure and some form of democratic or participatory decision-making. An organizational actor with a base of informal or formal power can project an attitude outward into the organization. A very critical factor would be leadership style, capacity, ethical characteristics and skills, as well as the effective use of these. An alternative situation is leadership abdication – thin or minimal leadership, and the activation and assertion of other informal sources of power. Negatively discriminating categorizations can spring from small beginnings and become accommodated into the organizational culture in time. If they merge into part of its logic for survival, to try to resist this system of logic becomes tantamount to questioning the legitimacy of the organization and its main decision-makers.

Discriminatory thinking is indeed closely linked to routine processes of categorization, ordering and ranking, which are basic preliminary steps for decision-making, including hiring decisions. Discriminatory patterns and categorizations are also potential vehicles for the distribution of privilege in certain ways. Applied in hiring and promotion processes, they are a singular mechanism for clustering resources, or, to use Tilly's (1998) concept, 'opportunity hoarding'. Employment is indeed a significant value-producing opportunity for individuals, as it is for society as a whole.

A key supporting condition is the decision of other members of the organizational collectivity to acquiesce, adapt or be blind to discriminatory practices. Tilly's (1998) model of durable inequality refers to processes of 'adaptation' and 'emulation'. It is important to note that these systems might not be the direct product of individuals' racial and cultural encounter. They might be lodged in protective energies around common or individual interests and be reinforced in a social capital network, for example. Eventually practices that discriminate can become lodged in the institutional or organizational culture, at which point such practice can take shelter in the procedures, regulations and the very mechanisms that are formally supposed to eradicate such phenomena.

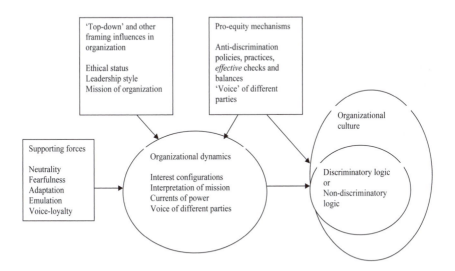

Figure 5.1 Logics of discrimination in organizational culture

In Figure 5.1, organizational dynamics are the main field of action but are impacted upon by many different forces. Leadership style, mission and goals, and ethical status frame and ideally guide organizational action. In the central field of dynamics, configurations of interests, including individual and group interests, have a bearing on how the mission is interpreted and translated into decision-making. Different actors in the organization use voice[1] and, depending on the organizational environment, are able to debate and contribute input into processes from different perspectives, and take a concurring or a dissenting stance. Organizational processes of decision-making are also subject to the play of power, both formal and informal.

Organizational actors who are not actively participating in the dynamic field still have a very weighty role. They might disengage from the processes for various reasons. Fear of reprisal is sometimes a well-grounded reason. The 'voice-loyalty' group are those who, in Hirschman's (1972) pyramidal model, 'speak up' but select the loyalty option over exit. The neutral actors form a de facto supporting force for the legitimizing of whatever decisions emerge out of the central field of organizational dynamics.

Equity mechanisms are critical in moderating and balancing internal processes. These are left at a formal level if not implemented into effective and functioning instruments of checks and balances. When equity structures are not in place or lie dormant, the responsibility for equity promotion is devolved to individual voice and action, and can be thereby externalized from institutional responsibility.

The argument made here is that the logic for discriminatory or non-discriminatory practice emerges from organizational process and dynamics before becoming established in organizational culture. If the discriminatory outcome is occurring frequently across institutions, it is a reflection of formal but not substantial equity. This is experienced by immigrants as systemic discrimination. It is interesting to note that wider discriminatory phenomena do not necessarily reflect general attitudes, but can be the *default outcome* of different combinations of dynamics in organizations, or the lack of effective equity mechanisms.

Equity promoting and positive action measures are the most critical interventions in the area of immigrant access in order to operationalize formally legislated equality. A wide range of anti-discrimination mechanisms for organizational application is available: such mechanisms have been shaped, demonstrated and are being used in different settlement settings. Equity promoting mechanisms can in actuality function as instruments of empowerment and reinforcement for leadership and pro-equity voices and actors. The need for systems of equity and accountability in labour market practice is clear. Without effective mechanisms, newer citizens' access is likely to be subject to processes that are contrary to the principles of social citizenship.

---

1   See Hirschman (1972).

Closing Comments

The phenomena of inequality and discrimination which are scrutinized in this chapter are generally disturbing, especially since they exist alongside legislative frameworks and within institutions that proclaim opposing principles. A gap between declared principles and practice can be interpreted in many ways, and thereby addressed through various approaches. The strategy using leadership in an equity and social justice-promoting function has been given less weight compared to the conventional focus on management, efficiency and areas of decision-making related to the mission of the organization. It is argued here that major responsibility as well as accountability for the promotion of equitable practices should lie with leadership, rather than being devolved to the level of the very individuals or groups who are affected by unequal conditions.

Chapter 6
Practice Modes for Settlement Social Work

The themes in this chapter open up the arena of intervention. Skill areas that deserve special emphasis in the field of immigrant settlement and integration are organized according to the three-tiered category of macro, meso and micro levels. The macro/meso/micro frame has always been a straightforward approach to organizing practice levels in social work. The scale of the client constituency to a large extent guides our approach and choice of strategy, in addition to which we pitch our work to reach different audiences in order to shape effective interventions. There is overlap in the macro, meso and micro areas as is evidenced in the Person-In-Environment approaches, empowerment, systems and ecological models, with their focus on individuals, the environment/social structure and the transactions and relationships that connect the two. Ecological approaches emphasize the goodness of fit between people and their social environment, and the role of the practitioner in working for and with resources in order to promote better synchronization of individuals with their environment. These approaches recall core questions in sociology that focus upon the linkage between structure, agency and process.

In this chapter, the macro section covers social action strategies and roles that include policy advocacy as part of policy practice, participation in the public discourse and coalition building. Interventions that involve wider engagement with political actors and decision-makers are less common in the field. In settlement practice, this area of activity would add value and reinforce the range of other settlement interventions. The full potential of settlement work spans societal arenas which are not within conventionally perceived social service provisioning but are important sites of participatory engagement in settlement, making an inclusive approach to practice an imperative for effective and holistic interventions.

In the meso section, I engage in the discussion of community and types of community as the immediate environment of the person and an area in which interventions can be targeted at the level of the collectivity. The community is discussed as an arena with an infrastructural fabric of human relations and as a field of affective and productive action. The total community, in all its complexities, is far greater than the sum of its parts, and is a collective level actor in the settlement and integration process. Community work offers practitioners the opportunity to broaden their base of contextual knowledge and to build 'emic' perspectives on the settlement experience of immigrant communities.

The micro section focuses on psychosocial facets of integration and personal processes of adaptation. The inter-related strengths, empowerment, resilience and ecological approaches are discussed in this section. In connection with the focus on strengths, the final section looks at sources of power and 'forms of capital' as resources for settlement.

Macro-level Settlement Practice

Advocacy is one of the time-honoured modes of practice, and its salience grows with the high profiling of the political role of the profession in promoting social justice (Haynes and Mickelson 1991). Satka and Karvinen (1999) write of the Finnish context that the problems which social workers currently deal with are very complex, to the extent that they often require more interpretation and advocacy than diagnosis and prescription. Advocacy is significant in settlement work, where client communities are often without channels of 'voice' in mainstream society, and with low rates of participation in the political process for a long time. In many settlement contexts they are also weakly represented at social and institutional levels from which their interests could be directly articulated and promoted. Advocacy brings issues and ideas into the public domain, where policy initiatives are sparked, contested and given preliminary direction. Jansson (2003) states that policies rarely emerge suddenly, but take shape through a developmental process. Policy advocates need both to understand this process and to be able to work skilfully within it. In the pursuit of social justice in the twenty-first century, social workers need to acknowledge the political dimensions of all levels of practice and to engage in multifaceted struggles to regain influence in the public arena (Reisch 2002). Advocacy is a prime tool for addressing this area in which effective participation often eludes newcomers.

Advocacy is understood as the act of directly representing, defending, intervening, supporting or recommending a course of action on behalf of one or more individuals, groups or communities, with the goal of securing or retaining social justice (Haynes and Mickelson 1991). It is a process by which people are given a previously denied say on issues that concern them, and this can turn paper entitlements into real rights (Bereford and Croft 1993). Advocacy signals the necessity to validate the experience of clients and patients and ensure that their rights, wishes and needs are met (Leadbetter 1998). It can be seen also as an empowerment approach since it is concerned with a shift of power or emphasis towards meeting the needs and rights of people who otherwise would be marginalized or oppressed.

Jansson (2003) makes a distinction between policy practice and more closely targeted policy advocacy. According to Jansson (2003) the more encompassing area of *policy practice* comprises the efforts to change policies in legislative, agency and community settings, through establishing new policies, improving existing ones, or defeating the policy initiatives of other people. Thus by this definition, people of all ideological persuasions, including liberals, radicals and conservatives, can engage in policy practice, and indeed the observation of the tactics of the opposing side can be highly educational. It is in the interest of practitioners to become skilled in policy practice as this will increase the odds that their policy preferences will be carried forward.

Policy Advocacy

Policy advocacy is seen by Jansson (2003) as a subset of policy practice, referring to policy practice that aims at helping powerless groups and minorities to improve their resources and opportunities. Policy advocacy is focused in this sense on a certain area of need or disadvantage among groups with less power. Jansson (2003) states that since social workers usually work with people who are relatively powerless, policy advocacy is the level of policy practice which is generally undertaken. The lack of power in immigrant client constituencies largely derives from their positioning in society as newcomers, and the fact that they have not previously been in the active circuits of social citizenship. In time, settling groups build their social resources and expertise base for directly addressing their interests through citizenship channels. Ideally they begin to acquire the types of power needed to ensure that the interests of their communities are addressed as part of the spectrum of concerns in the national agenda. This process is determined in large measure by the pace of integration into the societal and institutional structures.

Ezell (2001) differentiates between policy advocacy and case work advocacy which is carried out in the course of any practice setting in which caseworkers or micro-practitioners undertake advocacy efforts. There is some overlap, but many direct work interventions do not extend to or reach the scope of policy advocacy.

The process of bringing issues forward to agency, community and legislative decision-makers involves a series of policy advocacy task areas. Drawing on the work of Jansson (2003, 13, 73) these can be briefly outlined in six areas. *Agenda-setting tasks* occur when practitioners gauge whether the context is favourable for a policy initiative, and engage in proactive strategy to have it placed on the policy-makers' agendas. *Problem-analyzing tasks* employ the use of pertinent social science research on the cause, nature and prevalence of the specific problems. This is a significant tool in building the rationale for policy initiatives although the link is weak in the sequence of processes through which research results find their way into the arsenal of information needed by policy-makers and policy stakeholders. (This is discussed further in Chapter 10.) *Proposal development and writing tasks* involve creating solutions to specific problems, by developing legislation or proposals for the improvement of social programmes. *Policy-enacting tasks* are carried out by developing strategies for having a policy approved. Strategies might consume much time and effort, since they invariably involve a degree of negotiation and compromise. Policy advocates need to be vigilant to avoid compromises that would diminish the substance of the policy being proposed. However, on favourable occasions, the strategy to gain approval of a policy might simply involve presenting a position at one critical meeting. *Policy-implementing tasks* may give rise to considerable conflict as interest groups such as unions, professionals, civil servants, legislators, state officials and other stakeholders try to influence the priorities and directions of social programmes. Finally *policy-assessing tasks* consist of evaluating policy and identifying necessary changes when evaluation so recommends.

Jansson (2003, 74) also identifies four basic skills for undertaking effective policy advocacy. Analytic skills are needed for evaluating social problems and for assessing their severity. This is the basis for the development of policy proposals and creating strategies for overcoming barriers to policy implementation. Policy advocates require political skills to gain and to use different types of power as part of their political strategies. Interactional skills facilitate participation in task groups, committees and coalitions. Interactional skills are a great asset in persuading others to support specific policies. Value-clarifying skills are needed for identifying and ranking relevant principles when engaging in policy practice.

The general task area of gathering and mediating information strategically involves the responsibility of informing state policy-makers on matters related to policy proposals. Jackson-Elmore (2005) sets out the following related task areas:

1. Targeting information to legislative aides and the staff of legislative committees
2. Inviting legislative staff and legislators to workshops and policy forums in order to inform them of agency and project goals and public policy implications
3. Identifying and working with local grass-roots organizations to learn about findings and results from innovative projects
4. Partnering with national and local ethnic associations to inform policy-makers about demonstration and community project goals and corresponding policy recommendations
5. Translating research findings to policy briefings, bulletins and other mechanisms for informing practice and policy-making
6. Building meaningful relationships with legislators who have prior experience and expertise in a particular policy area.

Since a large part of the necessary information is often not widely available, and not yet generated in research or more grounded situational analyses, legislators, including ethnic minority legislators, must turn to alternative sources. Of particular importance in sourcing requisite information are grass-roots organizations, ethnic associations, conferences and annual meetings, local branches of state or national organizations, and the internet. Significantly, legislators are more likely to rely on information obtained from sources with which they have the most in common (Jackson-Elmore 2005).

Ezell (2001) refers to *agency advocacy* as a set of tactics and activities which are used to bring about changes in programmes and agencies for the benefit of clients.

Frequently targeted aspects are ineffective intervention and service approaches; inappropriate behaviour by workers; the failure to co-ordinate programmes with other services; inadequate or misdirected outreach; and lack of accountability on service use and outcomes. The target of change might be an individual agency or group of agencies, their policy and practice, or the municipal and national levels (in the case of more tightly co-ordinated systems).

Advocacy brings a singular opportunity for engaging in the public space in action that is rooted in the client constituency's concerns. The process benefits from a strong issue-focused thrust and from grounded synergies that lend much authenticity to its mission. Policy-makers are often far removed from the lived experience of citizen groups, and especially that of newer groups. Involvement in advocacy activity, moreover, is a prime training ground for settling groups to acquire civic insights and skills of value for resolving other integration-related issues. In the process of defining and documenting problems, community members can also discover a commonality of interest across groups. The capacity-building element comes to the fore in advocacy on behalf of and in partnership with immigrant client communities.

Sheafor, Horejsi and Horejsi (2000) offer some very practical guidelines on the human skills required in the political arena. The guidelines would have policy advocates hold to their principles without being ideological; be political without being partisan; be respectful of those with whom they disagree without being soft or compromising; and be active and engaged without being used and manipulated.

In immigration and settlement matters in particular, policy advocates need to be prepared to encounter and deal competently with opposition from persons and groups with opposing views and sometimes hostile attitudes and mistaken beliefs about the nature of specific immigration and integration issues. Countering misinformation in the public sphere is indeed a part of the settlement practice portfolio, since practitioners possess a base of authentic practice-based knowledge on the actual settlement situation of immigrants and refugees. This also puts them in the position of knowing how policies and programmes could be made more effective. Participation in the wider immigration debate requires entering societal discourses around questions of national identity, values, culture shift and societal change.

Change Agent: Social Action Models in Social Work

Social action models take on significance in the course of advocacy in settlement matters. Familiarity with these can assist us in shaping issue-relevant approaches. I draw here on Haynes and Mickelson's (1991, 8) three models of social action: 'citizen social worker', 'agent of social change' and 'actionist'.

Citizen social worker calls for the social worker to use information and knowledge gained through practice to inform the wider society of needed programmes and policies. The citizen social worker in this capacity confronts problems of civil rights and equality of opportunity, for example, as a concerned citizen, not as a professional obligation. Knowledge of social issues, problems, resources, policy and (as far as possible) on root causes of problems is an imperative. In this capacity the settlement social worker would not be pursuing narrow interest issues, but those of the wider field or the 'common good', such as, for example, the broad challenges of immigration in society and alternative approaches to this.

Agent of social change refers to roles that aim at producing change in institutional relations and policies, for example, to humanize social policies and bureaucratic procedures (see Needleman and Needleman 1974), doing this, however, through non-disruptive tactics. Social workers enter the political arena and develop skills in dealing more effectively with the community power structure. There is emphasis on working from within agency or community structures. Existing institutional arrangements are challenged through legitimate means (see Blau 1992). Disruptive tactics, such as protests or strikes, are seen as counterproductive in that they obstruct the operations of the target system.

Actionists believe that social change, particularly for disaffiliated people or groups, can be achieved only through the development and use of political, economic, or social pressure. Without being opposed to co-operation and collaboration as strategies, the actionist has more often been identified with attempts to develop power strategies. The professional's identification with organizations and with social sanctions is rejected by actionists, who instead hold conflict and bargaining to be superior strategies for bringing about change. Actionists place more importance on the sanction of the group with which they are identified, rather than the social sanction of the profession. This model holds appeal through its ideological identification with society's 'victims'. It emphasizes the need for social work to support the efforts of the disaffiliated to develop power and fulfil their needs. As such it also falls into the category of empowering practice.

Haynes and Mickelson's (1991, 8) model thus offers tools for conceptualizing approaches to settlement issues in the public sphere. The role of agent of social change generally tends to be the preferred mode of the profession. The first has the practitioner in the role of an informed and politically active private citizen, and the third as a member of a temporary coalition.

Coalitions

Working with or managing inter-organizational actors comprises a competency area of growing importance for settlement work. It is an approach to collaborative engagement with the spectrum of institutional actors who are stakeholders and potential stakeholders in settlement and integration questions.

In their study of 40 diverse social change coalitions in the metropolitan New York/New Jersey area, Mizrahi and Rosenthal (1993) found social workers and other human services leaders to be increasingly leading or representing their organizations on coalitions. Social change coalitions open up the possibilities of cultivating and deepening working relationships among and across diverse groups. The authors emphasize that success depends as much on creating an inclusive and flexible process as on a fixed structure or realistic goals. Coalitions are dynamic, and are fuelled by the sustained commitment and contributions of people, the strategic use of relationships, and competent leadership. Their findings affirm that sophisticated and experienced leaders are necessary for sustaining and using coalitions as vehicles for community improvement and social change.

Bacharach and Lawler (1980) state that the pragmatic bases of coalition formation are usually categorized on the one hand as a quest for resources and power. On the other hand, the ideological bases of coalition formation usually include some specific value-based commitment to a cause or to a general concept of the 'public interest' or the 'common good'. This dual motivation of pragmatism and ideology thus drives coalitions. Issues related both to ideology and utility need to be appreciated and addressed, since the organizational stakes in joining a social change coalition are related to both these motivational factors.

Coalitions can be seen as located between single-issue organizations and social movements (Mizrahi and Rosenthal 1993). When understood as forms of political behaviour, coalitions can alternatively be categorized as social movement organizations (McAdam, McCarthy and Zald 1988). A social movement is defined as a sustained campaign of claim-making, using repeated performances that advertise the claim, based on organizations, networks, traditions and solidarities that sustain these activities (Tilly and Tarrow 2006). Social movements employ contentious politics. According to Tilly and Tarrow (2006, 4), 'contention involves making claims that bear on someone else's interests', while contentious politics involve interactions in which 'actors make claims bearing on someone else's interests, leading to coordinated efforts on behalf of shared interests or programs, in which governments are involved as targets, initiators of claims, or third parties. Contentious politics thus brings together three familiar features of social life: contention, collective action and politics.'

McAdam (1995) has pointed out that the seeds of social movements take root in the fertile ground of pre-existing social networks where people communicate every day, develop close affective ties, and share cultural values and practices. In a similar vein Taylor (2000) observes that it is important that those seeking to create a social movement keep in mind that movements take root in the everyday networks of participants This is what gives social movements in complex society their hidden quality.

Some coalitions can be formed as a mechanism for maximizing existing bases of collegial and expert power to exert pressure from an organizational platform. The members of the coalition need not all be organization based. However, in some situations a significant representation of organizational actors has a greater chance of being 'heard' in institution-based decision-making circles.

The Meso Level in Settlement Practice

Generic approaches to community work lend themselves to meso-level settlement work. This section will focus largely on perspectives on the activities, relationships and functions of ethnic communities which represent microcosms of settlement and integration processes. The ethnic communities are the sites of informal structures which usually develop spontaneously many years before formal organized activity. Individuals and families locate circles of compatible people. In the initial period of settlement immigrants often interact more frequently with fellow countrymen for obvious reasons of shared language and culture. Networks based on common ethnic origin tend to arise naturally in the new home society. A comparable level of interaction with other groups and with the majority society – Kallen's (1995) 'primary structural integration' stage of integration – becomes feasible as immigrants grow in understanding of the culture, learn new social behaviours, and find areas of commonality that lead to meaningful interaction.

Interaction and mutual assistance flourish in ethnic circles and sub-groupings, and are especially valuable in the early settlement period when other contacts have not yet been made. The informal social group of fellow countrymen and countrywomen has a very pragmatic role. Practical help of all kinds is exchanged, with newcomers being generally readily admitted into these circles of social interdependence. Through its field of transactions and links, the social group can provide much tangible and intangible support. Interpreting, assisting with official transactions, help with caring for children, household assistance in sickness and other problem situations, financial help and emotional support are some of the forms in which mutual help is rendered.

In some cases, the vibrant social interaction can be attributed to folk ways in the original culture, where reciprocity and interdependence are important aspects of culture. These mechanisms are part of the time-honoured institutions that have sustained communities over time (Graham 2002). The coming together in the settlement environment of communities' own institutions of interaction and interdependence and the formal helping system in the new society can achieve the synthesis of a very robust arrangement that contributes to the quality of life of immigrants in settlement. The private and social spaces of life can be sites of productive and meaningful relations that help to meet tangible and less tangible needs which do not and cannot fall into the portfolio of more specialized formal service provision. Policy debate has at times pointed to the risk that social capital in community life will be crowded out by extensive state-mandated professionalization of helping and by human services which are based often exclusively on individual relations to formal helpers and systems of help, displacing the webs of lateral relations that denote 'thick' community (see, for example, Pennington and Rydin 2000). There is a risk of losing sight of the distinct and vital role of non-formal mechanisms and actors in the overall generation of welfare and well-being. The settlement field might be the site where the processes of intermeshing of formal and non-formal helping become acknowledged and shaped into inclusive approaches and methodologies that are truly facilitating of integration and respectful of the productive diversity in helping that can be brought into a '*welfare matrix*'.

The interaction in groups can also be seen as a type of social strategy or a collective response of people having to cope with similar adaptation challenges. Shared perspectives and approaches to settlement tasks and challenges can help individuals to problem-solve against a backdrop of collective support in the difficult situations that are encountered during settlement. The social interaction taking place in social collectivities of fellow countrymen and women can moderate acculturation stress and serve a very important psychosocial function.

Communities can constitute an important outreach mode to establish contact with those who are unattached in terms of conventional social systems (employment, family and school). Members of ethnic communities are often aware of nascent risks and problem situations. Individuals needing help are not always ready to seek out formal mechanisms, especially if they do not come from societies with highly organized social service systems and have been accustomed to obtaining help from kin, friends and other close circles. Settlement transitions have brought a break with individuals' original support systems, even though new relationships can replace these to some extent. In difficult situations, which are not amenable to the informal level of helping but require direct professional intervention, outreach into communities is a very valuable tool for identifying areas needing intervention. Outreach also allows for a preventative approach to integration problems.

The web of 'multiplex' relationships that develop in geographically based collectivities has the potential to alleviate many of the difficulties faced, for instance, by elderly immigrants if they are not fluent in the language of the new country and are reliant on the assistance of others. 'Multiplex' relations are those characterized by multiple and overlapping content, in which individuals are interacting with each other in many different roles (as opposed to discrete and specialized roles).[1] Proximity of residence, combined with traditional helping customs, create for them a secure living environment and reinforce the positive aspects of their settlement. Residential concentrations that are well serviced can be humane settlement environments for vulnerable groups such as elderly people. These concentrations of fellow countrymen and women have distinct advantages, provided that individuals otherwise have choice, and access to societal participation and opportunities on a par with others. (This is also discussed in Chapter 9 in the section on ethnic residential concentration.)

In the case of numerically small settling ethnocultural groups, proximity to other groups can afford an opportunity, when needed, for participation in larger communities with whom there is affinity. For numerically small groups, contact with outgroup and majority populations is critical from the outset of settlement. Small communities rapidly come to face acculturation situations. There is a possibility of isolation when cultural distance is perceived or real, and if the policy of resettlement, for instance, in the case of refugees, is one

---

1   See also Herberg (1993) and Hall (1976a) in high and low context cultures.

of geographical dispersal. The momentum of secondary migration to larger concentrations of the immigrant community can be understood as deriving partly from such factors. At base, the importance of contacts with other groups in the majority society comes to the fore. Immigrants' participation in life in the public space, such as that which is made possible through employment, for example, has major relevance for integration outcomes.

The settling community functions as a repository of culture, as well as an arena for culture valorization and cultural continuity over time and between generations. It is a locus for collective articulation of culture. It can also be a bulwark for identity in the new environment, especially if there is a desire to resist real or perceived social pressure for conformity to majority mores. Culture-based meanings are often vital elements of individuals' schema and world view.

An often overlooked but critical function of ethnic communities is the buttressing of wider community relations. As the experience of group members accumulates, the range and depth of perspectives on settlement, settlement processes and the new settlement environment grows stronger. The pooling of experience and perspectives across the group can foster and reinforce positive and balanced outward views on the new home society and a well-informed stance on different issues. The experience of the ethnic community, and the stocks of integration information, when tapped, can prove to be an important asset in developing inter-community relations. Seen as the locus of major collective coping mechanisms of resettling persons, the community constitutes a fundamental core of integration resources, which can be beneficially aligned with the formal settlement service system.

It is necessary to distinguish between the concepts of 'community' and 'category'. Using Calhoun's (1999) distinctions, 'community' is characterized by dense multiplex networks of interpersonal relationships, or is, in other words, a social subset of the larger ethnic collectivity, which would fall under his classification 'category', or people who share largely similar cultural styles. Thus at the level of collectivity, cultural similarities are used to demarcate very large categories of people not linked by close interpersonal relationships. A 'public', on the other hand, is the wide collectivity that forms around the functions and processes of public discourse and the positions taken on issues.

Community Organizations

The multiplicity of associations that are founded within any one of the ethnocultural collectivities or categories reflects the presence of great internal diversity. While its members share a historic, cultural and political background, the differentiation lines within ethnic communities might at times be seen as being of the same order as the cultural difference between groups. Divisions can be deep, as in the case of those refugee groups whose flight has been caused by civil war and the breakdown of trust. Insight into the diversity in ethnic communities is important for settlement practice. This underpins the shaping of interventions based on individualization and respect for distinctiveness.

Community organizations are a manifestation of 'active' citizenship and heightened civic participation of members. Associations constitute a base for becoming formally positioned in the wider institutional field, and for taking part, as well as having a stake, in processes and the public space of society. Fennema and Tillie (1999) have coined the term 'ethnic social capital' to denote participation in ethnic associational life. These authors argue that the denser the network of ethnic associations becomes, the more political trust the groups members will have and the more politically active they will be. The community organizations can serve as a formal platform for forms of active citizenship in the wider society.

Alliance with community helping networks and actors is important for strengthening culturally competent interventions by professionals. The emic or insider perspectives on the difficulties, problem-solving and coping processes in settlement are part of the stock of settlement and integration experience lodged in communities. Recognition that the resources in ethnic communities are vital to the shaping of appropriate, respectful and efficacious interventions leads us to assign value to this source of knowledge and expertise as important components of interventions. This constitutes a first step in adopting the idea of *partnering* in a service-oriented network. The peripheralization of non-professional expertise and even possible exploitation of such contradicts the equity principles espoused by professionals. The risk of such processes is present when professionalization is seen as threatened. This can result in a general exclusionary thrust that, in practice, marginalizes valuable non-formal helping mechanisms.

Facing the need to strengthen the culturally competent base in service provision, settlement practice needs to clarify its position on the professional–'ethnic paraprofessional' relationship, including work and power-sharing dynamics and principles. Involved in a process of partnering would be the planning and implementing of appropriate training and education of individuals, peers and future peers from the communities, as well as a fair system of rewards and human resource development openings in settlement service provisioning as a whole. Thus a commitment to occupational mobility paths would also belong to such arrangements. As has been demonstrated in, for example, the Canadian ethnospecific community organization sector, immigrant community organizations can function as providers in many areas of settlement support services operating out of the organizational sector and in an official capacity (see Chapter 9). The core question here is one of including immigrant actors into the established preserve of formal services.

There are several weighty reasons behind initiatives for admitting individual actors and community organizations into a role in the settlement service provision area. This would be a strategy parallel to that of the formal professional education route to entry, which can be slow and impeded by different factors. In most countries, immigrants are not represented in professional education institutions in numbers proportionate to their presence in the population. This is not entirely due to the length of time it takes for groups to become acculturated and oriented to the institutions of the new society. There are many 'technical' barriers and predispositions relating to admission criteria which inhibit immigrant applicants in their pursuit of higher education. Moreover, the capacity of qualification equivalency processes and procedures is often limited, as a result of which, the pool of training and education in immigrant cohorts remains underutilized. Suitable individuals of immigrant background would provide urgently needed cultural competence in the services, bringing as well the requisite language skills. Many of the settling groups are not familiar with formally organized helping and more readily turn to fellow countrymen and women, or to social circles or existing community groups for assistance. Channelling resources to these community collectivities would make sense in terms of settlement resource utilization and maximization.

Micro-level Approaches to Settlement Practice

Within organized settlement service systems, the social worker is one of the first frontline representatives of formal social services to establish a working relationship with settling individuals, families and groups. This service interface takes place during a critical life transition for settling groups. The working relationship has the potential for laying positive groundwork for meeting the challenges of settlement. An understanding of newly settling groups' circumstances of migration or flight, as well as of the social conditions in the country of origin, is part of the frame of reference that constitutes the starting point of a holistic approach. In working with new groups, and in particular with those from cultural backgrounds hitherto unfamiliar to us, we accept that there are aspects of the client context and background characteristics which are not understood from the outset. Social work with immigrants, like other areas of social work, engages the worker in a learning experience. The recognition that workers are yet to gain additional insight and understanding in the course of the working relationship with the client and that clients possess expertise on their own situations, engenders greater understanding and equality in the relationship (Sennett 2003). Sennett (2003, 177) points out that client autonomy embraces, at one and the same time, the aspects of connection and strangeness, closeness and impersonality.

Usually, attitudes of settling persons are strongly geared toward investing effort and energy in settlement. This resolve to forge ahead with settlement tasks is present even though there might need to be an interim adjustment period, for instance, in the case of some of the refugee groups whose circumstances of departure from their country have involved hazardous journeys and precarious transit conditions before being resettled. Settlement does present challenging and indeed problematic situations for individuals and their families, yet it is a practice area characterized by its clear solution-focused potential. The approaches to many of the issues arising can be understood as the challenge of problem-solving in a different environment, and sometimes very unfamiliar cultural context. Through a learning process, immigrants and refugees navigate their new environment. Settlement is an interactive experience with a strong thrust towards building and developing resource networks.

The settlement practitioner has a part to play in facilitating access for immigrant clients and groups to those areas of activity which are significant in the early settlement phase, and to others which assume greater significance from the point of view of long-term integration. Examples of the latter are trade unions, professional associations, legal aid services and educational institutions. The field of immigrant integration spans sectors and spheres of society, crossing disciplinary, professional, occupational and other boundaries. The portfolio includes working with clients to overcome barriers, to locate alternative strategies and thereby to resist exclusionary dynamics and the downgrading of social roles, personal goals and individual vision in settlement. In this light, practice can be seen to be centred on the active promotion of immigrants' participation in society, the negotiation of barriers to access, and the support of increased recognition of immigrants' potential roles and inputs.

Building a robust role in the community and society has been identified as being critically important for the subjective well-being of settling individuals in the long run. A robust role is one based on clear status and is affirmable before others. It can be justified in the face of hostility or prejudice, since it implies competence in some area as well as usefulness to the wider society. In other words, it is a reflection of solid forms of societal participation (Valtonen 1998). Coping with the challenges and obstacles in settlement calls for different strategies, all of which are part of the adaptation and adjustment process. The primacy and power of information to open doors and minds transforms settlement work into a positive educational role, as well as a learning experience.

The settlement transition involves for immigrants the cognitive tasks of reframing as a part of adjusting and seeking understanding of the new socio-cultural environment and its dynamics. Social adaptation can be seen as the range of cognitive and behavioural processes comprising individuals' adjustment to new arrangements. There is great individual diversity in the manner, pace and style of adjustment. Individuals bring their own schema, skills and capacities to bear on the process. Values, beliefs and personal or family life goals moderate the process. Adaptation is at the crux of integration at individual level, and is very much a personal relationship with change. From the individual/personal perspective, it features a complex interplay of competencies and ongoing development processes which involve resilience, strengths, competence, coping skills and self-efficacy in engaging with the environment. Support factors in the environment impact on the process. As settlement proceeds, individuals' positions, ties and roles vis-à-vis the surrounding society are established.

The subjective nature of adaptation is such that its features are frequently not outwardly evident. Smolicz's (1981) concept of culture comprised 'core' as well as outer elements of culture, with the former referring to enduring values, principles and beliefs which are intimately tied in with the individuals' life philosophy, and not easily relinquished. Core values might be outwardly articulated much less frequently. Initially they are not as 'accessible' as the more easily recognizable outer, or so-called 'pragmatic', elements of culture, such as dress, food, music and certain modes of behaviour. This frame suggests that a 'thicker' concept of individual adaptation would be a better tool for understanding adaptation. When new groups adopt the more peripheral elements of the new culture, a positive impression of integration activity and effort is given outwardly. For example, the manner of dress and social behaviour modes can be adopted early on in settlement out of choice or for various pragmatic purposes. This does not mean that those groups who do not follow this path are not making adjustments on other dimensions, for example, by devoting much observation and effort to understanding and making sense of the core culture of the new society before they embark on definitive changes to their own world views and lifestyles.

Other facets of adaptation need to be appreciated. Even though the concept of acculturation subsumes many aspects of this activity (especially when culture is understood in the broad sense), the distinct strands in this process are not always identified. When we speak of a transition between one culture and another, we might refer to a crossing between cultures that are very dissimilar in the first place. Settlement can also represent, for the individual, a change from, for example, a traditionally organized to a 'modern' society, from rural to urban conditions, from patriarchal arrangements to one of advanced gender equality, from informal economies to heavily formalized and regulated economies, from decades of civil war and disrupted institutions to stable conditions and specific social expectations, and so on. The last condition might be the most demanding in settlement. For instance, some younger cohorts of refugees have neither known about nor lived in stable conditions in their countries of origin.

Culture, Politics and Religion: High Profile Markers in Immigrant Groups

In the settlement field, groups who cling to their original culture usually arouse concern among those involved in integration services. This phenomenon draws the attention of majority society to what would appear to be a chosen path of separation from the main society (see Berry 1988). Individuals are perceived as not seeking interaction with members of outgroups, while retaining very strong cultural identity. Some might not make the level of effort required for learning the new language, preferring their own ethnic media when available, and otherwise withdrawing into the cocoon of the familiar culture. They are thought to be failing to become integrated or to be refusing to become part of the wider society. Meanwhile there has been a marked shift over time in the attitudes toward cultural retention among ethnic minorities. Scholars and policy-makers alike have come to acknowledge not only the enduring function of culture and the meaning of cultural identity in individuals' lives, but also individuals' right to self-determination in highly valued areas such as culture and religion.

Refugee cohorts include individuals who, having been involved in politics and political life in their home country, often retain this strong orientation and keep abreast of developments. In most receiving countries, political inclinations and affiliations are taken to be matters in the private sphere. However, in cases when political crises are triggered in relations between the host country and the immigrants' country of origin, settling groups find themselves placed in a highly vulnerable position. They can be the target of scrutiny and controls on the part of officials, facing as well the different types and degrees of hostility in ethnic and societal relations.

The policy implications of the events of 9/11[2] were complex in the US. Triandafyllidou, Modood and Zapata-Barrero (2006) state that they signalled that migration, and by extension globalization itself, concealed a potential for terror attacks and a threat to security. The wide reaction of caution in the society and official measures connected with the 'war on terror' have had implications for civil liberties. Muslim groups, groups assumed to be Muslim or people from the Middle East are vulnerable to being indiscriminately generalized as constituting a security threat. Writing from a European perspective, Modood (2006, 47) states that 'the military and civil liberties aspects of the "war against terrorism", even more so than at the time of the Satanic Verses affair, has seen a vulnerable and besieged group assert itself publicly, and at times defiantly' (ibid., 47).[3] He further observes that the 9/11 events, and the 'war on terrorism' that has followed, are having negative implications for domestic, political multiculturalism in the UK. Parekh (2006, 181) writes that 'European anxiety about the "Muslim threat" ... arises out of the belief that Muslims cannot and do not wish to integrate and are in fact engaged in a quiet but sustained conspiracy to subvert Europe'. Parekh (2006, 185) points out that 'despite the rhetoric and murderous deeds of a militant minority and the cultural confusion and ambiguity of some others, the large majority of European Muslims can, wish to and have made sincere efforts to integrate'. Among the reasons why an influential body of European people think otherwise, Parekh (2006, 185) suggests, are that some concentrate on the militant minority, and either ignore the others or erroneously interpret the latter's silence to imply that they share or feel sympathy for the views of the militant minority. Anxiety over the rise of Islamic fundamentalism in different parts of the world is unfortunately projected onto all Muslims, including European immigrants.

---

2   The attacks on the World Trade Center and the Pentagon on 11 September 2001 in the US.

3   The publication of Salman Rushdie's book, *The Satanic Verses*, in the UK in 1988 was taken by some as an attack on Islam. A fatwa was declared, and Rushdie had to go into hiding and received police protection for a number of years.

The post-9/11 social repercussions for wider categories of persons of similar but not necessarily the same ethnocultural and geographic background can be understood as constituting a clear integration risk for the groups in question. As the presenting threat of danger is otherwise real rather than perceived, there is a wide reaction of caution in the society. Indiscriminate generalization undermines and threatens the position of specific groups. It is menacing also from the perspective that these dynamics are sometimes society-wide.

Religion has become one of the more prominent group markers in settlement environments. Religious affiliation is often understood as an aspect of core culture and can also be a social descriptor for individuals and groups. Moral values and beliefs can be anchored in structures of religion. As well as constituting a social marker in the public space, religion can be a vehicle for explicit articulation of positions on social, socio-political and ethical issues. There has been increased research interest in the role of religion in settlement and integration processes.

Hirschman (2004) writes on the American context, portraying some of the functional aspects related to religious affiliation. He points to the important socio-economic role of churches, synagogues, temples and mosques in American society and gives a reminder that the creation of an immigrant church or temple often provides ethnic communities with refuge from the hostility and discrimination from the broader society, as well as opportunities for economic mobility and social recognition. Additionally, churches and other religious organizations play a key role in the creation of community. They generate social and spiritual comfort which in previous times was provided through the extended family. Generally having a long tradition of community service, they can be a major source of social and economic assistance for those in need.

Herberg (1960), writing earlier on the American context, argues that immigrants could find meaning and identity by reaffirming traditional beliefs, while the certainty of religious precepts serves as an anchor in the face of change in many aspects of life. Religious values, moreover, underpin other traditional beliefs and patterns including customary familial practices which become threatened with adaptation to the new, seemingly amoral American culture. Handlin (1973) observes that for immigrants, religion can create linkage between the old world and the new.

Manifestations of strong cultural, political and religious adherence are at times perceived as rival affiliations and assumed to defer and even derail integration. It is important to be cognizant of alternative understandings that offer more balanced views. These areas of affiliation and engagement provide domains of continuity that mediate disruptions in other spaces. They also constitute, in the broader sense, core areas of culture which individuals do not relinquish in the short term, nor are they expected to have to relinquish. At the psychosocial level, such affiliations function as frames from which individuals draw their systems of meaning and standards of integrity. Not least there are also tangible and intangible benefits to be had from affiliation.

At the macro level, as different forms of diversity gradually find their niche in the public space, differentiation in groups and group processes can be understood as a significant part of integration, and indeed as an indicator of a more mature and collective phase of societal inclusion. Integration can thus be seen as a gradual introduction of new collective features into the public domain, and a way in which diversity becomes legitimized. The settlement-related actions and efforts of immigrants are thus catalysts for qualitative changes at societal level.

Strengths and Ecological Approaches

A central focus of settlement practice is on transition-related change events and understanding the nature of change which settlement entails for clients at personal, family and community level. The personal and social resources in new groups are not always given prominence in interventions, nor are they explicitly validated as part of the arsenal of skills and qualities which have great significance in settlement undertakings. Strengths and empowerment methodologies allow for settling persons to build personal power by mobilizing their energies and distilling past experience into resilience-based approaches for dealing with tasks in short- and long-term settlement. The process is thus one of deploying strengths in new spaces, and also of further building of those personal competencies which will be salient to settlement situations.

In drawing a general distinction between power and strengths, power is closely related to the degree of influence that can be wielded by individuals and groups, including influence over their own conditions and the policies that affect them. People are said to be empowered when their personal, interpersonal or political power is increased as a consequence of which they are able to take action to improve their life situations. Strengths are originally person-based or group-based qualities and attributes. Strengths can be a source of power, and alternatively in some classifications are described as 'personal power'. Strengths also overlap with the concept of 'capital' – economic, social, cultural and symbolic – which constitute a type of social currency due to their quality of fungibility or convertibility to other needed forms of 'capital'. The 'powerlessness' of immigrant and refugee groups should be clarified as a condition strongly related to recent arrival into the citizenry. This is juxtaposed with their positioning which, in turn, is also affected by the state of social equality and/or ethnic relations in the society. Thus, the categorization of groups in society as 'powerless' does not preclude their having and employing reserves of innate strengths.

Empowerment can be understood as the process by which people, organizations and communities gain mastery over their lives (see Rappaport 1990). This can involve achieving a position of greater equity in resource distribution and enhanced social positioning vis-à-vis other groups. It conveys the idea that people who are relatively powerless are able to gain more power (Spicker 1993). Empowerment also implies that individuals and groups will progress through stages of personal capacity building to gain control over their own situation.

The ecological approach adopts a systems framework and focuses on the mutual interactions between individuals, their families, communities and the wider society. Using this approach, assessments consider the balance between stressors and supports, or risks and protective factors. The ecological approach can serve as a frame for understanding the web of social interactions which help in shaping personal behaviour, and which should be considered in constructing preventative and therapeutic interventions (Jack 2005). This approach is useful in charting the relationships and balance between the settlement-related stressors experienced by individuals, and the availability of appropriate supports to mediate coping processes.

Germain and Gitterman's (1995) typology of stressors includes difficult life transitions, traumatic life events and environmental pressures. This framework is well suited for understanding the settlement and acculturation experience of individuals and groups.

The authors base their interventions for dealing with life stressors on the ecological principle that the purpose of social work is to elevate *the goodness of fit between people and their environments*, particularly by securing basic resources. 'When a goodness-of-fit exists between an individual's concrete, social, and emotional needs and available resources, it buffers intrapsychic, interpersonal, and environmental pressures' (Gitterman and Shulman (1994, 9)). The ecological perspective is operationalized and specified in the Life Model which offers a view of human beings as in constant interchanges with their environment (see Germain 1973).

Furuto (2004) stresses the suitability of the ecological, strengths and empowerment approaches in working with immigrants. The ecological approach adopts a holistic perspective in assessment and intervention by focusing on transactions between the immigrants and their environment, and on the 'goodness of fit'. The ecological approach takes into account the functionality, expediency and appropriateness of the transactions, as well as any subsequent adaptation of these. In one sense, the ecological model brings the processual dimension into the Person-In-Environment context. The immigrant's past is important for understanding the dynamics of transactions in the present. The strengths approach emphasizes the identification of strengths on many levels and the belief that trauma and difficulties can strengthen the immigrant. Individuals are encouraged to achieve their full potential. The strengths perspective is based on the principle that resources are to be found in all environments (Saleebey 1997).

The empowerment approach, moreover, posits that power exists in many forms, and that there are various means and strategies through which powerless groups can attain power. Empowered individuals can better exercise control over their circumstances and shape solutions for problem situations. Furuto (2004) concludes that when used in combination, all three theoretical approaches can be a powerful, holistic method for working with immigrants in their communities.

The emphasis on empowerment is central at this time when many immigrant populations now include the second generation. It is becoming more evident that 'immigrant' collectivities themselves will also have to participate in the work toward a shift in power relations in the interest of equal citizenship. They will also have to be seen as actors in change processes.

Power and Sources of Power

Although types of power have not featured widely in connection with the discussion of empowerment, it is nonetheless well recognized that power exists in many and different forms. The concept of power has come to be more prominent, especially in the critical social work theory approaches. The construction of typologies of power involves 'commodifying' power and forms of power. The risk lies in over-commodifying power which can lead to a situation where we speak of power in a dichotomous mode, with individuals either having power or lacking it (see Pease 2002).

Focus on the instrumental dimensions and implications of power are helpful for facilitating the analysis and conceptualization of dynamics in settlement situations. In this respect, scrutiny of types of power is helpful. Social interactions, transactions and relationships can be understood as featuring a dimension of power, especially when purposive activity is in question. It is useful to scrutinize power and its different manifestations since settlement and integration themselves are fields of purposive action for all the main stakeholders. Moreover, understanding of the types of power can be valuable in assessing situations and contexts before embarking on interventions. Power can be understood as being lodged in the person, in structures or in situations. Power as a concept also has relevance for the strengths perspective. Some of the sources of power are scrutinized here. (Power of position in the institutional setting is discussed in Chapter 9.)

Mayer (2000) identifies two general categories of power: structural and personal. Structural power is lodged in the situation and people's objective resources such as the formal authority they hold, or the real choices which exist. Personal power refers to individual characteristics, such as determination, knowledge, wits, courage and communication skills. I adapt and present Mayer's (2000) well-elaborated frame of specific types of power which originally were discussed in the context of conflict resolution.

Formal authority is the authority given by an institution, a set of laws or policies, or by virtue of an individual's position in a formal structure. *Information* is an important source of power. People can discover information, for example, or they can decide to share or conceal it. *Expert power*, the power deriving from having relevant expertise, is a variation on the power of information. *Association* refers to power deriving from an individual's connection with other powerful people or organizations. Mayer (2000) observes that *political power*, a variant on this type, stems from people's ability to bring the power of others to bear in a political context, while the *power of neutrals* partly derives from their ability to maintain an association, with all parties making themselves valuable to each of them.

Resources may be either tangible or intangible. Tangible resources such as money or personal property are important, but it is sometimes the intangible resources – such as reputation, ability to handle stress, and physical endurance – that are more critical in some situations. *Rewards and sanctions* refer to the ability to provide or withhold meaningful rewards. The ability to impose negative consequences on others or to prevent those consequences are twin sources of power. *Nuisance power* is the ability to interfere, harass, irritate or disturb, but it falls short of the ability to impose significant consequences or penalties. *Procedural power* derives from the ability to control or influence decision-making processes. This is separate from having control over outcomes, although they are very often heavily related. *Habitual power* resides in the position taken in trying to prevent change as opposed to fomenting it. This is sometimes referred to as inertia. *Moral power* derives from an appeal to the values, beliefs and ethical systems of others or from an attack on the values.

Personal characteristics derive their power from the broad range of personal characteristics of individuals. These include, for instance, intelligence, stamina and strength, concentration, perceptiveness, determination, empathy, communication skills, endurance and courage. *Perception of power* refers to the belief which individuals hold about their own power and that of others, which is often as important as the power itself. *Definitional power* is the ability to define the issues and potential outcomes. This is a significant base of power in negotiations, and in institutional settings. Mayer (2000) states that very often the essential question is not how much power individuals have, but rather how they choose to use it.

Forms of Capital

Forms of capital and sources of power have some common features. They both refer to social resources which can be brought to bear on individuals' pursuits in social life, and facilitate purposive activity oriented to personal or collective goals. Examining forms of capital and sources of power can open up a new field of resources in that it is likely that previously unidentified and latent personal and social resources will be recognized.

A study of Bourdieu's (1986) different forms of capital is useful from at least two perspectives. Bourdieu's (1986) model of forms of capital provides the conceptual breadth for exploring the different types and dimensions of social resources which come into play in settlement processes and which need to be built to pave the way for long-term integration (including that of the second generation). Thus this frame is sensitive to the types of social resources which are needed to underpin participation in the mainstream institutions. Ideas about forms of capital also provide a conceptual model that has relevance for the strengths perspective in social work. As stated before, strengths are largely person-based assets. Capital, on the other hand, refers to social resources that partly derive their value from social structures, and can be harnessed as assets to be used in the individual's favour. 'Capital' thus conceptualizes individual or group assets in societal space, that is, in terms of their utility in, for example, improving life chances or establishing an advantageous role or position in the community and wider society. It is a framework that recognizes different types of tangible and intangible assets which can be mobilized and utilized.

Used in settlement social work, the forms of capital approach embodies the idea that the individual or group can develop those forms of capital or assets that would be in the long-term interest of integration. The term 'capital' implies that these are products of previous investment. We can link the idea of capital to the individual's capacity building to enhance life chances and opportunities.

Bourdieu (1986) proposes that there are immaterial forms of capital (cultural, symbolic and social) as well as material or economic ones. Capital is distinctive in its property of 'fungibility' or 'convertibility'. Different forms of capital are exchangeable or replaceable, in whole or in part, by other forms of capital. Calhoun (1995, 68) points out that the concept of fungibility is not straightforward. While it is possible for individuals to convert one particular form into another, the aspect of convertibility is not without its problems, since the extent and ease of convertibility is likely to be quite different in different contexts.

Resources, or social resources, is a similar concept, defined as 'the wealth, status, power as well as social ties of those persons who are directly or indirectly linked to the individual' (Lin, Ensel and Vaughn 1981). Forms of capital are understood as social resources which promote citizens' capacity and ability to exercise full membership and rights in the society. The notion of multiformity and convertibility of social resources links in with ideas of mutuality and reciprocity in ethnic networks and communities.

According to Bourdieu's (1986) model, *economic* capital corresponds to material wealth and is directly convertible into other goods. This is often the most common understanding of capital. *Social capital* is defined as the sum of the actual or virtual resources which accrue to individuals or groups by virtue of possessing a durable network of more or less institutionalized relationships of mutual acquaintance and recognition (Bourdieu and Wacquant 1992). Social capital is thus understood to consist of the resources of social relations and networks of relations which are useful for individuals and which facilitate action through the generation of trust; the establishment of obligations and expectations; the creation and enforcement of norms; and the formation of associations (Coleman 1990). Social capital involves mobilization of people through connections, social networks and group membership (see Peillon 1998).

The vibrant flows of social capital in many immigrant networks underpin much early settlement activity. Reciprocity of transactions in social capital networks constitute mutual helping activity, through which network members generate for themselves vital forms of assistance. Some immigrants arrive to join kin or friends in the new country, but for the most part, they leave behind such basic sources of support. Networks would ideally extend out into other groups. The building of social capital in the new home society is a sign that an individual is developing links to the society. In well-established networks, interdependence can develop, which actually reinforces the network.

Information exchange in networks is of central importance in settlement groups. Granovetter's (1973) concept of weak ties and strong ties proposes an explanation of how valued information might travel. 'Weak ties' are distinguished from strong ties. 'Weak ties' are defined as those that bridge outward into other circles and areas of society. Granovetter (1973, 1371) states that 'those to whom we are weakly tied are more likely to move in circles different from our own and will then have access to information different from what we receive'. 'Weak ties' can be contrasted to 'strong ties' which may exist in close circles that do not bridge, but rather sustain the individual in 'multiplex' relations.[4] Granovetter (1973) argues that the fewer indirect contacts individuals have, the more encapsulated they will be in terms of knowledge of the world beyond their own friendship circle. 'Weak ties' are productive of information, and should be recognized as a form of social capital with significance for newly settling individuals and groups.

Shapiro (1986) states that, in network terms, it is possible to differentiate between densely knit, bounded, solitary networks, and sparsely knit, ramified, multiple networks. The density or sparseness of a network refers to the degree to which network members are connected to each other. This has been expressed as the ratio of existing to possible ties. Dense networks tend to be more bounded, involving multi-stranded ties and with members tending to rely considerably upon each other for resources.

As Wellman (1981, 186)points out: 'strength is not always a virtue in ties ... Weaker ties often provide more diverse support, because they access a greater number and variety of [different] social circles ... Where close friends tend to hear about the same things at the same time, weaker ties are the source of novel news.' Granovetter (1973) suggests that the existence of weak ties is not necessarily alienating; indeed in some cases it may be more 'liberating' than strong, multi-stranded ties.

Wellman (1981, 191) points to the need to have more differentiated conceptions of networks as well as of ties, since the norm of a single, densely knit network has too often led analysts to treat complex, ramified networks as tattered residues of defunct solidarities. Wellman (1981, 191) states that

---

4   'Multiplexity', or multiple contents in a relationship, indicates a strong tie (Kapferer 1969, 213). Individuals interact with each other in many different roles, and social relations are highly interwoven.

we would do better to remove the normative idealization of density and inquire into 'what effects different structural forms have on the availability of supportive resources to network members'.

Apart from settlement networks, there are also those that connect migrants in origin and destination areas through bonds of kinship, friendship and shared community origin (Massey 1999). From the perspective of migration, networks can facilitate international flows in that they reduce the costs and risks of movement. Drawing on social ties to relatives and friends who have previously migrated, potential migrants gain access to knowledge, assistance and other resources that ease the migration process.

The aspects of social capital that are dysfunctional to settlement relate to its use to protect privilege and insider interest in bounded circles. Generally, social capital has been studied in the migration field from the perspective of its capacity to facilitate integration. However, it also lends itself to the scrutiny of excluding mechanisms that are potentially inimical to settlement.

Cultural capital, broadly speaking, refers to the general cultural background, knowledge, disposition and skills that are passed from one generation to the next. The theory of cultural capital holds that each class possesses its own set of meanings or cultural framework, which is internalized initially through socialization within the family. This 'habitus', or socially constructed system of cognitive and motivating structures, shapes perception, thought, taste, appreciation and action. The habitus of children from the dominant class equips them with cultural capital which is translated into academic attainment and occupational achievement (Bourdieu and Passeron 1977). Habitus is defined as a series of cognitive schemes organized as networks of meanings (Strauss and Quinn 1997). The theory of cultural capital was a frame focusing on the perpetuation of the class structure.

Parents' cultural capital can be seen as, in one sense, having an instrumental role in the second generation's acquisition of 'human' capital. The concept of cultural capital should be distinguished from the concept of 'human' capital which refers to those attributes which makes workers more productive or competitive in the labour market. These attributes include knowledge, ability and skill, and are generally the result of investment in education and training (Becker 1962).

MacLeod (1987) has used the concept of cultural capital in a less restricted sense, taking into account factors that are not class-based, such as ethnicity or ethnic background. In this usage the concept is useful as an analytic tool in settlement and integration studies. MacLeod (1987) has employed Bourdieu's theory of cultural capital in an ethnographic study of youth aspirations in a low-income neighbourhood. Considerable variance in attitudes to education was found in two groups within the same lower social stratum. MacLeod (1987) states that the objective probabilities for social advancement were perceived and internalized very differently, and concludes that different anticipations of social immobility or mobility do not arise simply out of social class, but are the outcome also of intermediate factors that mediate the influence of social class on aspiration formation and opportunity. MacLeod (1987) suggests that ethnicity could be a key factor in making a visible minority group more receptive to the achievement ideology. MacLeod (1987) concludes that, although social class might be of primary importance, intermediate factors are at work which shape the responses of the two groups and produce quite different expectations and actions.

Symbolic capital is, broadly speaking, a kind of advance or credit extended to those holding the required symbolic and material guarantees. Credit is granted to individuals who give or are likely to give the best material and symbolic guarantees. Symbolic capital is found in networks of relationships that are sustained by commitments and debts of honour, rights and duties which can be accumulated even over generations, and can be mobilized in extraordinary circumstances. Based on psychical trust–commitment complementarities, symbolic capital can occur among parties who might otherwise be only loosely linked, but it is nonetheless one of the mechanisms which makes capital flow to capital. Symbolic capital might have more flexible scope for convertibility, in that direct reciprocity is not the prime dimension.

While aspects of credit and trust are also features of the *social capital* construct elaborated by Portes (1998), the distinguishing feature between social and symbolic capital is found in the characteristic of group 'closure'. Social capital forms are situated in more 'bounded', demarcated collectivities. 'Closure' may even be a prerequisite to the emergence of some of the forms as, for example, those arising from enforceable trust, bounded solidarity and internalization of norms. Symbolic capital can be understood to be operational in the wider, more diffuse, societal context, as opposed to close-knit collectivities with the strong ties[5] and the multiplex relations associated with the emergence of social capital.

Symbolic capital is understood to reside in the recognized legitimacy of capital, of whatever form. This recognition might be founded in an individual's outstanding attainment level in an area such as sport or art, in some professional field, or possibly might be based on gratitude aroused by benefits that are accrued over time.

The forms of capital model projects an idea of the types of social resources which individuals and groups would utilize in establishing membership in different spheres of society. It projects the idea of strengths as also being environment and social structure- based, thereby opening up the strengths perspective to meso and macro level conceptualization. Perhaps most significant of all is the capacity for this frame to be used to generate greater

---

5   Granovetter (1973, 1361) states that 'the strength of a tie is a (probably linear) combination of the amount of time, the emotional intensity, the intimacy (mutual confiding), and the reciprocal services which characterize the tie'.

understanding, from a multidimensional perspective, of the differential outcomes of various areas of individuals' and groups' settlement activity.

Closing Comments

This chapter has situated settlement and integration work in the macro, meso and micro levels of practice. Within the section on the meso level, the roles and function of the ethnic community have been examined. At the micro level, focus has been directed to the social resources, power and strengths which can be mobilized by settling individuals as they deal with challenges in the pursuit of integration goals. The perspectives on social resources, power and 'forms of capital' have been drawn from bodies of sociological theory. These broaden the conceptualization of strengths by embracing a range of structure-related assets that are relevant for the integration process. Emphasis is given to the benefits of identifying or developing resources which are useful to settling persons and groups in the public space.

Chapter 7

Practice with Family Systems

The Immigrant Family

The functions of the family in settlement, its coping systems, its acculturation and adaptation as a basic unit, and its culture-based resources rank high in importance as elements in our work with immigrant individuals, families and their communities. The family is the institution that bears the main impact of migration and settlement initiatives, challenges, actions and outcomes. It is often the crucible of adaptation processes. Immigrant families and their members undergo periods of transition of varying intensity as they deal with relocation and/or displacement/settlement. As part of the migration experience, families devise innovative arrangements for the purpose of managing in a new culture. The family is a long-term locus of personal, interpersonal and social engagement with the activities and tasks of settlement. It is called upon to nurture the adjustment processes and undergo the collective experience and trials of its members. It is often at the heart of integration activity. Settlement practice has a major stake in this institution and in its welfare and well-being.

Most people live their lives in connection with 'family', albeit in different ways (Foner 1997). Families are the seat of long-term commitment to their members, even though the nature of commitment changes as members' needs and resources change and develop over time. In settlement transitions the family retains its central functions throughout the process of adaptation to the modes of settlement. It is grounded in the particular needs of its members. The importance of the family is even more marked when the settlement transition is demanding due to large cultural difference, or the necessity of dealing with the aftermath of refugee experiences of violence and uprooting, for example. Moreover, the family role retains its significance when settling communities are from societies, cultures and socio-historical backgrounds in which the family plays a strong, central and unconditional role in looking after the well-being of its members.

The extended family and wider kin can comprise a matrix of natural helping. The plurality of close ties in many larger family units, and the advantages deriving from these, can make for a difference in the quality of life and settlement of immigrants and refugees. When the family unit is contained within the two-generation 'nuclear family', the responsibility for well-being of family members undergoes a significant shift.

The ability of individuals to migrate and settle in the context of family is affected directly by the settlement country's immigration policies. In her work on family-related migration, Kofman (2004) states that in classic societies of immigration such as Australia, Canada and the US, family migration was encouraged and a wider range of family members was allowed in and sponsored. Even though employment-led migration has become more important in the US, it is significant that family migration still constitutes two-thirds of immigration into that country, and between a third and a quarter in Canada and Australia respectively (SOPEMI 2000). In contrast, in European states the criteria based on family ties have not been a priority in immigration policies and a highly restrictive definition of the family has been used as the basis of entry. This is normally limited to spouses and dependent children within the nuclear family. In policy terms, family migration has been treated as a secondary type of migration consisting of female dependants who come in the wake of the male breadwinner as the primary migrant, a gendered view reflected by immigration legislation in many countries. Family migration is seen as having few repercussions on, and only indirect relations to, the labour market which constitutes the 'motor' of international migration. The view that migration is initiated by economic motivation, with family migration constituting the related social dimension, still prevails in policy (Kofman 2004).

The mechanisms of concentrated family responsibility and support which are described above feature in the cultural backgrounds of many of the newer groups settling in the larger countries of settlement. Ties of responsibility retain their significance even over distance. Transnational ties and transactions represent for the family a strategy to overcome some of the consequences of separation. Many strategies have had to be devised to deal with intervening distance as a factor in immigrant and refugee family relations. The enduring quality of such relationships is reflected in the flow of remittances back to relatives in the countries of origin. Strategies of survival are conducted in the context of an expanded social field, as demonstrated, for example, in Chamberlain's (2006) studies of the Caribbean diaspora. Nonetheless the vibrancy of transnational connections cannot be seen as justification for the lack of immigration policies that would recognize the integrity of family systems as an important life quality criterion for its members.

From the perspective of long-term acculturation processes, Alba and Nee (1996) note that family patterns and values among some immigrant groups will affect notions of what is considered 'normal' behaviour in mainstream America and, over time, will become part of the standard repertoire. Migrants bring new dimensions that can in time possibly become part of the profile of family patterns in host societies.

This chapter looks at changes which affect family life, as well as changes that take place within the family system and require family adjustment and reorganization. These changes also take place at a 'deeper' level since they must be underpinned often by radical realignment of values and normative frames. Family roles, its support systems and resources for handling settlement, as well as its coping mechanisms, are examined.

Migration as Change

Hulewat (1996) describes migration as an experience that throws a family into a state of crisis. This experience offers them a wide range of opportunities and at the same time exposes them to many risks. Adaptation and coping with change is one of the foremost settlement processes, even when a crisis dimension is not emphasized. Mead's (1978) categories of cultural change derive from the perspective of anthropology, and capture the dimensions of sequence and the pace of change taking place in immigrants' lives. These categories also hold high relevance for the dynamic of change in intergenerational relations internal to the family.

Mead (1978) describes three different categories of cultural change which vary according to the magnitude and rate of the change. The first is *postfigurative* change, in which the change process is slow with the future repeating the past. The second is the *configurative* type, where change is moderate and the present can still serve as a guide to future expectations. The third type is *prefigurative*, when change is rapid, and in practice forces elders to learn from children about experiences which they themselves never had.

The case of settlement transition falls largely within the second and very frequently into the third category. In the third type, individuals are adapting to a very unfamiliar environment. It can be especially demanding when the integration and acculturation process requires deep change, calling for values and beliefs, core aspects of culture, to be examined and honed in the light of settlement tasks and contingencies. Mead's (1978) frame introduces the pace of change as having direct impact on how responses, including attitudinal responses in the family, would need to be shaped for effective adaptation. The pace of societal change in the settlement environment itself is also likely to have an effect on majority attitudes to immigration.

The immigrant learns about the new society through a wide and rich range of experience, interaction and transactions with other members of the society. When the space and opportunities are open, immigrants are genuinely able to exercise agency in the settlement process. The settlement practitioner or human service provider/client interactions function alongside other forms of interaction and strong outward-reaching ties with society. This is to the common advantage.

A critical part of settlement for immigrants who move into a new language area is acquiring language skill, which is held to be key for integration. In the case of those who do not, or cannot, learn the language in the settlement country, the mediation of kin, friends and others is critical if they are to be able to manage their affairs effectively, and to maintain viable links to the social environment. Language proficiency, on the other hand, is quickly gained by the younger people through education and interaction with peers at school. Adults, however, depend on the availability of language training. When language training for adults is supported financially and individuals are thereby free to participate in training for a stipulated period, this greatly facilitates the whole process. Language training is one area of services that will clearly be to the advantage of all settling groups when it is arranged from the start of settlement. Such training is often organized through the state or other designated organizations. Language skill and fluency is obviously of prime importance for participation in the main spheres of activity such as employment and education. Additionally, through the medium of language, many settlement barriers can be overcome, misunderstandings reduced and broad interaction in the social environment facilitated. The wide availability of such training is a very desirable feature of settlement programmes. I argue here that if all of its members are able to access language training early in settlement, the family as a whole will derive benefit and be an empowered unit for taking on settlement challenges. This could moderate the risk of an uneven pace of adaptation among different family members which has been found at times to generate problematic situations in family relations.

Family Roles and Supports

The family constitutes a unique bundle of roles. Even though there are limits on the extent to which the family can meet need in absolute terms, for its members it is often a first resort resource, so wide is its range of responsibility and, in particular, its potential for flexible response. Family responsibility and family work remain largely non-amenable to commodification. Although social policy does cater for some facets of its functions, as Foner (1997) observes, family relations and decisions are not reducible to rational economic calculations. Its dynamics are propelled by a constellation of forces from responsibility and 'primordial loyalties', which, according to Geertz (1971), are the pillars of social existence deriving from immediate contiguity and kin connection, to mechanisms of reciprocity and free choice. Members of a family often take actions that are not privately beneficial, but which will be best for the economic well-being of the family unit. Borjas (1990) states that tension arises between individual and family well-being, yet it generally remains the first and basic collectivity in the true sense of the word.

In the family, nurturance, socialization and education are important to the development and growth of children and adults. Each family member plays certain roles, and the expectations of these roles can 'mould' the family's functioning (Balgopal 2000). The pace and nature of adaptation to settlement conditions can unsettle the pattern of individual roles in the family, for example, those connected to breadwinning, childrearing and socialization. Family members must adapt their patterns of roles and responsibilities to meet resettlement contingencies. Women may take on main breadwinning roles even as this sets a precedent in the family. Children readily acquire language skill and come to play a new central part in communicating outwardly in the new language. The family system, in order to function well, must undergo a type of *role metamorphsis* in which individuals adapt and adjust former roles, and learn new ones that are valid and functional in the context of settlement.

Family roles are in many ways generic across cultures, but in settlement situations they acquire the dimension of socio-cultural adaptation which can either be a background or a more prominent factor in its processes. Family roles are examined here in the areas of:

1. Income security
2. Long-term care
3. Socialization/moral development, norms and values
4. Culture-building at pragmatic and instrumental levels

The fourth category reflects specific tasks in settlement. These categories of functions are not discrete, but intermeshed at many levels. Additionally, the family should be seen to be symbiotically connected to the informal and formal institutions in its environment.

Income Security

Ensuring income security, or looking after the economic welfare of its members, is a basic function of the family. Mature welfare systems have developed policies to reduce risks of poverty and to guarantee at least minimum income support/security for citizens as part of the package of social rights to which they are entitled. In societies where social rights are not developed, individuals and families are heavily dependent on earned income for meeting needs.

A novel aspect of migration is found in how the concern for economic welfare of kin retains its salience over distance, as the literature on remittances demonstrates. Geertz (1971; 1973) speaks of the 'moral economy', which generates long-distance support, provided as a moral obligation, and done to the limits of the resources available. A parallel understanding is that immigrants try to extend economic security over borders in the context of family roles and responsibilities. By not relinquishing ties of obligation and responsibility to the original circles, immigrants establish forms of cross-border social security (Valtonen 1996).

Employment carries central significance and far-reaching consequences for the settlement process of the individual and for the family. Immigrants' experience in the search for employment is highly variable. The best case scenario is when settlement occurs during a time of high labour market demand and individuals find employment in a relatively straightforward way. Employment itself is a very empowering part of the settlement process. The experience is one of an undiluted sense of satisfaction, achievement and challenge. This was expressed in the words of one refugee settling in Finland, who expressed the meaning of accessing employment in the words: 'When I got this job, I was so afraid that I would not know Finnish well enough. But now I am there at work, I can learn more and more' (Valtonen 1999).

When women are able to obtain suitable employment in settlement, this can be a very positive opportunity for their active participation in public life, especially significant if this was not possible in their former environment. Migration itself can change individuals' prospects radically. For some, these prospects are evident and even liberating. For others, settlement throws up challenges that draw on the individual's life skills, flexibility, creativity, strengths and resilience. The entry of Vietnamese women into the Finnish labour market in the early 1990s is one example of a positive outcome at the confluence of a number of effective social services (Valtonen 2004). The state-organized settlement arrangements include universal language training for all adults in refugee groups, as well as income support during the training period. Child care facilities are widely available and subsidized, which permits both parents to participate in language training courses, as well as labour market training. For this group of women, this proved to be a very suitable opportunity to enter the labour market and participate formally in activity in the public space. It is also evident that facilitating this process was the fact that labour demand was high at the time. Additionally, prior to their arrival, women had often had to assume responsibility for economic matters and the home in the context of the prolonged civil warfare in Vietnam (Hitchcox 1993).

For many immigrants, entering the labour market is a challenging experience, featuring a lengthy job search, retraining and often yet more retraining, encounters with various closure mechanisms and discrimination, occupational downgrading or unemployment. These take a serious toll on settlement for the individual and for the family.

Unemployment or severe occupational downgrading can bring about difficulties in status and role change. At times the more rapid insertion of women into the labour market can also create difference in the rate of adjustment, which can be a source of family strain. The shift of main income earning roles and status between spouses potentially entails adjustment of power and authority levels, and the corresponding role and relationship changes on the part of all family members. Adjustment processes test the collective as well as individual capacities for handling change and uncertainty. Marital relations can undergo severe pressure in acculturation. On the other hand, there is evidence of gradual and positive adjustment to familial role changes from the findings of longitudinal research conducted with refugee cohorts in Finland over a five-year span between 1994 and 1998 (see Valtonen 1999).

The effects of unemployment (which are covered in Chapter 5) attest to its multilayered linkages to life quality and to overall well-being in settling families and communities. Settlement social work has a stake in this aspect of the integration process. A systematic scrutiny of this problematic is needed in settlement social work, with a view to developing suitable approaches based on the range of available professional methodology.

Long-term Care

The family is generally the institution that provides long-term care for its members to varying degrees over the life cycle. For immigrants, in addition to the meeting of physiological needs, the family can offer irreplaceable forms of caring in the new country in the area of affective, nurturing and supportive elements (see Sogren 2004). Foner (1997) speaks of the family as providing a place where solace and support can be found in a strange land and where family members can pool their resources as a way to advance.

The support mechanisms of the family constitute the natural caring system in settlement, which is supported by existing formal family and welfare service mechanisms and guarantees. Many of the newer groups come from societies where the scope of formal social services is narrower than that of the countries of settlement. Natural caring systems in family and close circles are often central to people's lives and retain their meaning for individuals. The importance of kin can be demonstrated by the example of Asian Americans. Gellis (2003) states that Asian Americans share a common thread of family-centred social support systems in which emotional, financial and instrumental support are given. These support systems are maintained through a cultural sense of family loyalty and the predominance of group over individual concerns. There is also great respect and obligation offered to family members, especially parents.

To recognize the immigrant family system as part of the welfare matrix is to engage in holistic assessment of settlement strengths and to build a dimension of value into settlement practice. If there is family breakdown during the resettlement period, its members are deprived of a very important support system, which is hard to replace in the new home society. Individuals are left in a position of vulnerability, while their main resource unit is diminished, since the wider kinship resource base which was often of central significance is missing.

The family is poised to exercise important protective functions for its members. Building connections outward into the society and its institutions usually entails meeting, to some degree, prejudice, resistance or discrimination, and can entail difficult experiences for individuals. Family and social circles serve as protective mechanisms for resisting the effects of prejudices, and in particular for the prevention of their internalization. Ethnic communities function also in this respect when they have been established. Findings from Alitolppa-Niitamo's (2004) study of Somali youth in Metropolitan Helsinki identifies youth as being in a role of African-Muslim 'icebreakers' in cases where there are no previous co-ethnic communities to cushion the acculturation process. Settlement can bring to immigrants new unforeseen roles of cultural 'icebreakers', which they carry out in the pioneering of different aspects of 'multiculturalization' processes.

In the case of refugees, the way in which children handle experiences of war and violence depends, to a large degree, on the way in which their parents deal with these experiences (Bek-Pedersen and Montgomery 2006). The role of family support in the individual's interpretation of, and response to, violent events is critical. Familial attachment and positive modelling of coping behaviour have been found to buffer stress and to combat the influence of trauma and disruption. The benefits of family integration and attachment were found to extend to both children and adults (McCallin 1992; Ager 1993). The healing processes associated with family integration and attachment underscore the significance of family reunification programmes and processes.

While difficult adjustment and settlement conditions undeniably constitute 'threats' to be overcome, family functioning increases welfare and well-being, freeing its members for engagement in the arena of societal interaction, with its distinct opportunities for learning, self-development and, not least, expanding life skills and resilience mechanisms.

Socialization as the Honing of Civic, Social and Life Skills

In addition to the building of life skills and social and civic competencies, developing strategies for survival and assisting its members in the process of adjustment is a key role of the immigrant family. While socialization in the majority society involves a process of 'enculturation', when individuals learn the cultural patterns of the ethnic collectivity to which they actually belong, the socialization of the youth in immigrant families is simultaneous with socio-cultural adaptation of the whole family to the new culture. This is a qualitatively different task.

Rapid language skill acquisition and a different pace of acculturation among youth can raise the risk of intergenerational distance and family conflict. Studies have shown that a major area of conflict in immigrant families is that between parent and child (Balgopal 2000). Tension arises from double expectations of youth, who are encouraged to pursue achievement at school and outside the home. This must generally happen, however, at the cost of adopting the ways of the new society, a cost which some parents are not ready to pay outright. Parents are unwilling to accept, or are apprehensive in accepting, that young people gradually give up principles and values that comprise the core of the original culture which has sustained and structured their own lives.

The potential of a rift in relations is encountered around issues of parental authority versus family democracy, the boundaries of adolescent freedom and behaviour outside the home, including sexual relationships, and the use of alcohol, for example (see Balgopal 2000). Children start to negotiate two cultural spaces early in settlement, since their schooling brings them directly into public roles and cultural spaces. For their parents, with firm roots in the original culture, the transition is likely to be more subtle and gradual.

Stein (1986) observes that many of the first generation might have seen migration as having been for the sake of their children or their children's future. Improvements of the second generation's prospects and their well-being have commonly been one of the hopes of the migration process. The second generation can be much more tenuously rooted in their home culture and influenced by the need for peer acceptance. Their acculturation is rapid. Parents need to reconcile pride in children's progress in the new society with distress at the gradual loss of the original culture and respect for the 'old ways' (Stein 1986).

The strains arising from problems in the socialization of youth can result in dysfunctional outcomes. In settlement countries which prohibit physical disciplining of children, the use of corporal punishment has been one of the reasons leading to children being taken into protective custody. Incidences of children being taken into care can lead to family breakdown in settlement situations. The resort to physical disciplining of children constitutes one problem area that calls for the development and adequate implementation of culturally sensitive, effective and proactive service responses in the area of cross-cultural child socialization issues. Aronson Fontes (2005) states that as professional helpers work towards safeguarding and promoting the welfare of children in ethnoculturally diverse families, they meet the challenge of how to work to the same standards regarding thresholds for intervention. Aronson Fontes (2005) points out that there are inherent tensions for professionals in working with culturally diverse families in a multiracial context where there are different conceptions of what constitutes harmful behaviour.

Roer-Strier and Rosenthal's (2001, 276–7) concept of the 'adaptive adult' opens up a perspective on the functional roots of culture and can throw light on why the first generation might not be willing to relinquish its values, principles and beliefs without very good reason. Goldman (1993) sees that every culture can be seen as a statement of the adaptive values it has evolved in the course of the struggle for survival and striving for well-being under a given set of physical, social and cultural environmental conditions. Roer-Strier and Rosenthal (2001) propose that the organization of child-rearing and educational ideologies is derived from an image of a metaphorical 'adaptive adult'.

The image of the 'adaptive adult' may vary significantly between societies and across cultures, while there could also be common features. This concept of adaptive values justifies why culture retention might have a very pragmatic function, and why it should not be dismissed simply as unwillingness to change, or as arising from a narrow moralistic perspective on the part of the first generation. Before abandoning the 'old' adaptive values, parents/adults must have newer adaptive values to put in their place.

Using the concept of the adaptive adult, Roer-Strier (1996; 1997, 277) suggests that there are three styles which parents employ in coping with socialization responsibilities. The traditional 'uni-cultural' style is represented by the kangaroo image because of its tendency to protect its offspring in a secure pouch. Families perceive themselves as the primary socializing agents of their children, preserving the image of the 'adaptive adult' of their culture of origin, and erecting barriers against outside influences. The 'culturally disoriented' style accommodates the rapid assimilation of children. It is represented by the metaphor of the cuckoo which lays its eggs in the nests of other birds which then take care of its young. Roer-Strier (1997) states that families adopting this style tend to disqualify themselves as effective socializing agents in the new culture and entrust the socialization of their children to the agents of the new system, even though they retain their own image of 'adaptive adult'.

The 'bicultural' style is illustrated by the chameleon and its ability to change its colour to blend in with the environment. Families choosing this style appreciate the significant differences between socialization practices in the two cultures and encourage their children to live in harmony with both cultures as far as possible. Although efforts are made to maintain, at least partially, their 'old' image of the 'adaptive adult', they seek to understand the characteristics of the adaptive adult in the new society in order to help both the child and themselves to cope with the new environment.

The 'culturally dis-oriented' style includes a risk dimension. This approach is likely to be based on parents' belief that the settlement environment generates mechanisms and supports which will lead to positive socialization outcomes. Such an assumption could be derived from previous experience in the country of origin, where this approach would have been valid for conditions in which wider social control and social responsibility constituted the norm in high context[1] communities and societies. In settlement, the rationale underlying this type of socialization choice to accede to more localized socialization forces could be based on inadequate assessment of settlement environments. Parents require deep understandings and insight into the new culture as part of their resource base for socialization tasks.

The family and the home in settlement become important sites for renegotiation processes as family members fashion approaches and choices to meet challenges of settlement. This process comes to involve so-called 'deep change', entailing as it must some transformation or compromise of values and beliefs. Meeting settlement challenges can be an empowering and very enlightening experience from which individuals learn and through which all members of the family derive valuable knowledge. As Foner (1997) points out, immigrants are not passive individuals who are acted upon by external forces. They play an active role in reconstructing and redefining family life.

Socialization can be understood from the perspective of the family's responsibility for the 'moral development' of youth. The settlement context of this task might be different from the environment in the country of origin, where it might have been possible to draw upon specific social resources that played an important function in this area. The core of the 'old' culture, imbued with specific values, beliefs and principles, provided unfailing signposts for living. Additionally, sources of informal social control and socialization were generally available in the environment through immediate and wider kin circles, schools, religious and other institutions. In the absence of such mechanisms for socialization, the

---

1   Herberg (1993) has adapted Hall's (1976a; 1976b) ideas of high and low context cultures for application within societies extending Hall's original cross-national meaning. Herberg (1993) states that in 'high context' cultures, kin relationships, established at birth, define who one is and one's lifelong mutual rights and obligations. At the other pole of the continuum of 'context' is 'low context', where very little of one's identity, obligations and rights derive from family. Rather, the individual is expected to develop his or her place or context in each new situation and must go through that development activity on a lifelong basis.

family mobilizes its strengths and available external supports in this most critical responsibility area. Socialization includes not only inculcation of behavioural patterns but the dimension of 'moral development'. The return to religion and possible intensification of emphasis on religious forms might be part of this concern with core culture and its innate significance for living. Herberg (1960, 12) claims that immigrants must confront the existential question of 'Who am I?' In a new social context, immigrants might be able to find meaning and identity by reaffirming traditional beliefs, including the structures of religious faith that may have previously been taken for granted.

Moral development is a basic dimension of socialization. Kohlberg (1963; 1981) proposed that individuals progress through six stages at three levels as they develop a set of principles regarding what is right and what is wrong. At the preconventional or premoral level, behaviour is governed by external controls, through rewards and punishments. At the conventional level, moral thought is based on conforming to conventional roles. The opinions of others become important, and behaviour is governed by conforming to social expectations. The postconventional level refers to the development of a moral conscience. Moral decisions are internally controlled, and go beyond what others might say. Morality involves higher-level principles beyond law and even beyond self-interest.

Using Kohlberg's (1963; 1981) model, we can appreciate the influence of the immediate social environment on the first two levels. When the value frames of the settlement environment are different or as yet unknown, it is likely that parents experience the need to exercise extra caution in their role as the prime socializing agents for their youth. In these scenarios, the role of the ethnocultural community, kin and social circles (in close proximity and even over distance) assume great importance during settlement. Parents and adults often have renewed or intensified interest in the role of the religious congregation to assist in the moral development of youth. They must locate and work with socializing agents to whom the development of their youth can be entrusted. Some acculturation issues are, at least in part, linked to concerns about moral development.

Building the skill set needed for fulfilling the moral development responsibility of socialization also requires intimate knowledge of the mores and culture of the settlement society. In this respect the support and input of other socializing agents in majority society would be critical in some instances. For example, parents who do not learn the majority language are at a disadvantage when it comes to picking up new cues on parenting styles in the new environment. The mediating function of ethnocultural communities is also of value in transmitting information and the benefit of experience.

Acculturation as Part of Socialization

Acculturation is a process of adaptation and becoming competent in another culture. The challenge in acculturation is twofold: to arrive at an understanding of the new culture and to make sense *again* of the old. This is the preliminary for arriving at a well-informed synthesis of cultural elements that will be of relevance for settlement challenges. The process is one of reaching a workable balance of old and new that will serve the family unit and its members in settlement – enabling them to draw on strengths from the old and new, in order to manage change and adjustment successfully. It can be seen that settlement entails the building of multidimensional frames of understanding of both the new and the old environment.

Fong (2001) points out that in the original home environments, immigrant and refugee children and families had quite functional cultural values and practices which operated as strengths and bound them to their countrymen. But in journeying to a new host country, many of these cultural values have been re-evaluated, because the receiving country's culture either fails to understand them or disagrees with their priority. Practitioners ought not only to acknowledge that cultural values of clients are strengths but also learn to use them in social work assessments to guide treatment planning and intervention implementation.

Chamberlain (2006), who has studied Caribbean families in diaspora, speaks of the transmission and transformation of values which have proven by custom to be efficacious. Referring to them as part of cultural capital, she draws the conclusion that the generation of this type of capital is perhaps the most valuable function performed by families. Such a process provides the individual with a sense of value, and the community with a shared and distinctive culture and identity. Chamberlain (2006) places emphasis on the values that surround and support the importance of kin as both a practical element of family life, and as a symbolic element of belonging.

Adaptation and Acculturation in Refugee Groups

One of the more subtle sources of settlement stress among refugees is the burden of seeing their society fall apart in political and civil turmoil, and witnessing the human and social costs of this. Refugees have to come to terms with this shadow side of their settlement process. This experience can be intense and long-lasting for persons who have been actively involved in, or have waited for, political changes to bring positive developments in their own country.

The experiences related to displacement can impact subsequently on adaptation and settlement. Harsh living conditions and social disruption prior to flight range from restriction on mobility, school closure, general breakdown of law and order, to military conflict, political persecution, imprisonment, terror and violence, with the consequent fragmentation and separation of families. The duration of conditions needs to be considered as an integral aspect of the experience. Refugees include those who have lived in zones of turmoil and pervasive conflicts through prolonged civil wars and those who were displaced in violent uprising (Barudy 1989; Dannreuther 2007). Some groups have been long-stayers in camps. For example, Fong (2001) discusses the situation of refugee families who have experienced camps and long stays in unfamiliar transit countries. Undocumented immigrants have endured sometimes desperately grim passages on boats. These transitional experiences can both directly and indirectly impact on the identity formation of children and the coping adaptations of families. Social workers need to be competent in assessing the various contexts and social environments encountered in the emigration journey and in understanding their influences on the adaptation behaviours of their clients.

The dynamics of displacement differ from those connected with voluntary planned migration, a process for which individuals try to prepare themselves in advance. Most refugees have had little chance to plan. Any physical or mental preparation for flight of necessity was conducted in conditions of great uncertainty as the circumstances of the journey have not been predictable. It is not uncommon for refugees to have to deal with varying degrees of culture shock, which is the type of physiological and psychological stress experienced when familiar cues are no longer present. This stress, which is common to any anxiety-producing situation, may be severe or mild, may last several months, or appear only fleetingly (Stein 1986).

The families of persecuted individuals have faced stress as a consequence of forced disorganization and brutal changes to family structure and functioning. In settlement, adjustment strives toward a new equilibrium aimed at the survival of the family as a system. The process of equilibration, however, is frequently overcome by the intensity and rapidity of events which can constitute a risk to the stability of the family (Barudy 1989). With regard to prevention and intervention in the interest of refugee mental health and well-being, Ager (1993) proposes a more general preventative approach focusing on minimizing stressors and bolstering ameliorative factors within refugee experience, rather than discrete psychosocial interventions.

Most individuals in exile do not cut off ties with their homeland when residing in another society. Many bonds endure physical distance and separation. These are those with kin, friends and countrymen and women, as well as cultural ties. Refugees strive to manage concerns over distance, and to come to terms with the fact that there are problem situations affecting close circles, over which they have little control. The disparity between their own condition in settlement and the distress of those in the home country might be very unsettling. Cambodians resettled in European countries and North America, for example, tried to retain connection with siblings who were living in camps along the Thai border for years, in desperate conditions and with ultimately bleak prospects. These situations present an inverted and troubled version of the standard relative deprivation theory. Marsiglia and Menjivar (2004) state that all family members sooner or later feel the stress of a legacy of war, acculturation and the pressures of living in two worlds.

Loss and separation are part of the complex experiences of refugees. Lyons, Manion and Carlsen (2006, 70) state that multiple or compound losses are common after mass violence, including 'loss of loved one, home, workplace, school, pet, emotional and physical safety, comfort in daily life, trust in the future, financial stability, sense of fairness, control, identity, meaning and hope'. Family relations must bear the factor of separation. Refugees who have had to leave family members behind live with uncertainty regarding family reunification, the outcome of family reunification application procedures and processes of orderly departure from regions still in the throes of social upheaval. Such situations affect family relations and also the process of settling into the new environment.

Coping Skills in Settlement

Lazarus' (1984) and Lazarus and Folkman's (1984) classic work on stress and coping provides a useful framework for understanding how immigrants and refugees might manage stress from settlement and acculturation processes. Lazarus' (1984) work was also adapted by Anderson (1991) into a heuristic model for understanding acculturative stress of black Americans. I draw here on this body of work, and that of Snyder (1999), to present a framework for understanding stress and coping styles as applied to settlement contexts. According to this framework, the manner in which individuals cope with different types of stress is influenced by their own personal characteristics, and how these are brought to bear on the stress-encountering experience. In other words, situations of stress are managed by individuals via the mediating effects of their own personal characteristics. As an outcome of this process, individuals come to select and adopt different forms of coping. In applying this frame to settlement and integration conditions, we can use four categories of stressors:

1. Life events: these can refer to migration itself, as well as significant migration-related events. In the case of refugees, this would include pre-flight events, the breakdown in civic structure or long stays in camps.
2. Life transitions: examples can be found in the different facets of acculturation and settlement, such as having to learn a new language of communication; encountering and living in another cultural environment; rebuilding social networks; and finding employment.
3. 'Hassles' or problems in the environment: these could be represented as cultural misunderstandings or as prejudiced attitudes, for example.
4. Loss and separation: most significant examples may include separation from kin and family, but also loss of cultural milieu, social circles, social status.

There is variation in individuals' range of capacities and dispositions for engaging and managing stress-causing situations. Individuals are different in how they make *appraisals* of situations and how they assess their chances of overcoming presenting difficulties. Previous experience of engaging with and successfully overcoming stressful situations may have built up an individual's personal resources and a *sense of self-efficacy* in being able to handle difficulty. Other personal characteristics which promote coping and which function as strengths in this process relate to *identity* and *self-esteem*. A strong ethnocultural identity has been found to be a resource for integration, particularly for the second generation, for example, in Portes and Zhou's (1993) study of ethnic communities in the United States. It is likely that immigrants would have had chances to build a sense of self-efficacy when of necessity they have had to face new situations and engage in continuous problem-solving. Their sense of self-efficacy could also be built on past success in working through adverse situations. In this case, such a quality would constitute or be bordering on *resilience*.

Categories of coping include:

Emotion-focused coping which is largely focused upon managing distress rather than changing the problem situation. The types of strategies identified in this type include distancing and escape-avoidance strategies, which refer to the individual's efforts to divert attention from the stressful situation, and to disengage mentally from it; deciding to accept responsibility or blame; exercising self-control over the expression of feelings; and selective attention strategies aimed not only at diminishing the negative emotional impact, but generating positive emotional responses as well. Selective attention strategies include making positive comparisons, cognitive restructuring, employing comforting cognitions, as well as positive reappraisal. Antonovsky (1979) refers to the ability to control and use emotional and affective responses to stress, a coping mechanism roughly parallel to the emotion-focused strategies listed above.

Coping through social support is based on support-seeking and using social support resources. Generally the benefits of social support involve practical, material help and emotional support. This form of coping can contribute in powerful, important ways to assist individuals to deal with, and recover from, stress (Baumeister, Faber and Wallace, 1999). Compton and Galaway (1999) refer to the network of family, friends, neighbours and colleagues as a supporting social system, which can also provide information and other resources in a time of stress or crisis. In general, coping strategies also reflect basic dispositional tendencies within the individual.

Problem-focused coping is a coping process which is directed at changing the situation that is causing distress, or alternatively focusing attention on the problem in an effort to prevent or control it. In order to change the situations in the social environment, the individual can engage interpersonally and even confrontationally in the effort to remove barriers. In problem-focused coping, the problem-solving process might involve acquiring different attitudes or learning a new skill set, as well as being able to generate solutions in one's personal or social life spheres.

Coping reflects how individuals respond to a particular class of events. Ideally they would have the capacity to use all styles appropriately, depending on the stress-causing situation. No single mode of coping is superior since they are context- and contingency-related. Individuals will have developed their own repertoire of coping styles and applications. Without emic perspectives on problem situations, it is difficult to appraise the reasons behind the coping selections which are made by individuals in different situations. For example, after careful consideration, an individual might come to the conclusion that emotion-focused coping in the situation might be the only feasible course at the time. To outward appearances, coping responses might not yet have been deployed, yet the reality might be different.

In social work and settlement practice, the potential exists to intervene at many, albeit not all, points in coping processes. In the area of life stressors, practitioners work, for example, to create conditions and mechanisms that facilitate settlement and integration-related life transitions and acculturation processes, as well as carrying out anti-discrimination and anti-oppressive interventions. Empowerment approaches valorize and seek to foster client strengths and personal qualities. Tangible and intangible supportive and professional mechanisms of various kinds constitute valuable inputs into individuals' and families' coping efforts. This framework can be adapted for understanding the collective processes of family coping in settlement. Coping skills and incremental experience in coping are the basis of resiliency in families as well as individuals.

Closing Comments

In this chapter, we have discussed the immigrant family as a crucible of adaptation and coping processes in settlement. Its members engage in reflective tasks as they re-think and re-appraise their roles, relationships and responsibilities. It is important for practitioners to conceptualize the family both as a dynamic system in itself, and also as a unit within its vitally important social and societal environment. The immigrant family, like its members, must find its place in the wider society in order to function optimally.

Chapter 8

The Second Generation

Introducing Second Generation Issues

The life conditions of the second generation constitute a powerful indicator of the longitudinal impact of policies and programmes. Studies from the USA, Australia, France and Canada indicate that many of the second generation of migrants can encounter grave problems of social exclusion despite having lived all or the greater part of their lives in the new home society. The scrutiny of second generation issues raises some troubling questions about current settlement processes and intergenerational inequality.

Second generation immigrants already make up large percentages of the generation of young adults in many of the countries of settlement. The percentages are not likely to fall as international migration is forecast to continue at a high pace throughout the twenty-first century. In Europe, the populations are aging and shrinking while economies and labour markets are becoming increasingly interconnected. Large socio-economic inequalities between nations drive labour migration flows. Peoples are displaced and dispersed over great distances by political wars and repression. The second generation will be a vital part of the populations of tomorrow in countries of reception.

Defining the second generation can be complex when the multiple strands of present-day migration are taken into account for policy and demographic purposes. Vogel and Triandafyllidou (2005) observe that 'in many sociological studies, foreign born individuals are called "first generation immigrants", while their offspring – born in the receiving country or having migrated with their parents at an early age – are called "second generation immigrants"'. Another definition is offered by Suarez-Orozco and Suarez-Orozco (2001) who propose categories of 'immigrant children' and 'children of immigrants', a definition which was originally developed in the course of their work on Central American immigrants in the USA. 'Immigrant children' refers to those who have migrated to the settlement country with parents or other adults, and are not born there. 'Children of immigrants', on the other hand, refers both to foreign-born children and those born in the settlement country of immigrant parents. This definition does not probe the age, immigration status and mixed parentage factors that would be otherwise necessary for purposes of policy or research. The first definition, referred to by Vogel and Triandafyllidou (2005) above, is used in this work.

This chapter looks firstly at identity issues which have been foremost among studies focusing on the second generation. In the latter section of the chapter, the structural aspects of settlement in the second generation are examined in the light of Parekh's (1997) parameters of 'equal citizenship' and their implications.

Ethnic Identity, its Formation, Refashioning and Politicization

An evolutionary view of ethnic identity offers us a clue as to the popularity of the concept. Gans (1979) points to a new kind of ethnic involvement which emphasizes concern with identity. The new involvement can be understood to be minimal or even 'an ethnicity of the last resort'. It does not require traditional ethnic culture or institutions, but does give central importance to symbols. When ethnicity is altered to symbolic status, it should not constitute a barrier to social advancement, can be seen in positive terms, and can be sustained without 'cost'. It has the potential to persist indefinitely. We can understand that this new genre of ethnic involvement can be a mode that would readily fit with the advanced stages of acculturation in the second generation. In their case, rapid or steady acculturation cannot accommodate the dense ethnic involvement more characteristic of many immigrants of the first generation. Identity holds appeal to researchers and some policy-making circles as a focal point for understanding the changing nature of ethnic involvement. Identity, thus, is the embodiment of symbolic ethnicity.

Furthermore, contrary to the idea of identity as an a priori entity, and according to which people would or would not be members of ethnic groups, Calhoun (2003) proposes that, in actuality, people participate in ethnicity to varying degrees. From another perspective, identities declare not some primordial identity but rather a positional choice of the group with which they wish to be associated. Identity choices are more political than anthropological, more 'associational', and thus less ascribed (Modood et al 1997).

Studies have focused on how identities are being refashioned to take on instrumental roles in political life, as demonstrated by the 'new veiling' movements. The process of establishing identity also involves the individuals' journey to self-understanding and understandings of how the world is organized. This project of establishing identity can have an activating effect (Calhoun 2003).

The refashioning of identity to take on instrumental roles in political life is a process of increasing salience for social citizenship. Modood (1997) observes that, for some, ethnic identity has become a primary focus of their politics, similar to the way in which other groups have politicized identities based on gender and sexuality. He refers to an ethnic assertiveness that grows out of feelings of not being respected or not having access to public space, and seeks to bring out positive images to fight the effect of traditional or dominant stereotypes. Modood (1997) states that this movement does not simply pursue tolerance of ethnic difference, but aims to challenge existing power relations and seeks also public acknowledgement, resources and representation.

The consequences of inequality and its effects into the second generation is a longitudinal process. The second generation's positioning in society is different from that of their parents or elders, who could attribute differential positioning and treatment to their brief period of social citizenship in the new home society. The succeeding generation must itself fashion its tools to address the contingencies in their particular social situation. Ethnic identity can be used as a political resource (Solomos 1998). Wimmer (2004) identifies a downside of this activity, stating that the process of 'racialization' (or, in the German- and French-speaking world, 'ethnicization') can create those very cultural barriers that are the focus of multicultural 'integration' policy.

Identity is constantly adapted in the context of the dynamics of relations to the surrounding society and its institutions. The well-accepted understanding of the process of identity formation and adaptation through the frame of internal and external definition has particular salience in settlement situations. In his work on ethnic groups and boundaries, Frederik Barth (1969) stated that personal identity is located within a two-way social process, an interaction between 'ego' and 'other', inside and outside. It is in the meeting of internal and external definition that identity, whether social or personal, is created.

Immigrants, especially visible minorities and newer groups, undergo continuous processes of scrutiny and categorization in the course of building relationships outward and becoming positioned in the new home society. These categorizations might be derived from impressions gained over quite brief periods of interaction and co-existence. Although categorizations might not necessarily be negative, they might be misleading or based on superficial criteria. In the case of negative stereotyping or labelling, which might also be on a public level, negotiation between the inside and outside images is a critical process. The consequences of the internalizing of stigmatizing public images can lead to a circle of disadvantage and marginalization which is induced by the interaction of the negative self-image of a stigmatized minority with impacting effects of discrimination and exclusion (Franklin 2003; Jenkins 1994; 1996). At the same time, individuals would be in a decisively better position to dispel such stigmatizing mechanisms if they are not encapsulated in their own ethnic community circles. The resistance of negative stigmatization calls for the deployment of strong coping capacities by individuals and groups. In this situation it is important to build the capacities for 'having – or choosing – an "identity" that enables rather than hinders' (Franklin 2003, 470).

For the second generation the possibility exists of developing the mechanisms for facing the challenge of negative categorization on a collective basis. That this can constitute a potential source of power is demonstrated by the rise of 'identity politics', political engagement grounded into the settlement environment and with ethnic minority members as the central actors for change.

Identials

David de Levita (1965) proposed the *idential* concept, which is a useful analytic frame that can assign a legitimate place for the broad range of socio-cultural and other characteristics existing in newer groups, which are otherwise often crudely subsumed under the category of 'difference'. Identials refer to all the identifying particulars in individuals which may constitute their 'identity'. Identials are the salient components or material of identity. The unintentionally ascribed identials refer to those pertaining to sex, date of birth, ethnicity, and possibly also to social class. They are the given categories with which an individual is furnished at birth, and which he or she can do very little to change. These categories are crucial with regard to self-definitions and definitions of others. *Intentionally attained identials* can be understood as pertaining to membership in groups, collectives and organizations to which the individual builds purposive affiliation. Identials are associated with a series of structural properties and roles. They can be referred to as the 'substantives' or 'nouns' of identity. They constitute identity's kinds and categories. They pertain to its contents.

Identials is a comprehensive concept and can help to counter overriding emphasis on culture in identity formation. Through the concept of identials we can understand the composition of identity as involving a selective dimension. Nazroo and Karlsen (2003) point out that gender and class are also important markers and in certain situations might be more important aspects of identity than ethnicity. Ahmad (1996, 190) states that when culture is stripped of its dynamic social, economic, gender and historical context, it becomes a rigid and constraining concept which is seen to mechanistically determine peoples' behaviours and actions rather than providing a flexible resource for living, and for deriving meaning.

Findings from Nazroo and Karlsen's (2003) study of patterns of identity among ethnic minorities suggest that ethnicity as identity is an important, but variable and context-dependent, aspect of people's lives, and more sensitive measures of ethnicity should be developed that can take account of this. The authors emphasize the inter-related nature of each different aspect of identity and how an experience of ethnicity is influenced by other aspects of our social identities. Ethnicity is just one part of who we are and should not be viewed as operating independently of other elements. Ethnicity and religion function as central visible markers of identity in the field of identity politics. This needs to be juxtaposed with the holistic concept of identity as a matrix of identials. The former is a politicized understanding of identity, the latter is an understanding of identity that encompasses the different facets and categories of its substance (Nazroo and Karlsen 2003).

Identification

In distinguishing between identity and identification, identity refers to self-perception, while identification, in the context of ethnicity and culture, refers to the extent to which individuals view themselves as involved with an identifiable group and also on the strength of their investment in (or stake in) the particular culture of the group. Interaction with the specific culture, as well as changes during life, moderate the identification process (Cetrez 2005). Identification is an individual-level process. Ongoing social learning is involved but the settling actor ultimately retains autonomy.

Segmented Assimilation

Immigrant youth is not the sole group in societies bearing the risk of unequal citizenship. Segmented assimilation is a concept that refers to the idea that succeeding generations of immigrants become incorporated into different segments of the society to which they are exposed. If not integrating into the mainstream, succeeding generations might become affiliated to, or part of, other groups to which they are exposed and which might be positioned in society's margins. Segmented assimilation is a concept that retains the early idea of immigrants' momentum toward assimilation in the new environment, but incorporates the possibility of divergence in the direction of this process. It seeks to explain the divergent destinies of the immigrant second generation (Zhou 1997, 984; Portes and Zhou 1993). Segmented assimilation of subsequent generations would seem to suggest that for certain groups integration no longer seems to be simply a matter of time and the sequence of generations (Esser 2004, 1126).

Waldinger and Feliciano (2004) have studied second generation Mexicans, the largest second generation group in the US and predominantly of working class origins. There are early indications that this particular cohort is not experiencing 'downward assimilation'. The researchers' evidence suggests that the experience of today's second generation is consistent with the earlier pattern, in which the children of immigrants progressed by moving ahead within the working class. They warn that as the patterns of cohorts change, there are likely to be different outcomes.

Equal Citizenship

Parekh (1997) looks beyond the technicalities of immigration and settlement policy and procedures in liberal societies to make an important point. Using Britain as an example, he claims that two main assumptions underpin the relations between the wider society and its immigrants, forming the basis of an unspoken moral covenant. The society expects that its immigrants will identify themselves with it, and in turn it undertakes to treat them equally with the rest of its citizens. Parekh (1997) states that identification and equality lay the basis for fair terms of co-operation, by bringing together the legitimate claims of the wider society and the immigrants in a reasonably satisfactory manner to create the conditions for a cohesive and fair society.

Immigrants who have chosen to come to settle in a country would be committed to it and strive to become a part of it. They would value their membership of the community and accept its corresponding obligations. Parekh (1997) goes on to say that identification extends to a moral and emotional attachment to the community, although identification for immigrants does not entail the surrendering of cultural identity which would be an unacceptable price of membership. Identification with the wider society and the individual's more particular identifications can co-exist.

This is otherwise a principle that is gaining increased recognition in settlement and integration policies in many countries.

I draw here on Parekh's (1997) frame for equal citizenship in a multicultural society. His work focused on the British context, but it has wider relevance for societies of settlement which are experiencing increasing cultural heterogeneity. It is particularly relevant as a frame that takes the principle of equality, the pillar of social citizenship, and shapes it to capture dimensions of equality that are especially salient in the context of contemporary societies in which the population comprises a significant number of non-majority groups (or the culturally diverse groups of the multicultural mosaic).

Second generation immigrants comprise a core part of the non-majority groups. The status of full citizenship is theirs, but in some of the most critical participation-related aspects, rights and membership remain at formal and non-substantive level. Contemporary modes of immigrant integration recognize difference and cultural integrity in addition to the principles of universal equality. Parekh's (1997) frame transposes equal citizenship into a workable mode for multicultural societies. The author points out that while citizenship is based on the principle of equality, the traditional discussion of equality has largely been predicated on the assumption of a culturally homogeneous society, and does not grapple with issues of inter-cultural equality in the present day societies of immigration. These original understandings and ways of interpreting equality do not readily lend themselves to newer groups' pursuit and achievement of substantive equality. We thus need to approach equal citizenship from a different perspective if we are not to weaken the quality of membership of newer groups. Parekh (1997) proposes five parameters of equal citizenship in a multicultural society:

1. The elimination of discrimination
2. Equality of opportunity
3. Equal respect
4. Public acceptance of immigrants as a legitimate and valued part of society
5. The opportunity to preserve and transmit their cultural identities.

Parekh (1997) observes that different societies address these five areas of equality differently and create their own distinct patterns of equality, making cross-country comparisons difficult and possibly meaningless. The parameters touch on aspects of equality and inequality which frame settlement and integration processes on the ground. Should these be pursued only through the provisions for formal equality, there is a greater risk of longitudinal and persisting inequality with its intergenerational impact on integration.

It used to be assumed that the second generation would have overcome most of the integration obstacles which commonly are faced by the first generation. Of late, however, the problematic plight of second generation cohorts in traditional receiving countries has been raised in the media, public discourse on immigration and by some researchers. The parameters of equal citizenship are discussed in the light of studies on the second generation, as well as in the context of settlement situations and issues.

The Elimination of Discrimination

Parekh (1997) states that as long as minorities are liable to deliberate or unintended discrimination, they are clearly not treated as equal citizens. Discrimination can occur for newer groups in different areas and across the spheres of participatory activity. Differential access to welfare mechanisms or to educational opportunity signifies that the scope of membership is reduced in the short term and possibly also in the long term.

In the case of the second generation, however, more attention has been focused on aspects of labour market discrimination, and its associated risks of marginalization and social exclusion. The work of Portes (1994) and Rydgren (2004) illustrate aspects of this phenomenon. Rydgren's (2004) study explains phenomena which occur widely across the spectrum of societies of settlement, and are not features unique to its particular location.

In Rydgren's (2004) study of second generation cohorts in Sweden, inferior employment outcomes are found to have most affected those individuals with a non-European background. For those with one Swedish-born parent, the risk is twice as high as it is for Swedes of the same age who have two Swedish-born parents. For those with both parents born in a non-European country, the risk is more than three times as high. These employment outcomes occur regardless of the fact that individuals born in Sweden would have acquired language skills, knowledge about Swedish 'culture', norms and established ways of doing things to the extent that they would be able to harmonize with working teams (Rooth and Ekberg 2003). With regard to the labour market in general, Rydgren (2004, 712) states that the difference in labour market outcomes between migrants and native Swedes suggests 'the existence of rather extensive ethnic discrimination in the Swedish labour market'. Rydgren (2004) refers to the processes and mechanisms that lead to such outcomes. Key actors who hold gatekeeper positions in the labour market discriminate against migrants in a twofold way: by making recruitment decisions based on stereotypical (and often prejudiced) beliefs about group-specific characteristics rather than on individual skills; and also by selecting persons known to them or who otherwise have been recommended for vacant positions by someone they know. Rydgren states that neither of these mechanisms involves much reflection, implying that the actors in gatekeeping positions discriminate often against migrants without being aware of it. Additionally unintended consequences of state programmes and legislation may lead to institutional discrimination.

Portes (1994) refers to labour market conditions which have affected immigrant employment in the US. He draws attention to the fortunate combination of circumstances brought about by the expanding economy and scarcity of labour early in the twentieth century, which allowed the European second generation to move steadily upward on the economic and social ladders. Academic theories extrapolated on their successful experience, resulting in the development of the concept of the linear process of assimilation. In contrast, the children of migrants who settled later in the last century were much less fortunate. The second generation of Puerto Rican migrants faced extensive discrimination. The changed economic situation blocked the mobility of these migrants' children and confined many to the same inferior jobs held by their parents. According to Portes (1994), the perpetuation of these negative conditions later led to an inter-related set of urban pathologies. Portes nonetheless emphasizes that immigrant families and communities commonly possess material and moral resources that confer advantages on their young as they seek avenues for successful adaptation. This has been demonstrated, for example, by MacLeod's (1987) ethnographic study of youth aspirations in a low income neighbourhood, and the finding that ethnicity could be a key factor in making a visible minority group more receptive to the achievement ideology.

Equality of Opportunity

Even if there is no problem of discrimination, immigrants are hindered by obvious economic, political and cultural 'positional' disadvantages inherent in the situation of new groups. Parekh (1997) argues that appropriately targeted interventions and the implementation of these are critical if they are to exercise their rights of equal citizenship and develop a sense of identification with the mainstream society. Immigrants would need well-targeted forms of help in order to exercise the rights of citizenship equally and to build the requisite capacity for this. Forsander (2002) states that ethnic inequality is a problem if it is transferred to the next generation, because at that point there is a risk that it will become a structural problem. The principle and practices of equality of opportunity are often not far reaching or powerful enough to impact on processes in favour of fair outcomes. As seen in Chapter 5, the principle of equal worth would call for individuals with different needs to be considered for different resources. This distribution would be in accordance with their treatment as equals rather than as being administered equal treatment. Such an approach recognizes the existence of individual and group differences, and that identical treatment for all will not necessarily achieve a just set of outcomes.

Parekh (1997) points out the need for policies and interventions to overcome the lack of economic, cultural and political 'leads/advantages' generally held by longer standing members of the citizenry. Appropriate measures with an affirmative thrust would be critical in initial stages to enable newer citizens and their children to bridge such 'gaps'.

Regarding well-being, Raz (1994) states that the principle we should uphold is simply that every individual should have access to an adequate range of options to enable him or her to have a successful life. Access implies fair chances to be able to obtain and take up the opportunity, not simply to be eligible to apply for it. In other words, problems of inequality might be more far reaching than opportunity disparity. Gibelman's (2000) work on affirmative action is discussed in Chapter 5, while Nussbaum's (2006) capabilities approach is presented in Chapter 10.

Equal Respect

Equal respect is central to the individual's sense of dignity. This principle reflects the universal right to human dignity. Individuals remain outsiders if they are subjected to offensive treatment and degrading stereotypes. Equal respect is not implemented in situations where groups hold devalued status in society. Prejudice and racism with associated negative stereotyping have corrosive effects on the process of positive identification with the society. On the other hand, equal respect implies recognition of diverse identities, including ethnic identities, within the society and the citizenry itself.

Jenkins (1994, 218) describes identity as the product of two interacting but independent dimensions: a name – the nominal, and an experience – the virtual. In terms of racist oppression, Jenkins (1994) states that the external imposition of a characterization will affect the social experience of living with that identity and also affect the self-image of individuals so defined. In this way, racist oppression can actually structure an individual's own identity, and correspondingly affect the way in which the individual with that identity interacts with others. Defining who we are, both by name and in experience, is dynamic, relatively ambiguous and will be heavily influenced by the wider society. While internal factors (agency and the construction of identity) might be the focus of emphasis, the structuring of identity by external social factors remains critically important. If minority groups are accorded devalued status in the society, there is increased risk of becoming marginalized.

Public Acceptance of Immigrants as a Legitimate and Valued Part of Society

Minorities will remain on the periphery of society if they are in practice excluded from the public space and have no representation or presence in, for example, institutions of state and the media. Parekh (1997) states that if immigrants are resented, if the dominant definition of national identity excludes them or if the institutions of government, the media and official ceremonies of the state do not reflect their presence, they remain peripheral to the wider society, in it but not of it. To be part of the citizenry of a country denotes membership. Walzer (1983) states that to be without membership is to be alienated, and to be at risk of marginalization and oppression, the enemies of civic and moral strength. Individuals need to belong to the community as responsible and valued members.

Attention to the first generation immigrants' positioning in the public domain is crucial, lest the task of establishing a position in the public space and public spheres of life be shifted on, to become the responsibility of the succeeding generation. Contrary to the idea that disadvantage in first generation migrant groups is corrected over time and length of residence, deferred structural integration can be a longitudinal experience into the second generation. Blocked integration in the first generation could establish conditions of longitudinal risk for social marginalization and peripheral status, which can interact with other exclusionary and exclusive elements to constitute a situation of social exclusion.

Proactive policy instruments which declare and confirm national level commitment to settlement and integration, and timely provision for and implementation of anti-discrimination mechanisms, confirm the place of newer groups in the society. Without substantive principles, guidelines and measures, formal rights remain at the level of remote and abstract ideas with weak connection to actual settlement conditions and conditionalities. Immigration and settlement is above all a civic matter, lodged in multiple and ongoing relationships and transactions that take place in the civic context. The integration visioning in the policy and planning process would need to be more widely inculcated in civic structures and principles which effectively frame the field of settlement dynamics.

The activation of the second generation is crucial to Europe's future civic life. If they are active today, they are more likely to stay active in the future and they are the parents and potential role models for their children (Vogel and Triandafyllidou 2005). Political mobilization and claims-making based on ethnic identity are modes of activism and, from this perspective, valuable efforts to create a presence in the public space. As settlement proceeds, the second generation is the actor cohort which can take up the responsibility for raising challenges against inequitable conditions.

The demonstration of disaffection in the public space by the second generation, which has taken place in several larger settlement countries such as the UK and France, indicates that the current conditions are not implementing parity in areas critical for minority groups. This is not a positive indicator of integration, and specifically contradicts the assumption that settlement gains will accrue in a longitudinal fashion. Second generation protest in the public space is in the first place a call for outstanding issues to be addressed, albeit from a reactive stance. Public policy and practice responses to voiced dissatisfaction would entail valid intervention that would involve genuine consultation, analysis of problem issues, participatory approaches in planning and implementing measures to redress problem issues. If we look beyond to try to capture the meaning of protest, we can understand claims-making in the public space by the second generation to be a gesture of willingness to engage with the structure of decision-making and power in the society. It is in itself, at base, an initiative for communication and action, regardless of the form of articulation which such communication might take.

The first generation might in general use more acquiescent modes of coping with less than equal conditions of social citizenship. The dynamic of their arrival and settlement is quite different from that of their descendants whose positioning was not shaped in the circumstances of migration. The second generation can choose the route of articulation and action to claim missing aspects of substantive and equal citizenship. This type of activism could be interpreted as reflecting a situation of powerlessness, but the mode of coping that is selected would definitely suggest otherwise. Protest in the public space conveys a strong message of engagement with the structure – that groups are trying to bring about change in conditions, which in principle constitutes a very active mode of participation in civil society.

The Opportunity to Preserve and Transmit their Cultural Identities

Minority members and groups are entitled to retain valued aspects of their culture. This can include their languages, cultures, religions, histories and ethnic affiliations. Identity is integral to individuals' sense of who they are, and a basis of self-respect and sense of community. Parekh (1997, Foreword) says:

> Some of their values and practices might be unacceptable and then they need to be changed, by consensus when possible and by law if necessary. However, this is quite different from asking them to abandon their cultural identities as a condition of their acceptance. The identities are integral to their sense of who they are, nurture their self-respect and sense of community and provide the resources on which they rely to find their feet in the new society and to feel secure enough to interact with it creatively.

The idea and principle that individuals are entitled to be self-determining in matters of culture and identity have become accepted gradually, along with the decline in assimilationist values in settlement. The original culture of immigrants is recognized as a potential base of resilience or hardiness in the face of new problems and challenges.

People who settle in new cultural environments face a process that has different facets. On the one hand the liminal condition is evident. Suarez-Orozco and Suarez-Orozco (2001, 92) comment on the difficulties of remaking identities, observing that: 'Immigrants are by definition on the margins of two cultures. Paradoxically, they can never truly belong either "here" or "there".' Hall (1992) proposes that migrants live in cultures of hybridity which are the products of their interlocking histories and cultures. According to Hall (1992, 310), in this process migrants are 'irrevocably translated', a condition which can be understood as that in which the old and new cultures are combined, potentially satisfactorily, to reach a degree of cultural integrity for individuals. This process starts at the outset of settlement and is continuous. The second generation's acculturation has, in one sense, its point of gravity in the new home society, and in their case we can speak simultaneously of enculturation. Their informal as well as formal relations and transactions in the society should be reflective of mainstream status.

Institution-Based Initiatives for Equal Citizenship

Settlement conditions can be examined in the light of these markers of equal citizenship. These are key areas for ensuring that newer immigrant groups will be included under the provisions for equal citizenship in a society to which all groups belong. The state itself holds the key responsibility, invested as it is with the prime authority and the resource base. The implementation of the principles and structures of equal citizenship is a national-level project closely linked to higher levels of decision-making. Initiatives for such arrangements for inclusion should be taken within the relevant institutions formally associated with the realization of different areas of citizenship rights.

In the case of addressing the first parameter relating to removal of discrimination, the state's approaches are critical. If states place more weight on public opinion and its changes, rather than on protecting individual immigrants from discrimination, there is likely to be deferral of definitive action, with the responsibility for initiative being devolved to the organizations in the labour market (trade unions, employers and their associations), or to the settling individuals who are affected. The state's role as the protector of minority interests is weakened as a result (see Graham and Soininen 1998). When the enactment or implementation of anti-discrimination legislation is deferred for decades, the first generation cohorts do not benefit from this. Yet second generation mobility is not tied solely to the educational and enculturation inputs, since parental situation also features alongside other impacting factors. The tardiness in addressing discrimination problems might also have a strong effect on second generation integration outcomes.

Policy implementation arena   Under the existing policy implementation purview of the organizational level, many existing policy structures would in actuality allow for the accommodation and implementation of practices more salient for promoting participation of newer groups. Some of the difficulties of access are institution-based. Policies come to be circumscribed within certain limited practice interpretations to ensure 'standardization' and a level of accountability in institutional practice. These more limiting interpretations can become habitual and limit the scope of action and the conceptualization of this. Policies, however, are meant to be flexible and usually designed for broader utility as frames for contextual decision-making. Yet many of them are used in a prohibitive sense, with established practice tending to draw the boundaries of their application.

Changes could be initiated at the point where policy is revisited in the light of changing conditions, with a view to seeking innovative solutions. Policies are themselves general statements or understandings which are designed to guide or channel thinking, decision-making, courses of action and eventually behaviours. They are meant to contain some flexibility, and set broad guidelines for decision-making. Weinbach (2003) states that policies should be explicit but innately flexible, general and broad enough to cover most situations, even those that have never occurred before and may never occur again.

At the organizational level, matters are compounded if policies are not written but simply implied by the actions of others. Many policies, principles and practice are based on incremental understandings and previous precedents, which can weaken considerably the situation of newer citizens. In this case, the drawing up of policy would be the course of action when situations warrant this. In certain cases, it would be necessary to shape new legal and policy instruments in order to change or modify the frame of social citizenship to accommodate all groups in the citizenry. Existing policies might simply not have the scope or capacity to include the interest of newer groups.

In sum we see, first of all, that within institutions policies could be revisited and re-interpreted to assess their capacity for accommodating different needs or catering for the needs of different groups. Secondly, the institutions associated with the implementation of citizenship rights would be the spaces in which new policies could be shaped to keep abreast of the changing profile of groups in the citizenry. The third possibility is that the initiative is left to the groups themselves who are negatively affected by conditions of unequal citizenship. The protests of immigrant youth in the public space in different settlement countries are a manifestation of this scenario, in which responsibility for conditions of inequity and equity is devolved onto the shoulders of those who are in the situation of disadvantage.

A responsibility of leadership with wide ramifications in the social services is the interpretation of policy. As stated earlier, policies have been developed historically in their own contexts. More importantly, their interpretation and applications have been tailored to even more particular situations. Social work leadership with grounded experience in settlement conditions would hold the expertise for conducting competent appraisal of the adequacy of current policies and policy applications for addressing access and other settlement issues. Long-established practice and approaches might not be suitably pitched to redress situations where participation is blocked. There is a need to work within the spirit in which policies were originally shaped. Policy evaluation needs the emic input of immigrant service users and clients as well as the institutional and structural insight of policy practitioners. Neither party can reach a full understanding of the efficacy or impact of policy and programmes on their own.

Closing Comments

Identity questions and policy issues regarding integration in the second generation have been examined in this chapter. Upward social mobility is frequently taken for granted as a characteristic feature of developed economies in settlement societies. However, in terms of the realization of universal substantive citizenship, closer scrutiny of the situation of immigrant groups and their second generation cohorts would be necessary as part of valid exercises in accountability and programme evaluation. Attention would need to be directed to the actual effects of policy on the conditions of newer groups and the second generation, in order to generate accurate information on the processes of exclusion and inclusion.

The personal and social investment of first generation immigrants into the well-being and future of the second generation is usually considerable. Migration has at times been understood as a situation in which reaping the rewards of settlement efforts is deferred to the succeeding generation. This is one aspect of migration that calls for serious efforts to be made to address problems of intergenerational inequality.

Chapter 9

Developing and Implementing Social Policy and Social/Settlement Services

This chapter presents different national integration policies, in order to locate settlement programmes in a broad cross-national context. It is not possible to do justice to national models here, but fortunately there is available a wealth of recent research into these contexts (see, for example, Hatziprokopiou 2003; Gowricharn 2002). An overview of settlement service components is followed by discussion of policy processes and impacting dynamics in organizational and bureaucratic settings. In the final section, the formally non-planned phenomenon of secondary migration of settling groups and a community organization model of service provision are examined.

Policy Models – Integration Principles and Policies in Different Reception Countries

Settlement and integration policy and policy implementation constitute a challenge even in societies with comprehensive welfare systems. Integration policy goals need to remain integral to the wider national policy frame, yet must be facilitative of the particular thrusts of settlement and long-range integration. Settlement services moreover need to be responsive to the need profile in immigrant cohorts of increasing diversity. Migration flows have become global, originating from nearly all states and comprising many different types, including involuntary migrant groups. Papademetriou (2003) notes that immigration makes change the rule, whereas most organized societies are built around the concept of constancy. Furthermore, in the context of large-scale immigration, the receiving society faces examination of its own sense of identity. Immigrant settlement and integration tend to expose the weaknesses of its social and economic governance, and of its capacity to enforce its laws – factors which are a potential source of political contention.

The thrust of national settlement and integration policies can be understood as directed towards inclusion, equality and equity. These social citizenship principles underpin either explicitly or implicitly the policies and the thrust of their implementation. The participation of settlement social work in public and social policy processes entails not only contributing expertise but also representing the interests of a stakeholder constituency of newer groups that is not positioned strategically for promoting its own interests in the highly competitive national policy agenda.

Welfare states, with their emphasis on citizenship rights, are often held to embody prime instruments for inclusion and equality. However, their potential for promoting the inclusion of immigrants is not straightforward. In the first instance, as Freeman (1986) states, national welfare states are by their nature meant to be closed systems. The logic of the welfare state and thick rights of citizenship imply the existence of boundaries that distinguish between the entitled and the non-entitled – those who are members of a community and those who are not. The welfare state structure is nonetheless open, at least partially, to its external environment, and to the currents of international trade, the mobility of capital, and increasingly to the migration of labour. A feature of the system is thus an ongoing dialectic between the distributive logic of closure – mutual aid undertaken by members of a community according to socially defined conceptions of need – and the distributive logic of openness – treatment according to one's performance in the marketplace without regard to membership status or need (Freeman 1986). Yet if the welfare state in a settlement country is to remain faithful to and abreast of the contemporary patterns of need in its citizenry, it has to avoid institutional stasis. Giddens (1998) points out that the welfare state needs to be as dynamic and responsive to wider social trends as any other sector of government.

As services are extended to settling immigrants and refugees, they are generally accommodated within the prevailing blueprint which the society uses to arrange social provisioning for the majority. In very centralized systems, the settlement services tend to be outgrowths of these structures, although there is devolution of some kind to the Third Sector. Despite the undeniably well-resourced foundation of services in a welfare state, more decentralized patterns of services within this model can have the advantage of being more receptive of partnership modes of service provisioning. With more permeable boundaries, there is likely to be greater scope for immigrants' agency in roles other than service consumer. The involvement of settling groups in the service provision arena is a powerful factor in working toward the appropriateness of services from a socio-cultural perspective and their convergence with actual settlement needs on the ground.

National Models for the Incorporation of Immigrants

The original assimilation approach to incorporation, which was fashioned in its own historical context in the USA, has languished. It is discussed more fully in Chapter 4. Multiculturalism principles and approaches, even if not formally declared, have influenced settlement approaches in many reception countries. Different societal settings give their own stamp to national models, a few of which are discussed below.

Canada The development of multicultural policy in Canada which is described here is drawn from Lindström's (1995) work. Lindström states that Canada's population has always been composed of many cultural groups, with the cultural modes of French and British colonizers being dominant in its history. Immigration policies were originally Eurocentrist. In the 1950s and 1960s, racist immigration policies were becoming difficult to defend, and were in conflict with Canada's efforts to build an independent national image as a liberal, humanitarian and modern nation interested in playing an important role in the then recently founded United Nations and its refugee organizations. The point system of admission, introduced in 1962, emphasized education, training and skills as criteria for immigrant selection and admission.

In the course of fostering French–English bilingualism, it became evident that other cultural groups likewise craved official recognition in the public space. Two years after the Official Languages Act was passed, the federal government introduced Canada's first multicultural policy that had a twofold aim of helping minority groups preserve and share their language and culture and removing the cultural barriers they faced. It took ten years before multiculturalism could be institutionalized, and subsequently in 1988 the parliament adopted the Canadian Multiculturalism Act. Gradually in Canada, as in other societies practising a multicultural approach, it has been found that multiculturalism tended to be too narrowly focused on solving the 'problem' of cultural diversity as the way to inclusive citizenship. The focus needs to be directed more specifically on the tougher questions of equality and equity.

Australia Australian migrant entry and settlement policy, and the official construction of national identity, have shifted from a 'White Australia' identity and practice, through a short phase of assimilationism, to the present model of multiculturalism (Dunn 1998). The multicultural project has been a progressive attempt to transform service institutions, to shift the ideologies of national identity, and to embrace cultural difference in Australia (Fincher 1997).

Jordens (1999) states that the Labor government that was elected in 1972 introduced an entirely new concept of Australian national identity as a multicultural society. It was responsible for the reconceptualization of Australian citizenship from membership of a society essentially British in culture and ethnicity, to a rights-based notion of citizenship. This involved the dismantling of the network of discriminatory legislation, which had perpetuated the conception of Australia as a nation still holding to citizenship principles originally derived from Britain. In 1973 the government also declared its intention to abandon discrimination on the grounds of race and ethnicity in the selection of migrants.

According to Jordens (1999), the redefinition of Australia as a multicultural nation and the ratification of a number of international instruments set new benchmarks for citizens' rights in Australia, and created a political environment favourable also to the Indigenous cause. Aborigines gained rights to equality before the law with the passing of the Racial Discrimination Act in 1975. This Act incorporated Article 5 of the International Convention on the Elimination of All Forms of Racial Discrimination and conferred on Indigenous Australians the right to manage their own property, a right that is binding at both Commonwealth and State levels (Jordens 1999).

By the beginning of the 1990s, approximately half of new immigrants to Australia originated from Asia. Some of the main source countries were Vietnam, Hong Kong, the Philippines, Malaysia, China, India and Sri Lanka. Asian-born immigrants made up 4 per cent of the total population by 1991 and roughly one fifth of the overseas-born population. In common with the USA and Canada, large movements have developed mainly through use of family reunion provisions (Castles and Miller 1993). Castles and Miller (1993, 227) state that the classical countries of immigration (Australia, Canada and the USA) have moved toward the multiculturalism model because it is seen as the best way of incorporating large groups of immigrants with diverse backgrounds in a relatively short period of time. The need for 'making immigrants into citizens' raises the pressure for multicultural policy. They can participate as voters and start to build their base in the society. Multiculturalism was nonetheless not readily adopted, but encountered resistance in all three countries (Castles and Miller 1993, 227).

Sweden Sweden's multicultural policy was introduced in 1975, and it was founded on three principles: equality, freedom of choice and co-operation or partnership. *Equality* refers to the goal of achieving the same living standards for immigrants as for the rest of the population. *Freedom of choice* implies the principle that members of ethnic and linguistic minorities domiciled in Sweden should be assured of having a genuine choice between retaining and developing their cultural identity and assuming a Swedish cultural identity. This should be safeguarded by public initiatives. The goal of *partnership* implies that immigrant and minority groups as well as the native population should benefit mutually from working together (Hammar 1991).

Odmalm (2004, 475) describes the measures taken by the state to foster migrant organizational activity. After Sweden was officially designated a multicultural society in 1975, the state has provided institutional arrangements facilitating the formal organization of migrant organizations. Migrant groups and religious minorities have a constitutional right to express and develop their cultural heritage. Their associations are intended to function as natural channels for information. In principle having the same status as other Swedish associations, they are recognized to a certain extent as formal partners and are expected to maintain the link between migrant and Swedish institutions. The Swedish model stipulates that different societal organizations are viewed as representatives of the different segments of the population and are to be assigned a significant role as the state's formal partners. Migrant associations are thus supposed to represent the interests of their particular ethnic group, region or multi-country federation. On the national level, umbrella organizations are provided with official channels through consultative bodies and advisory councils.

While responsible authorities exercise few restrictions on the type of organization that is to be set up, the local authority oversees that there should be as little overlap as possible between organizations in terms of similar purpose and activities. This means, as Odmalm (2004, 476) states, that 'organizational life in Sweden is highly regulated and tightly steered from above'.

Drawing attention to the dimension of social control, Schierup (1991) speaks of the Swedish model as 'prescribed multiculturalism' in which immigrants and their organizations are co-opted into the corporatist state but end up on the political margin. Graham and Soininen (1998, 534) also comment that it is debatable 'to what extent immigrant organizations can serve as channels through which to represent immigrant interests in the Swedish political system, other than the cultural interests of specific local immigrant groups'.

Ethnic organizations have been perceived as a vehicle to structural integration of their communities in the multiculturalism model and also in other systems that adopt this mechanism (see Lepola and Suurpaa 2003). Yet the results in time have shown that organizational activities have yielded many advantages but not achieved this particular aim. Immigrant organizations generally have not built up a base of leverage for any level of political negotiation, nor have they been delegated such a role. Basically they function parallel to the central structure but on a much more peripheral platform. Their relationship to central policy and decision-making is a consultative one (see Kernaghan's typology later in this chapter). Whether and how far issues are considered on the national agenda rests with the other political actors. Effective promotion of immigrant interests at the political and higher policy-making levels would require more powerful mechanisms of input.

Specific Policy and Programme Areas

Social Policy and Policy Practice

Within the wider national policy context, social policy plays a central role in shaping arrangements for settlement in such a way that the adaptation, agency and participatory activity of settling persons will be facilitated. Participation in social policy creation is a strategy that needs to be developed as a fundamental activity of settlement practice (Delap 1997; Washington and Paylor 1998). Social policy comprises plans and programmes in education, health care, crime and corrections, economic security, and social welfare, which are carried out by government, voluntary organizations and citizens, depending on the particular welfare mix prevailing in the society. It is the range of policies and programmes organized by the state in relation to the welfare of its citizens (Hill 1996). Social policy can be understood as a range of principles and activities which derive from the society's value and customs, and play a large part in determining the distribution of resources as well as the level of well-being of citizens (Barker 1995).

Social workers, according to Ginsberg (1996, 5), become professionally involved in social policy through different routes. Those who work in administrative or policy responsibilities in voluntary and government agencies can propose, implement, or develop and promulgate social policies.

Some carry out their social policy mandates through participation in social action organizations and political campaigns. Others initiate contacts with legislators and administrators to engage their support for policies. Activity in professional organizations or carrying out policies effectively all constitute aspects of the policy mandate.

Policy practice, according to Gibelman (2000), is much heralded as an essential component of current social work practice and lays a sound basis for a more active leadership role in ongoing debate. It refers to efforts to change policies in legislative, agency and community settings, through establishing new policies, improving existing ones, or defeating the policy initiatives of other people (Jansson 2003). Policy practice is indeed of critical importance in settlement practice. The contribution of information recommendations and opinions on settlement issues are valuable inputs into the policy-making process. In this respect, the profession holds a very strategic position vis-à-vis this process. Practitioners are also called upon to counter negative views and often inaccurate information on problem situations or areas of challenge.

Policy practice, as an intervention that can be pitched to national or municipal level, is important across all types of welfare settings – from the mature to the laissez-faire. The field of settlement is relatively new and needs to be effectively brought onto the policy agenda even in mature welfare systems. Migration patterns are not static but feature considerable variation in groups, scale of flows, geopolitical origin, inter-group dynamics/ethnic relations. In the pursuit of substantial citizenship, policy practice seeks to bring the principles, values and meanings inherent in the state's social citizenship commitment to bear on actual settlement conditions. The goal is to work toward translating the principle of social justice into specific policies and modes of intervention, thus laying the foundation for full participation. This activity is high on the agenda of settlement social work which seeks to create integration-facilitating features and qualities in the environment. The task, skills and competencies necessary for effective policy practice and policy advocacy are discussed in Chapter 6.

Settlement Programmes

Immigrants ideally gain access to social service provision in the society on a par with others. Services that have pragmatic salience for settlement are, for example, in the areas of income support, child care, language training, health care including mental health, education and training, housing and comprehensive information services.

Income support has its inherent value as a basic security mechanism for individuals and families in the situation where adults have not yet obtained paid employment. In the case of immigrants, income support can allow individuals to participate fully in language training, which gives a strong capacity-building thrust to settlement programmes from the outset of settlement. Some settlement service models see entry to the labour market as critical enough to warrant early initiatives for the rapid induction of immigrants into the field itself. Arrangements for language training are synchronized alongside actual employment from the outset of settlement. Participation in these two areas extends to newcomers the immediate advantage of engaging in public life and forging links that facilitate all areas of settlement. It is a very empowering combination.

Child care services for children under school age have, in Finland, for example, allowed women, who normally bear the main childrearing responsibility in the family, to participate in language training early in settlement. This has been, for many, the opportunity to build, in a timely way, a key competency for settlement. There is great variation in the provisions for child care across different social service systems. Those systems featuring formal child care provisioning clearly will allow for greater access of women to participate in the labour market.

Language training has often been arranged on the principle of equal treatment. However, more purposive matching of different characteristics in groups of students – for example, by education level and age range inclusive of the elderly – with an appropriate level and medium of teaching, could yield greater benefits in the long run. More individuals would attain a functional or fluent level of language skill. In turn language skill fosters independence and a sense of control in being able to communicate and manage one's transactions with competence.

According to Bourdieu (1991), the ability to speak a country's dominant language fluently is a social resource that may be helpful in gaining access to the country's desirable goods and positions. Individuals who cannot communicate in the language of the country are in a situation of vulnerability, dependent on formal and informal interpreting and information brokerage. Additionally, they are unable to represent themselves favourably in official matters, especially in problem situations which otherwise call for almost advocacy-type support. Language skill would balance the interchange in acculturation processes, enabling the new groups also to be in active communication in roles as providers of information. Usually the ability to receive information is stressed in settlement situations, but language skill acquisition enables individuals to be in the situation of dialogue with the receiving society.

Health and mental health services are primary elements in settlement services. A serious shortcoming in the service can arise when standard procedures of self-referral do not prove to be an adequate response for meeting the range of actual need in the newly settling populations. One channel of contact of great importance could be established through outreach into communities. Cultural bridging can lower the threshold to formal service, through mobilization of individuals with cultural competencies, including professional, paraprofessional and laypersons. For those refugee individuals who need interventions relating to flight and trauma experience, the timely provision of specialized responses is critical. In this regard, the question of the availability of competent personnel would need to be addressed proactively. Moreover, consideration needs to be given to the fact that forced migrants lose their original support networks. Community support becomes significant, as well as the measures to organize, arrange and foster this response.

Settlement practitioners will often be called upon to carry generalist roles in case management, linking clients to essential resources and empowering them to function as independently as possible in securing the resources they need. 'Knowledge of resources, skills in connecting clients with resources and skills in following up to ensure that clients receive services and resources in a timely fashion are ... common to all case management roles' (Hepworth, Rooney and Larsen 1997, 456). Case managers are resource specialists who possess knowledge about community resources and employ skills in utilizing community resources to benefit their clients (Moore 1990). Settlement case management also requires practitioner competence in implementing all aspects of problem-solving processes (Hepworth, Rooney and Larsen 1997). Case management promotes a society-directed thrust for the development of clients' resource networks, and its principles are central to direct settlement social work.

Culture-related activities are usually in the domain of community organizations. Mother-tongue teaching will, for many families, be an important part of socialization for their children. When parents have time constraints due to work outside of the home, or if their educational background is weak, formal mother-tongue training is a valuable input into enculturation. It can also be arranged as part of the centrally funded school curriculum. Language is a significant part of the cultural heritage of an ethnic group, and providing instruction through mainstream activity could ensure that an important choice is available to those who wish to avail themselves of it.

Specific programme or service interventions responding to the needs of newcomers are in the areas of, for example, educational and vocational training, accreditation, and different forms of orientation information that would strengthen employability, as well as the ability to navigate in the new society. From a utility perspective, these programme interventions can be understood as investments in the human capital of individuals, and in the labour market and economy from the societal viewpoint. From a life cycle perspective, immigrants who arrive as adults are partakers of only a minor segment of the state's serial range of social and educational services. On the other hand, the service response to settling groups is recognized as possibly requiring qualitatively different slants or approaches if access and equality are to be attained as settlement service outcomes.

Accreditation programmes create a path for persons who have already acquired skills and qualifications to enter the labour market. One example of such an intervention is the work of the National Population Council (NPC) subcommittee in Australia which was given the mandate to elucidate systematically the principles, procedures and institutional structures needed to establish an efficient, fair and consistent system for the accreditation of overseas qualifications. Such proposals would need to be flexible enough to cover all occupations, and to respond to changing occupational and award structures (NPC 1988, cover letter). Effective accreditation programmes not only validate and help to 'commodify' immigrants' previously acquired qualifications and work experience, but they also provide information valuable for planning accreditation training modules and courses that lead to local competency.

Needs Discourse

The policy-making process can fail when actors or institutions engaged in public decision-making are unable to convert demands for change into action. Ewen (2006) sees the most obvious source of process failure occurring in the communication of information, which might be lacking, inadequate, misunderstood or misused. Moreover, effective policy-making is threatened when information is selectively appreciated, deliberately manipulated or falsely created for the advantage of specific groups on a consistent basis.

In promoting services and welfare mechanisms which will facilitate settlement objectives, we are called upon to create social policies that address selective needs within a universalist framework (see Titmuss 1958). Where universalism is a pronounced principle in social policy, the targeting of needs in specific groups should not be in contradiction. Parekh (1997) has argued that individuals or groups hindered by obvious economic, political and cultural 'positional' disadvantages inherent in their situation as new groups are in need of appropriately targeted interventions which are critical if they are to exercise their rights of equal citizenship and develop a sense of identification with the mainstream society. Policy practice in promoting the particular interests of newer citizen groups needs to present these selective needs within a universalist framework.

The framework of 'needs discourses', developed by Fraser (1989), provides a useful tool for promoting the interest areas of new and less powerful groups in the society. Expert needs discourses lend themselves to the strategy arsenal of policy practitioners. Fraser's (1989) critical theory of welfare and needs is based on an application of Foucault's (1977; 1982) discourse analysis. Fraser points out that 'concepts of need' enter into the political debate, social research and welfare policies in complex and contradictory ways.

Needs only become political, or subject to public action and contestation, when they are brought out of the sphere of private economic and domestic organization. Needs become publicly recognized with the acceptance that domestic and community structures do not have the capacity for providing certain kinds of support and resources. According to Fraser (1989) policies are not straightforward responses to the condition and needs of citizen groups. Policies are the outcomes of struggles between 'power publics' (Fraser 1989) – or sections of the population with different degrees of relative power. We can scrutinize settlement and integration policies in this light.

Fraser (1989) identifies three kinds of interacting needs discourse: expert discourses, oppositional discourses and reprivatization discourses, of which the first is of great interest in the policy practice context. Expert needs discourses are associated with the institutions of knowledge production and application, such as universities and think-tanks, professional associations and state agencies (Fraser 1989). These aptly serve as vehicles for translating politicized needs into objects of state intervention by re-defining them into categories of administrative service. This redefining process takes the form of 'translating a particular "expressed" need into a "case" of a more generalised social problem – unemployment, disability or homelessness, for example' (Fraser 1989, 125).

The process of redefining the need actually decontextualizes it from its class, gender and racial location and depoliticizes the conditions which gave rise to its expression in the first place. The redefinition of different and particular settlement service needs can promote their being identified in categories of need that are recognized as 'legitimate' within broad categories that are otherwise generally accepted. These needs can also thereby be associated with categories that are feasibly implemented. In this sense, it is a methodology for channelling appropriate service provision initiatives into mainstream need channels, and in this way, having them 'legitimized' for further implementation processes.

The other two types of discourse are also relevant to settlement practice. Oppositional needs discourses are associated with active social movements. Private concerns are brought into the public arena by action on behalf of disadvantaged or oppositional groupings. Fraser (1989) cites the political success of the women's movement in highlighting, for example, sexism, wife battering and job segregation. Previously private concerns would not have been the subject of intervention by state and pseudo-state agencies such as, for example, the police, the social services and the Equal Opportunities Commission. The oppositional needs discourse has resonance with anti-racist approaches in social work. Reprivatization discourses contest the rationality, efficiency and morality of public responsibility for need and seek to re-establish the boundaries between public and private, political, domestic and economic interests and to move responsibility for needs from the public into the private sphere (Fraser 1989).

Needs discourses can be used to bring out the needs of new groups which may not be recognized, acknowledged or associated with well-accepted categories of need in the majority population. They can work toward redressing the situation in which social policies prioritize some cultural patterns relative to others, or fail to recognize the salience of some cultural characteristics and culturally determined needs (Hill 1996).

'Needs discourse' should be sensitive to the parties who are receiving the information. This audience can include political and administrative decision-makers, the general public, and interest groups in the society, as well as other specific stakeholder bodies. Communication 'languages' include, for example, the language of administration (for example, statistical evidence, trends, cost information), the language of bureaucracy (for example, framing issues relative to how they feature in procedures, regulations, division of work), moral discourse and empowerment discourse. Facility in the use of different 'languages' of communication can increase the effectiveness of messages and the efficacy of the communication.

Issues relating to the insertion of settlement and integration-related needs of immigrant groups as part of the mainstream policy agenda is part of the wider mandate to identify and address the needs and issues of less powerful or under-represented groups. The importance of discourse needs to be emphasized here because of its potential to strengthen the impact of the voice of professional social work.

The *default outcomes* of ineffectual policies are observable and also articulated in statistics, levels of inequality, stratification, and so on. Chronic underemployment of immigrant professionals, segmented labour markets, disaffection in the second generation, high immigrant unemployment, disproportionate number of child custody cases in the immigrant population, are examples of default outcomes. Default outcome here refers to cumulative effects of deferring or eliding key settlement issues, and the consequences of ineffectual policies, skew in policy emphasis or paying lip service to policies. Default outcomes are reflected in individual-level restriction in the ability to exercise full membership in society. Default outcomes are accompanied by social and human costs.

The Cost of Social Services – A Dimension of Public Discourse

The settlement field is in some ways a contemporary immigration scenario for much earlier discussions on the deserving and non-deserving clients and 'others'. Service providers also routinely become involved in categorizations and eligibility justifications based on the criteria established for the particular policy period. Even in the absence of the so-called welfare backlash, social services and settlement services face encounters with overtly or covertly hostile task environments. It is proposed here that the use of rationales directly related to the production dynamics in society can be juxtaposed with humanitarianism and social justice-based arguments on the principles of distribution.

Depending on the context and target audience, social welfare – and by extension settlement service costs – can be justified in 'a way that is consistent with the international market economy and its dictates' (Dolgoff 1999, 298). Thus the provision of adequate education and health services safeguards the quality of the human capital in the labour force. In the cyclical downturns and periods of restructuring in the economy and labour market, social benefits moderate the stress and economic distress of unemployment, redundancy and layoffs, and low income (Dolgoff 1999). The social welfare system is a response not only to individual need but also to macro-level contingency. The system underpins social cohesion, safety and stability in society.

Lewis and Widerquist (2001, 2) comment that social workers might not be aware of it, but they produce goods. The economic definition of a good is anything that at least one person finds valuable, useful or desirable. Goods need not be physical, and include services. Thus, when social workers provide individual counselling, group counselling or community organizing, they are producing goods, similar to automobile workers producing goods when they assemble cars and to professional basketball players producing goods when they entertain audiences.

Corresponding arguments around settlement services are weighty. A period of investment in and support for settlement services, including language and labour market training, will produce new cohorts of workers. In the scale of social expenditure, there is a great difference between the investment in newer groups and that in other groups in the citizenry who go through all levels of schooling. Immigrants in the main comprise young persons and those of prime working age, a fact which is increasingly being recognized in countries with an aging population and impending issues around labour force renewal, with related social policy implications. At the level of community relations, immigrants expend their own considerable effort in pioneering multicultural attitudes and dispositions in receiving societies. This is an aspect that goes unacknowledged. Parallel with the higher profile campaigns for 'tolerance' are continuous processes of engagement in everyday life. Newer groups also play a significant part in internationalization processes and in the strengthening of the national social fabric.

Bureaucratic and Institutional Work Environment

The sphere of social work activity is decisively affected by how the profession (and its various professional bodies) sees itself and its own autonomy. The issue of the positioning of social work has always been problematic. Whether social work is lodged within or outside the bastions of the establishment, or whether it is successfully able to straddle both fields, are questions that are resolved differently in different situations. Many of the outstanding issues in settlement, such as those relating to substantial citizenship, equity and discrimination, are perceived as potentially threatening to the larger establishment of which social work is invariably an arm.

Stern (2004, 129) points to the strong ties which the social work profession has to bureaucracy. He states that social work has actually defined itself within the constraints of bureaucratically organized social service agencies. The agencies enjoy the sanction of the community, and are staffed by professional workers carrying out clearly defined roles within the agency. Scholars have questioned the future of social work's bond with bureaucracy. In the context of the British system, this linking of bureaucratic organizations and professional social work expertise has been referred to by Harris (1998, 197) as a 'bureau-professional organization'. Harris (1998) argues that the contradiction between clients' rights and the bureau-professional stance of social work has still not been addressed. Harris' (1998) observations have wider relevance for societies where social work is heavily linked to bureaucratic structures and where this link is taken for granted. It is suggested here that envisioning the profession outside of this context could be useful as a situational analysis exercise in strategic planning activity.

The dilemma along another dimension is described by Prilleltensky and Prilleltensky (2005, 98) in terms of the profession's pull for amelioration, wellness and the prevention of institutional unrest, on the one hand, and on the other, the pull for the critical change agent which involves transformation, liberation and disruption of unjust practices. These authors argue that in order for critical professional praxis to emerge, these two roles need to exist in tension and synergy, not in opposition. The need for social change is as great as that for specialized knowledge and ameliorative interventions. In the interests of wellness and liberation, people who work from inside the system are as critical as those confronting it.

Professional autonomy   Professionalism projects the image of an individual who is independent or, if working in an organization, is doing so in a relationship of equal partnership (Hugman 1996). This contrasts with the idea of being in an organizational employment relationship characterized by limited autonomy. Elaborating on autonomy, Derber (1982) proposes the distinction between two types of autonomy: 'ideological' autonomy and 'technical' autonomy. The former refers to the degree of independence for an occupation to shape its own objectives, not only at the operational level but also strategically and in the wider society. The latter refers to the degree of independence that is exercised by an occupation in selecting the practices or means through which it seeks to achieve its objectives. Significantly, the issue of professional autonomy is made problematic by the professional's organizational positioning relative to managers who are not necessarily professionally qualified or experienced in the areas of work for which they are responsible (see Pollitt 1993).

Even within constraints of particular work contexts, professional knowledge and ethics are assets which lay a basis of credibility which can be used strategically to champion settlement causes from inside the system. Professional and field knowledge provide a base for authority on settlement issues, and in particular from a policy practice perspective. If professionals enjoy credibility and authority in the area of their mandate, this could promote greater professional autonomy in the two senses proposed by Derber (1982).

The New Managerialism and Constraints of Bureaucracy

Leadership concerns have recently focused on the managerialist approach which, broadly speaking, is a set of beliefs and practices that assumes that better management will resolve a wide range of economic and social problems (Alford 1997; Davis 1997). The 'new managerialism' proposes an ideology of management as the panacea for shortcomings which might be identified in organizational functioning, performance and output. It is seen as threatening to the tenets of practice in the human service (Tsui and Cheung 2004).

The new managerialism discourse actually amplifies the issue of management in the social services, perhaps making it out to be a novel development in the organizational setting. The engagement with varied challenges of management in the human services is not new, and the professional/administrative divide at one pole in the management continuum is not unfamiliar. The role of participatory management, ethical and responsive leadership, training in related skills and responsibilities, asserting the position of professionalism, are a few among many approaches held to have potential for addressing management and leadership in the human and social services (Weinbach 2003; Joyce 1999).

Baldwin (2000) draws attention to the spread of managerialism, arguing that it is replacing clinical with actuarial expertise. Public assistance and income support have long had to battle with the contradiction between the primary focus being directed to the application of rigid eligibility criteria relative to the holistic approach. The real danger of the actuarial emphasis, important as it is from the perspective of effective distribution, is the way it can constrict vision which is so vital to the efficacy of interventions. Actuarial emphasis can be seen as another manifestation of the commodification of helping (McKnight 1995; 2000).

Dominelli (1996) observes that needs-led assessments and relationship building have given way to budget-led assessments, increased managerial control over practitioners and bureaucratized procedures for handling consumer complaints. This author sees these changes as being led by the purchaser–provider split in service provision, which is the British state's response to the market discipline imposed by increased privatization of welfare state services. These changes furthermore seek to reorient social work away from its commitment to holistic provisions and social justice in the direction of technocratic competencies which are the purview of the externally directed bureaucrat.

The advantages and disadvantages of the bureaucratic setting have been discussed quite extensively in the literature. The issue is relevant to the growing field of settlement and migration which requires from social work and social policy-making a vision that is unhindered by organization-bounded needs and is not limited to mere expansion of the structures that already suffice to address the needs profile of the majority. Wider settlement goals and the project of substantial citizenship calls for an initial outward thrust of linking interventions from the outset of settlement, in order to enable immigrants to establish working relationships in different spheres. For example, service components could be fashioned in concerted efforts with other institutions closely related to settlement, such as trade unions, schools, NGOs, faith-based organizations, and so on. The network of services and service transactions would be one in which societal actors would be engaged collaboratively, and sustain linkages that would serve settling groups as conduits to activity in the public space. Currently the main vehicle for structural integration of immigrants is seen to be employment. The potential for different forms of activity and participation in the public space has not been explored with a view to fashioning innovative fields of activity with value for integration.

Issues of Leadership and Power in Institutions

Selected facets of leadership are presented in this section because of the critical importance of leadership in facilitating progressive thrusts in settlement policy and practice. Texts of particular usefulness in this area include those of Northouse (2004), Sashkin and Sashkin (2003), Manning (2003) and Johnson (2001). A longitudinal perspective on the management and leadership situation in social work should at least take account of the uneven state of the field. Out of the discourse on the new managerialism in social work comes a keener awareness of our need to engage with the serious issues involved in developing organizational structures that will be equipped to meet the challenges of the present and future, which differ qualitatively from those of the past. This frame can be transposed to the settlement field.

The immigration and settlement field would need to be acknowledged as an area requiring distinct competencies and capabilities related to the nature of the issues. When regarded as another province in the wider public service structure, staffing at leadership levels in bureaucratic organizations often takes primarily into account 'standard' experience, qualifications and institution-oriented predispositions that can crowd out very critical areas of competencies which are vital for the field of immigration and settlement, its direction and its development. Default outcomes of ineffectual policies are likely to be linked closely with this phenomenon.

Leadership in social work is exercised in many capacities, contexts and levels although the cultivation of leadership qualities and skills is not often featured as a distinct part of the core curriculum. Since the late 1990s there has been greater recognition, in the US and the UK, for example, of the need for leadership qualities and skills to be emphasized in education and training programmes in the human services (see Manning 2003; Joyce 1999; Clawson 1999; Pinto et al. 1998; Gable 1998; Perlmutter and Crook 2004; and Proehl 2001). The need is recognized as being pronounced in the bureaucratic and hierarchical contexts in which so much practice is conducted at the present time. When social workers are under-represented in managerial and leadership positions in their own agencies, this constitutes a fertile environment for the spread of the so-called 'new managerialism'. Bureaucratic culture and hierarchies can have an adverse impact on the spark of idealism, the multilevel visioning and the human commitment that gives social work its special mark.

The crossing over into the leadership arena in social work is facilitated by the fact that many of the leadership skill areas are related to basic competency areas in social work. The human relations spectrum of skills which are systematically emphasized and built in social work education and practice are of central importance in leadership, where relationships are critical for ensuring collective engagement and commitment to goal-oriented activity. Leadership is a relation with subordinates that draws them into common ownership of the agency mission. The comprehensive frame of 'people skills' covered by Thompson (2002) is relevant. These include the constellation of interaction skills such as verbal, nonverbal and written communication, influencing skills, handling conflict, handling feelings and interviewing. Common to social work and the leadership field are skills of analysis and assessment as well as teamwork-related competencies.

Core leadership areas include:

- Good organizational design (organization rules, policies and regulations; organizational structure and design and the distribution of power; control of decision processes; access to and control of information) (see, for example, Northouse 2004; Clawson 1999)
- Human resource management competencies in recruitment, hiring and staffing; orientation and continuing staff development (education and training); performance appraisal and compensation management; as well as equal opportunity and labour relations (see, for example, Weinbach 2003).

Professional ethical codes resonate with those of leadership. Manning (2003, 8) states that the essence of leadership is ethics. A leader's ability to make a choice about good or harm is critical. The special qualities of leadership are the visions, values and moral positions that individuals bring to the role. These can transform the nature of work and the good (or harm) that is produced.

Leadership and Power

The structures and process of any institution or organization are potentially the vehicles for using and abusing power. 'Power' is often used in a negative sense, but in fact it derives its positive or negative qualities from how it is used. Leadership is inextricably connected to power. Leaders must develop a keen awareness about their power and its impact on others in order to be ethical leaders. Reluctance of leaders to acknowledge the level and influence of their power leads to harmful consequences for an organization and also for its members. Decisions and policies made by individuals in leadership positions can indicate the use or abuse of power.

Manning (2003) states that the ability to use power and influence positively is the essence of leadership. In order to develop an ethical framework which is effective in the workplace, leaders must learn how to use their own power in morally transformative ways. This requires an understanding of the nature of power in the workplace. I draw on Manning's (2003) work to describe the power that resides in position. This covers five sub-areas, the power to:

- Affect the lives and well-being of people materially (salary, rewards, promotions) and psychologically (policies that affect employee morale). The manner of resolving employee conflicts can be through a fair, interactive process of all involved. Such an approach provides a means to improve employee relations and establish ethical standards.
- Promote self-interest since leaders and managers are able to insulate

themselves from the impact of policies and decisions through the 'privilege of authority'. More power and value might be ascribed to individuals and to groups which leaders judge to hold similar values to their own. Manning comments that there is a temptation for leaders to believe that their power resides in the position and not in themselves. Personal values are never removed from occupational or corporate decisions. According to Manning, leaders and managers always put their moral stamp on a decision, and by default if no other way.

- Distribute resources. This requires ethical judgments about the use of resources which include access to revenue, technology, capital expenditures, personnel, space, furniture and so on; access to time; access to opportunity; access to communicate ideas with those persons who make critical decisions.
- Design and implement rules and policies and use latitude and discretion. The ethical quality of rules and policies depends on who has participated in developing them. Executives bear the ultimate responsibility for the gravity of policy-making both inside and outside the organization. According to Manning, the power to develop policy and the ultimate quality of the developed policy can impose moral and ethical dilemmas upon subordinates, reducing their latitude for being flexible.
- Be privileged, reflecting the ability of the leader to be in a position to promote self-interest.

Two Settlement Phenomena: Residential Concentrations and a Community Organization Service Provision Model

Ethnic Concentration through Secondary Migration

Secondary migration of settling groups to larger population concentrations, and to urban centres, makes for larger ethnic communities, and is also generally not a planned phenomenon from the settlement policy perspective. Such internal movement is fueled by a range of factors. In the case of refugee cohorts who have been settled along a dispersal principle, those from remote or outlying areas might seek proximity not only to the ethnic community but to larger centres which offer more avenues of participation and a greater variety of lifestyle and activity. Reasons for internal migration include employment and educational opportunities, as well as access to income-earning possibilities in ethnic businesses or in seasonal and temporary work. Individuals and families move to be near to religious congregations, which (as discussed in Chapter 6), also undertake social and secular functions, and are sources of assistance in important areas such as child socialization.

Amin and Thrift (2002) argue for the benefits of spatial communities in shaping human and ethnic relations. They note that much of the discussion on belonging has focused on the counterfacing of, for example, diasporic affiliations and national level belonging, often neglecting local modes of belonging. Neighbourhoods, streets and shopping centres are sites of interaction and interface, which comprise 'the prosaic negotiations that drive interethnic and intercultural relations in different directions' (Amin and Thrift 2002, 291). The authors propose that it is in the context of the density of racial or ethnic coding that can take place in daily life that individuals derive their experience and perception of the potential cultural compatibility of others and the capacity for sustaining a common or shared sense of place. Active and harmonious social relations in neighbourhoods, between native populations and immigrants – first and second generation – is seen as an important factor in integration (Simon-Barouh and Simon 1990). Viable communities can be the site of many crossover ties in the public space, which make for social integration at collective level.

Orum (1998, 7) states that 'the roots of our identity and the sense of our security are also tied up in neighborhoods both past and present'. The benefits of living in an ethnic neighbourhood are singularly suited, for example, to the needs of elderly immigrants, who have greater scope for interaction and transactions with countrymen and women. This aspect is especially valuable when the elderly have not become fluent in the majority language. In cultures where there is the tradition of mutual help and natural caring, the proximity of living arrangements facilitates such activities. There is opportunity for association and for collective activity and participation in the public spaces of the neighbourhood. The neighbourhood is also the site of dense social relations with fertile ground in which relationships of multiple content can thrive. Such multiplex relations are associated with strong ties, as opposed to single purpose relations in looser networks (Kapferer 1969, 213). Thus even if settlement occurs in wider so-called low-context societal environments where individuals generally interact with others in specific limited activities and for specific single purposes, the neighbourhood can offer the option of strong supportive networks for groups such as the elderly, who experience the need for this.

One example of this is the suburb of Varissuo in Turku, which has one of the highest concentrations of immigrants in Finland. In addition to a large number of ethnic return migrants from the Former Soviet Union, groups include refugees and immigrants originally from Vietnam, the Former Soviet Union, Iran, Iraq and many other countries of origin. The elderly form only a very small part of the immigrant population in Finland, which has experienced net in-migration only since the late 1980s. Neighbourhoods such as these, which house in their vicinity basic services, networks of acquaintances and kin, routine meeting sites in shops and so on, are significant for the quality of life of the elderly in particular, who are generally less mobile.

Dunn (1998) gives a portrayal of development in Cabramatta, Australia. He refers to fragmented ethnic collective actions, frequently undertaken by small collectives, which developed various places of worship, leisure, welfare, aged care and education facilities. These included churches, mosques, synagogues and temples; clubs, sports grounds and camping sites; child care facilities; classrooms and schools; archives, libraries and museums; nursing homes, retirement villages and self-care units; and welfare facilities. The outcome of this development of new urban and social infrastructure was based upon scarce material resources and indeed depended on ethnic migrant initiatives and on the collective willingness to foster this development despite difficulties in times of settlement. This new social and urban resource, developed by over 410 ethnic collectives in Sydney since 1950, can be understood as a form of 'ethnic community capital' (Dunn 1998).

Dunn (1998) points to the central premise of many theories which hold that ethnic concentration is an outcome of either marginalization or ethnic separateness. He argues that when conservative critics point to ethnic concentration as 'spatial proof' of the failure of ethnic diversity, it is an indication of 'the failure to detect advantages of concentration, and the dynamism of unassimilated cultural difference'. Based on his studies of areas in western Sydney suburbs, Dunn (1998, 514) states that the socio-economic deprivation and maladies of such areas are not directly related to the ethnicity of the residents but rather to more general problems of economic crisis and social inequality. Problems might be related not to ethnic concentration but unemployment. Viviani (1996, 23) points out that critiques of ethnic concentration in Australia might be functioning as smokescreens for other critiques: of immigration, of immigration from Asia in particular and of the social policy of multiculturalism. The development of secondary migration concentrations brings out the importance of adapting and shaping national and municipal policy to keep pace with the changing settlement and clustering patterns of newly settling groups (Anisef and Lanphier 2003).

The ethnic enclave is very different from a neighbourhood with clusters of residents of different backgrounds. The ethnic enclave is understood as an ethnic concentration with a high degree of institutional completeness, or self-sufficiency. Ethnic enclaves develop infrastructure which generates commerce, employment and services, in addition to being residential concentrations. These have at times been perceived as a counter-integration force. Ethnic enclave literature currently reflects three trends: increasing interest in them as a vehicle for integration; their contribution to the larger urban economy; and the risk that an enclave, in combination with long-term deprivation, could be transformed into a ghetto (Neymare 1998, 17).

The Ethnospecific Sector

Welfare systems can feature civil society prominently in service provision through large voluntary organizations. Governments can delegate the provision of welfare as far as possible to civil society organizations which collaborate with business and trade union organizations. This practice of state empowering through funding of both civil society and private enterprise is common in, for example, many southern European countries (Washington and Paylor 1998; Esping-Andersen 1990). Current trends in social development see elements of civil society taking a more commanding role in this social welfare policy and provision (Midgley 1995). This has implications for organizations of civil society, with welfare aims to be featuring more prominently in settlement service provision alongside mainstreams services.

An example of settlement service provision by immigrant community organizations in the Canadian ethnospecific model is presented here. The community organization sector, as part of the third sector, is an active service provider to immigrants and refugees. It has proven to be a distinct model of resettlement service which promotes the interests of settling groups in a novel way, and at the same time offers a response to practical needs on the ground.

Non-profit organizations within the third sector have always played an important part within the Canadian welfare state structure, and are heavily subsidized by the state to deliver quality, targeted services, education and advocacy. Their activities have been part of 'the national project to build the social and economic citizenship rights that helped shape the modern Canadian identity' (Shields and Evans 1998, 113). According to Lanphier (1996), NGOs enjoy a broad base of public support in the role of service providers to populations in need. NGOs are involved in the areas of social, health, educational, economic, cultural, research, financial and advocacy services to the whole of the Canadian population. Shields and Evans (1998) state that the sector offers a wide range of services which, in most instances, could not be adequately provided directly via the open market or through the state.

The immigrant community organization sector is administered and implemented by members of the immigrant communities who themselves are usually individuals who have resided for many years in the country. The sector thus possesses not only a unique level of cultural and linguistic competence to deal with newcomers, but also a substantial resource base of settlement knowledge and expertise. Organizations specialize in a wide range of services needed by individuals and families during the initial settlement period, such as interpreting, orientation to Canada, as well as counselling in initial settlement and transition difficulties. Services include referral to mainstream organizations and departments, an important component in those cases which require more extended or administrative interventions. The organizations have developed expertise areas which are complementary to those available in government offices, in particular in the area of needs assessment and service delivery (Lanphier 1996).

The needs assessment component is of particular value as 'on the ground' community service is a very sensitive instrument for identifying need. An inadequate level of cultural competence in mainstream service could lead to service responses that do not target the actual or underlying need. The immigrant organization model has shown that immigrants' own organizations can fill important roles in settlement and integration, and can be intermeshed with professional social service to reduce the client-community-worker distance. The community can be legitimized as a body for promoting interests of newer citizens, and for articulating needs on behalf of its constituency.

The state is the main funder of the community organization sector. This is done through project contracts to provide specific resettlement services. The organizations are thus part of the social service structure and not peripheral to the settlement field. Organizations take their place in the public space, working to promote substantial and equal citizenship for their constituencies. In Canada, funding has been customarily provided by the state to non-profit public interest organizations for the purpose of lobbying (Shields and Evans 1998, 100). It is thought that state funding to disadvantaged constituencies brings an element of fairness in the representation of the spectrum of interests in the society, and that non-profits can act as advocates, critics and participants in policy-making and policy-setting for such groups (Phillips, S.D. 1991, 187).

Training for the sector is provided by larger co-ordinating organizations and by educational institutions. Alongside professional social work, the community organization sector can be described as one that has mobilized the 'paraprofessional' arena and achieved working relationships within the formal service provision arena.

The educational level of personnel is strong in general as immigrants from various professional backgrounds have been attracted to the challenge of the settlement field, wishing also to have an opportunity to make a contribution to settlement. One challenge for the sector is to maintain consistent standards in service provision. Linkage with mainstream organizations ensures accessibility to specialized services as and when needed. The sector represents an innovative response to the needs of newcomers, mobilizing into the welfare state resources and skills that would not otherwise be available to the mainstream service provision system. It brings immigrant workers into the service provision arena. Lyons and Lawrence (2006) state that greater efforts need to be made in many countries to offer qualifying programmes to existing minority groups as well as to refugees who have arrived more recently. Some have qualified previously in health care, for example. Moreover, on the basis of their experience in settlement, they could form a valuable resource for the workforce if offered additional training.

The role of NGOs can often be seen as an ancillary one in service provision. However, it could be brought more effectively into the settlement service arena in receiving countries. Immigrant community organizations can become embedded into the mainstream service network as one locus of settlement services and also as an area of opportunity for immigrants' labour market participation. Shields and Evans (1998, 107) have observed that social partnerships between social service-oriented non-profit organizations and social policy ministries – involved in health and social welfare – are becoming more critical actors in the delivery of social policy.

Kernaghan's (1992) typology of partnerships is constructed along different degrees of differentiation in the distribution of power between each partner. The types of partnerships are:

- Consultative – when advice is sought from external actors

- Contributory – includes the provision of financial support, for example
- Operational – when work is shared, but not decision-making power
- Collaborative – the only group which is faithful to the real meaning of partnership. Collaborative partnerships entail joint decision-making power in addition to the sharing of human, financial and informational resources. This type involves some risk for the public official who must surrender a degree of control to an external actor/organization.

Closing Comments

In this chapter, national integration policies have been briefly presented. Effective policy practice – as a central component of settlement social work – is key to the development of effective settlement services, and fuels innovation in programme development. Examination of the bureaucratic and institutional work environment and its associated challenges (including the issues of leadership) is necessary if settlement social work practice is to develop to its full potential within existing organizational and service provision structures.

Chapter 10
Settlement Practice and Ethical Principles

This final chapter explores ethical principles in social work with applications to the settlement and integration context. The capabilities approach is discussed as one aspect of self-determination. The development of quality features and robust approaches to settlement practice, which is presented in the second section, draws on many of the insights discussed earlier in the work.

Ethical Principles

This section is devoted to examining social work professional ethics in the context of settlement practice. Clark (2000) defines a code of ethics as a frame of guiding principles, denoting a specific prescriptive scheme of obligations, and a course of action which may be defined as ethical or unethical when compared with such codes. Clark (2000) points out that there are two main aims, the prescriptive and the critical, in any field of professional ethics. As prescription, ethics seek to instruct how professionals ought to deal with morally problematic situations. The critical aspect, on the other hand, examines the premises and arguments on which prescriptions are based. Clark (2000) uses the precept of confidentiality as an example. The prescriptive arm of professional ethics holds that information acquired by the social worker about a client should not be indiscriminately disclosed to other persons, whereas the critical analysis of confidentiality considers the rationale and justifications for this principle of non-disclosure on the basis of general moral theory.

As a base for examining ethics in the settlement social work context, I use the four broad principles identified by Banks (1995) in her survey of the codes of ethics of 15 national associations of social workers. The principles are: respect, self-determination, social justice and professional integrity.

Respect

Respect, in the most basic and universal sense, is awarded to all other human beings on the basis of their inherent human dignity. Ronald Dworkin (1977), an important exponent of justice as rights, sets out, as a key feature of his theory, equality of concern and respect, a right which all possess not by virtue of birth, characteristic, merit or excellence but simply as human beings with the capacity to make plans and give justice.

Closely linked is the principle of non-judgmentalism, or avoidance of making moral judgments concerning clients. In settlement service settings, working relationships imbued with these qualities can be of considerable assistance in reducing distance between the immigrant client and worker. The ethical principles can be seen as inbuilt mechanisms to work against interactions being unduly obstructed by factors such as cultural difference and stereotyping, for example.

Weick et al. (1989, 353) state that the importance of acceptance and non-judgmental attitudes lies in the belief that people have an inner wisdom about what they need and that ultimately they will make choices based on their own best sense of what will meet that need. Weick et al. (1989) comment that it is not possible for even the best trained professional to judge how another person should best live his or her life. These observations bring out the contrast between the ethical principle of respect and an ethnocentric approach in practice, which carries the risk of undervaluing or disregarding settling individuals' and groups' personal choices, which are based on self-knowing/'knowledge of self' and their own adaptive logics.

Respect and non-judgmentalism are further related to the principle of individualization which requires that the social worker be sensitive to each client's unique history, characteristics and situation (Sheafor, Horejsi and Horejsi 2000). The contextual approach to practice is underpinned by respect and individualization. It emphasizes, as part of the holistic work approach, becoming familiar with the socio-cultural background in clients' country of origin and their background experiences (see Lyons, Manion and Carlsen 2006). These include, in the case of refugees, traumatic events leading up to flight, and experiences in the recent past in transit and refugee camps. In working with groups from different societal backgrounds who hold different perceptions of formal social service and its methods, it is especially important that the settlement practitioner appreciate the possible hesitation, unwillingness or inability of clients to participate in a particular intervention strategy, or even to accept help at all. One example of this might be therapeutic or group counselling, which in some cultures would be too invasive of individuals' private life spheres. In problem situations, individuals turn to more informal support circles from which they can ask and expect assistance in difficulties. Individualization and cultural competence requires practitioners not only to be flexible in how they work with clients but also, in the interest of effectively responding to diverse client constituencies, to be ready to develop or adopt alternative and culturally appropriate support mechanisms and interventions as part of their practice.

Al-Krenawi and Graham (2001) provide an example of the need to rethink the use of individual-focused solution-seeking strategies in working with clients who are from strongly collective cultures. Speaking about the value placed on collectivity in Arab culture, Al-Krenawi and Graham (2001) state that the definition of problems and the processes leading to their solution are invariably referenced to and involve the group. Individuals who are experiencing problems do not make a choice between alternative courses of action in isolation from others. Help-seeking is often collaborative, involving family members more explicitly at every stage of intervention (Al-Krenawi 2000; Al-Krenawi and Graham 2001).

It is not uncommon that family members see themselves as involved intimately in help-seeking and problem-solving. They do not see help-seeking as a non-contextual process based on an individual relationship with the formal or professional service provider/s. Adult siblings, for example, can take it as a matter of course (and indeed of common expediency) to take responsibility for the basic well-being of each other's children.

Significantly, the involvement and support of the social and kin environment is, in generalist practice, the elusive and valuable support factor that is critical for the success of many practice interventions. Fong (2004) speaks of contextual social work as integrating culture-based and culturally relevant mechanisms of settling communities into professional practice. In working with groups where the natural helping traditions occupy a vital place in social life, there is a unique opportunity to re-capture into practice the element of environmental support and strength, and to make this an integral component of settlement work with such communities.

Self-determination

Promotion of self-determination in work with immigrant clients can involve visioning alternative courses of action, as well as weighing ideas, perspectives and strategy options. Many immigrant clients would probably not yet have full awareness of a range of available, possible and realistic options. While final choices are not prescribed, the practitioner can share valuable insights to enable a client to make informed choices. Information on the potential implications and ramifications of certain choices of action can sometimes provide an important contribution to the decision-making process. The practitioner relies on ethical principles to guide this work process.

The principle of self-determination takes its cue from clients' goals which, either overtly or covertly, are fundamental to settlement efforts and plans. In a study of refugee groups from the Middle East settling in Finland, the broad categories of their reported goals list employment, education and training, and retention of valued aspects of culture (Valtonen 1998). When family reunification was outstanding, this priority was overriding. Goals of course reflect highly individual perspectives, choices and interests. In this study, the universality of emphasis on employment brings it near to the status of a value in settlement. Dependence on welfare is experienced as a negative factor in settlement, and strongly diminishing of self-reliance and the individual's life possibilities.

Settlement and integration processes are about change and adaptation. They are at base linked to personal priorities and goals. Life satisfaction and life quality are seen to be a function of the gap between personal goals and an individual's actual conditions (Ross, Eyman and Kishchuk 1986). When goals and life conditions are converging, this has a positive effect on life satisfaction. If individuals perceive little convergence even in the future, life quality is negatively affected.

In settlement, individuals do not expect rapid achievement of life goals, but are motivated by the hope that they are making progress toward objectives. The range of options becomes clearer as familiarity with the settlement environment grows. In this regard, information flows are critical.

'Achievement' is the point at which goals are brought to fruition. Sen (1985, 36) uses the term 'functioning' to denote achievement, and the term 'capability' to denote an ability to achieve. He defines well-being as the achievement of valuable functionings. Sen (1985, 16) claims that a just society has to centre on a person's positive freedoms to achieve valuable functionings as part of the wider choices of citizens. These choices are about 'what life we lead and what we can and cannot do, can and cannot be' (Sen (1985, 16). Nussbaum (1999, 234) sees the basis of the individual's political claim to the right to have 'the chance' – the power to exercise self-determination – to achieve valuable functionings as deriving from human dignity. The lack of internal and/or external power to exercise self-determination to achieve such valuable functionings is seen by Nussbaum (1999) as a form of oppression, and a condition which is brought about by both material constraints and social constructions. She argues that people living in oppression are not 'free to do as they wish', the result of which is the denial of basic liberties and meaningful equality of opportunity (Nussbaum 1999, 231).

Self-determination, the right of each person to shape her or his own life, is at the core of the capabilities perspective and plays a pivotal role in social work (Morris 2002, 371). The particular relevance of self-determination for settling groups is also brought out in Nussbaum's (1999, 234) statement that people should never have to lose their individuality by being considered only as part of an aggregate group or mean, since valuable functionings are vital for each person. If society is unresponsive to situations in which minorities (including newer groups of citizens) consistently encounter barriers in their efforts to access valuable functionings on a par with others, this can be understood as contrary to principles of self-determination. Nussbaum (1999, 234) states that valuable functionings are essential for each person and that it is 'profoundly wrong to subordinate the ends of some individuals to those of others'. This understanding of self-determination does not leave the principle as an open-ended concept but carries it forward to the actual achievement stage. It refers to a right that goes further than the freedom to decide for oneself on a specific issue and incorporates the idea of not being obstructed in the pursuit of achievement or 'functioning'. It is close to the idea of full participation and full membership in the society. This understanding of capabilities takes self-determination out of the individual realm and imbues it with societal level ramifications.

Nussbaum (2006, 286–7) states that it has been assumed, in one way of thinking about rights, that the inhibition of interfering state action would be the sole requirement for securing a right for a person. Fundamental entitlements have often been understood as being effected through prohibitions against such state action. The thinking is that once the state keeps its hands off, those particular rights are taken to have been secured. Thus the state is not expected to have any further affirmative task. Nussbaum (2006, 287) states that the capabilities approach, by contrast, understands the securing of a right as an affirmative task: this understanding is central to her own approach to capabilities, as well as that of Sen (1985). The right to political participation, the right to the free exercise of religion, the right of free speech and other rights are all:

> best thought of as secured to people only when the relevant capabilities to function are present. In other words, to secure a right to citizens in these areas is to put them in a position of capability to function in that area. To the extent that rights are used in defining social justice, we should not grant that the society is just unless the capabilities have been effectively achieved (Nussbaum 2006, 287).

Social Justice

Social justice is an overarching principle of practice. Its gradual adoption was the result of a long struggle, and took the core principle of social work beyond charity to that of social justice. Hagen (2000) points to ambiguity surrounding the term, even in policy circles. He states that while it is well recognized that social justice has to be promoted at all levels of government, from local to national, the concept is not defined in literature.

The social justice perspective is one of the strongest instruments for approaching settlement situations which relate to conditionalities in the societal structure which affect settlement. A sound understanding of this principle is the foundation for settlement practice. It is at one and the same time multilayered and able to capture many facets of settlement issues. Social justice appeals to civic values governing the relations between individuals as citizens and formal institutions. It is not easily contestable and overturned when used as a basis of rationale in the public sphere. In discourse, it is an approach that can offset the more contentious levels of engagement which are often pursued in the empowerment and moral modes of discourse.

Clark (2000, 147) observes that justice plays a similar theoretical role to the principle of respect. While respect is seen to be the key to right interpersonal relations, justice is held to be the key to right action for the public sphere and its institutions. I draw here on Clark's (2000, 148) five principal intuitions that animate the ideal of justice. These intuitions or primitive notions of justice provide a framework for understanding the 'range of ways in which it is possible to be wronged, cheated or duped' (Clark 2000, 147). The five intuitions are set out below:

Justice as due process Justice calls for decisions affecting people's interests to be taken according to rules and procedures that carry acknowledged authority and standing. A basic criterion for carrying out justice as due process is that those who are given the responsibility for adjudicating disputes should have no stake in the interests of the disputants. Moreover, prior to making a decision on a specific issue, it is desirable that the relevant framework of rules should have been put in place. Disinterested adjudication and independent rules are critical for ensuring that like cases are treated similarly, and for avoiding bias or favouritism.

Justice based on desert   This notion of justice holds that an individual's attributes, actions or failures to act have moral significance. Clark (2000) provides the example of a hard worker deserving recognition and extra pay, or similarly of a leading scientist deserving a prize. Justice calls for people to be rewarded or punished according to desert. Preferential access to specific resources and positions are awarded to individuals of particular merit. Access to jobs is normally on the basis of qualifications and skill, for example. The implementation of justice based on desert can present challenges in the settlement situation. Criteria of merit can contain dimensions of bias which can skew the selection processes. An example of this is unjustified emphasis on specific levels of language fluency in selection tests or procedures for education and employment areas where this feature would not be critical. Such procedures in practice block participation avenues for new groups.

Justice as human rights   This notion of justice is most easily appreciated in relation to paramount human rights including the rights to life, personal liberty and freedom of speech. This area of justice is at times disputable. It is complicated by the fact that precise delineation in the content of human rights is not possible. Additionally, if rights are grounded solely in the concept of respect, reasonable and competing rights of individuals still need to be reconciled by some additional independent principle of decision-making. Thus the principle of human rights is not without its problems of interpretation and implementation. However, the idea has high importance both politically and historically. (Human rights are discussed in Chapter 2).

Justice as fair shares   Justice as fair shares is about the equity or fairness of any person's treatment in comparison with others. It is embedded strongly in the context of existing conditions in which goods and resources are usually in limited supply in relation to the number of potential consumers and beneficiaries. Clark (2000, 150) states that we cannot expect that even distribution would be a workable solution in the long term since needs are unevenly distributed in any population. The challenge of justice as fair shares, and the focus of social justice, is to determine which uneven distributions would be the fairest.

Social justice is about need and response to need. Even the idea of basic needs, while not generally contested as a principle, is nonetheless difficult to define and quantify in a way that would be acceptable to all (Doyal and Gough 1991). Of the theories of social justice which use the stratagem of a social contract, John Rawls' (1973) version is the most influential. Rawls (1973) proposes a 'thin', or minimalist, theory of primary goods which are essential to human life under any circumstances. In order to avoid anyone knowing in advance whether he or she will be advantageously or disadvantageously endowed by nature and circumstance, the parties to the social contract confer behind a 'veil of ignorance' in Rawls' (1973) scheme. Rawls (1973) argues that the parties to the social contract would rationally agree to two basic principles of justice:

1. Equality in the provision of basic goods
2. Inequality in other respects is just if the effect is to increase the welfare of everyone, and especially the least well off in society.

Reisch (2002, 346) observes that the principle of justice as fairness as stated by Rawls (1971, 100) seems to be particularly well suited to the social work profession's goal of eliminating racial, gender and economic inequalities. According to Rawls (1971), undeserved inequalities call for redress. Since inequalities of birth and natural endowment are undeserved, these should be addressed by compensatory mechanisms. Thus, the principle holds that in order to treat all persons equally, to provide genuine equality of opportunity, society must pay more attention to those with fewer native assets and to those born into the less favourable social positions. This principle is one of redressing the bias of contingencies in the direction of equality.

Gal (2001) elaborates on this issue through an exploration of the different notions of social justice implied in the concept of compensatory social welfare policies. Gal (2001) maintains that social justice is defined in two fundamental ways. One definition reflects efforts to reward individuals for past services or contributions, or as a redress for 'injuries or losses inflicted unjustly on individuals or groups'. This definition is often in conflict with the view of social justice that emphasizes equality. Gal (2001) suggests that a way of reconciling this conflict is to use the social welfare system to ensure horizontal equality in meeting needs, while allowing the market to reward people for their efforts by 'providing them with their just deserts'.

Justice as liberation is based on the belief that conventional ways of apprehending human nature and capacity are radically wrong. Injustice is a consequence of faulty ideology, which incorrectly treats as natural fact what is really a constraint imposed by human error. Feminism constitutes the clearest contemporary example of this. Liberationist ideologies share a similar logical structure, and a thrust to emancipate humanity from obsolete views of human nature and capacity.

Professional Integrity

Professional integrity is a theme that has been otherwise well covered in the literature. I will present some aspects which should be emphasized in working with client constituencies of immigrant background. These include the need for building specialized knowledge in the settlement and integration field, the importance of immigrant client input into decisions and other work processes, and the working of settlement and integration elements into accountability frames.

Specialized knowledge   Working effectively with immigrant communities and individuals calls for development of the requisite knowledge base in more specific areas of settlement, its structure-based dynamics and related challenges at personal, family and community levels. I am using the term 'knowledge base' in a dynamic sense, indicating its evolutionary dimension as practitioners actively build their own stocks of information and experience and also engage in reflective appraisal of their own practice. In settlement social work, the diversity in client groups and needs calls for a dynamic knowledge base as advocated by Payne (2001, 134). He argues that the idea of the knowledge base as a crucial aspect of a professional activity might be flawed, and that it is more useful to see social work as a continuous process of constructing and reconstructing professional knowledge. Payne (2001) states that once we take this view, it is possible to study what interest groups and stakeholders contribute to that construction, and the processes and routes by which they do so. Clarke (2006, 12) writes that 'when migrants are excluded from knowledge production, their narratives are not told or are told in such ways that their voices can easily be appropriated for different interests'. Payne (2001) argues that the idea of a knowledge base can take into account the range of biases existing within the current knowledge base, and calls for the need for a more complex and fluid understanding of the structure of knowledge within social work.

While the professional values and principles seek to reflect what is thought to be of fundamental value and importance to human beings, practice approaches (including generic approaches) grew out of particular socio-historic conditions and processes that invariably impact on and restrict their applicability and universal generalization.

The practice modes of social work were heavily influenced by context. However, the symbiosis with theory helps us to focus on generic facets in approaches, while the centrality of the body of values and ethics promotes distinct standards. In much the same way, the terms of citizenship have been predicated on the life conditions and context prevailing at the time. The skill of settlement social work would be to derive settlement and integration-specific adaptations of the current approaches, as well as developing new ones. Thus at least in the same order of importance as selecting appropriate strategies is the challenge of innovating in the reflective practice mode.

Reflective learning processes are necessary in order to maximize and make the best use of the experience, knowledge and theoretical perspectives to guide and inform settlement practice (Thompson 2002). It is also especially well suited to the collaborative approach discussed below. Reflective practice is an active process of constructing solutions, rather than the simple application of technical solutions or a rote process of following procedures or guidelines. It involves building and adapting responses to suit the specific circumstances, rather than looking for ready-made solutions. Thompson (2002) suggests stimulating a creative approach by, for example, changing angle, and learning to see situations from other people's points of view in order to work more effectively together. Developing a vision would help to avoid deviating from objectives. At the same time, vision can also stimulate creativity and help to avoid narrow focus on a single way forward. Reflectivity also involves stepping back to improve and expand perspective (Thompson 2002, 243).

Immigrant client input into work processes   The building of collaborative principles into the approaches and phases of work has several critical implications. By including minority group members and their emic or 'insider' perspectives into work processes, the risk will be reduced that ethnocentric or culturally inappropriate action would endanger the effectiveness of interventions. Moreover, such collaborative activity can be the basis for developing methodologies that would enhance the skill profile for settlement practice. Genuine collaboration is also a step towards redressing the imbalance of power in client–worker relationships. In settlement social work the risk of power imbalance can derive from individuals' newcomer status and the social positioning of clients, as well as from cultural difference and membership of a cultural minority. One consequence of this situation might be that some needs and problems remain invisible. The capacity for collaboration in settling groups can be enhanced by structural provisions which would need to be made for the training and education of minority members. Collaboration would also include mechanisms for inclusion of minority staff in work roles.

It is essential to stress the need to incorporate emic or 'insider' perspectives into social work approaches in order to safeguard the appropriateness of actions. At points in critical interventions, such as in child custody cases (which are supported by legal authority), professionals exercise legitimate power. Our base of appropriate expertise is fundamental to the exercise of legal authority. I argue here that emic perspectives are an integral part of this expertise base when working with immigrant clients. *When proceeding with critical or invasive interventions in which emic representation in decision-making is weak or absent, there is a danger of stepping into ethically questionable terrain.* This has special relevance in settlement practice with groups whose cultural background has been hitherto unfamiliar. As Clark (2000, 23) states: 'It then becomes an issue whether good faith is a sufficient defence of inadequate or dangerous practice.' It would be timely in settlement practice to consider 'indigenous interventions of the client system and use them in planning and implementing services' (Fong 2001 , 6).

Accountability frames   Practitioners and scholars alike avoid the term 'successful integration'. In the first place, it is not possible to make a valid estimate of success except through the lens of the individual or group in question. Secondly, myriad conditions in the societal context have as great an impact as personal qualities on integration outcomes, giving rise to hesitation over how the concept could be operationalized. Statistical data generate information on, for example, employment/

unemployment rates, school performance, health status, income levels and so on. It would be useful if indicators of effective settlement could be developed to provide guiding information for the development of approaches in the field. Such a project would, at the same time, constitute a reflective exercise on the state of the settlement practice field.

In any scrutiny of settlement, there should be consideration of long-term integration. Such a perspective would take us beyond immediate and interim measures of a more pragmatic nature to dimensions that would reflect aspects of composite integration achievement or functionings, to use Sen's (1985) term. Long-term integration achievements can be regarded in the light of full and productive roles in society, and as well-being at the individual and family level. Well-being, as stated above, can be understood as being related to the gap between an individual's goals and actual conditions. One central concern would be to assess which types of intervention promote or have promoted long-term integration and clients' access to important functionings.

Building Robust Approaches for Settlement Practice

The dynamism in the field of social work with immigrants and refugees is reflected in its ongoing development of robust practice approaches and quality dimensions in interventions. Sound understanding of the scope and nature of settlement and integration, as well as recognition of the importance of affirmative tasks, are pillars of robust approaches at policy level. The following are some of the features of robust settlement practice:

Strong and Comprehensive Inter-sectoral Networking and Links

The linkages of settlement work with other sectors are functional along several dimensions. Information flow often involves supplying critical areas of information to colleagues in other fields, where orientation to settlement situations might be otherwise minimal. Other human service workers do not generally have the same intensity of transactions and tasks in settlement issues, and might be unaware of the context of referrals or requests for supportive services. Settlement practitioners can mediate valuable insights that assist other sectors in matters relating to immigrant client issues. It is also common that immigrant service users might not be able to present their cases with the requisite informational emphasis and input that would ensure effective response. As in networking in general, personal contacts work on the principles of social capital and can expedite matters greatly, especially when the qualities of trust and confidence are present.

Intersectoral networking is vital if we are to harness the range of information that is called for in settlement and integration practice. Our networks of information need to be wide ranging in the interests of keeping abreast of developments and potential opportunities both to strengthen immigrant participation and to expand our strategies.

Analytic Approach to the Structural Environment of Settlement and Structural Social Work Approaches

An analytical or critical approach to the structural environment will generate deeper understanding of the systems in which settlement activity is embedded. This approach can facilitate 'unpacking' of problem issues, and allowing for the more accurate targeting of interventions. New and innovative ideas can be sparked, thus broadening our perspective on possible strategies. Understanding the social systems that impact on settlement is an aid to planning strategically by taking environmental factors and their impact into account ahead of time. For example, understanding how and why a hostile task environment might react to a community initiative would allow for shaping responses to meet such challenges.

Above all, structural approaches in social work direct us to seek and address root causes of problem situations in the social systems and environment. For settlement, this would preclude the expectation that immigrant and refugee clients adapt to all the circumstances they meet in settlement. The structure-focused stance has implications for the settlement social work mandate.

Collaborative and Other Ties with Communities, Partnership with Ethnic Community Organizations, and Other Civil Society Parties

The advantages of establishing working links with ethnic communities are discussed in Chapter 6 and elsewhere. Emphasis has not been put on the fact that formal collaboration has a strengthening effect on the position of community and on its status. Collaborative activity helps organizations to become viable, purpose-directed collectivities. In the process, they also build infrastructure to accommodate collaborative tasks, thereby consolidating resources and energies of the community in a concrete way.

Other civil society actors take part in settlement activity in different capacities. The Red Cross is one prominent example, as it generally functions in important roles in reception services and also on a cross-national basis. Civil society organizations constitute resource bases for many of the areas of settlement which are not in the preserve of formal service provision. Some examples of activities vital to settlement processes are mentoring;host and other befriending programmes; sports, recreation and youth activities. Religious congregations have generally taken a very active role in assisting newcomers. Connections to civil society organizations can be activated through referral. The organizations function in their own way to facilitate the rooting of immigrants and refugees in the wider community. Additionally, civil society and its very diverse organizations function in an ethos of inclusion, which lends itself to the participation of newcomers.

Proactive Work and Proactive Organizational Culture: Using Community Channels

A preventative or proactive practice approach is crucial when working with groups who are not familiar with formal service provision and formal help-seeking. Linkages through members of the communities are invaluable for recognizing when early targeting of supportive services is needed. Situations that mature into difficult and intractable problems can have as their source lack of elemental understanding of customs and expectations, as well as sanctions in the new home society. In these cases, cultural interpreters or mediators play an important role. Al-Krenawi and Graham (2001) write of the role of the cultural mediator bridging the gap between a non-western community and professional social work practice. Cultural mediators are usually well-respected individuals in the life of their community. They mediate between the community – the cultural canon – and local social workers – the professional canon. They can also be involved in mediation between two or more parties. Many of the settling groups have folkways of mediating differences and difficult situations. It has been common for respected members of communities to function in this role. It is a role which carries weight in problem situations for which the solutions might be quite elusive in the frame of formal practice. Cultural mediators intervene with credibility, based on their position in the community, their understanding of human situations and their cultural expertise. These are bases of 'power'. It would be in the interest of settlement to bring in resources such as these to aid in interventions, also using a proactive approach.

Respect for Cultural Integrity of the Client Community

Invasive interventions need to be considered in the individual's or family's cultural as well as social context. Invasive interventions are grounded in serious ethical consideration in mainstream practice. In settlement practice, problem analysis and assessment would call for integrating culturally competent inputs into these work processes to take account of all impinging aspects of the problem situation. From another perspective, cultural integrity implies that the inclusion of newer groups in the society's fabric of solidarity would not be on condition of cultural conformity.

Transparency

In work with individuals and groups whose acquaintance with social work services is weak, individuals need to understand procedures, processes, implications and the rationale behind these. Cultural competence is one of the skill areas that facilitate this process.

Participation at Different Levels in the Immigration Discourse

The public discourse is an important platform where stakeholders engage in the preliminary phases of policy-making. Participation in the discourse is, in a sense, a proactive aspect of policy practice. In the context of ongoing discourse, settlement questions and issues do not remain invisible. It is possible to correct biased perspectives.

Policy Practice

Policy practice features in Chapter 9. In this section, emphasis should be given to the fact that greater engagement in policy practice by settlement practitioners will reinforce the voice and profile of the profession as a body and, at the same time, have the downstream effect of strengthening the individual voices of advocacy and equity in internal organizational discourses and decision-making. Policy practice entails systematic building of the relevant knowledge base on settlement issues, which indirectly underpins all practice areas.

Integration of the Social Work and Human Service Workforce – Minority Group Members

This fundamental issue has been discussed in earlier chapters. Integrating minority group members into the social workforce is a major step toward addressing the need to build cultural and linguistic competence in agencies. This would also facilitate the establishment of direct community connections for facilitating proactive and other approaches, as well as building emic perspectives into our practice. Equity principles in hiring minority members into the human services are at the heart of settlement activity.

Closing Comments

Ethics and social justice have been discussed in this chapter in the context of social work with immigrants and refugees. The discipline derives a compelling base of legitimacy from its roots in ethical and social justice principles. In order to mobilize this resource, we would need to unravel and identify the main strands that unite settlement and integration phenomena with these powerful principles. Robust approaches for settlement practice have been proposed as a platform from which practitioners can fashion methodologies and strategies that also incorporate their own stocks of practice knowledge.

Final Remarks

Settlement and integration are about substantive citizenship which would allow for unimpeded and full participation of immigrants in a given society. Some of the central tasks for settlement and integration practice relate to more extensive engagement with issues in the area of social justice. Immigrant integration is a question of long-term prospects for self-development, and the attainment of meaningful and productive roles in the life of the community and society. Valuable as it is, access to social services and benefits is not a total panacea, nor does it constitute a sustainable response to unequal chances in the society of settlement. Discrimination, non-commodification of immigrants' expertise and glass ceilings serve to disqualify significant numbers of capable and competent persons whose contribution is needed in a critical way in their communities and in society.

Low levels of representation of immigrants at higher levels of responsibility in organizations and in the professions are evident, even in societies with long experience of settlement and in those which otherwise have achieved advanced gender equality. This is a troubling situation which erodes the principles of solidarity and equity. Discriminatory processes have an adverse effect on individuals' identification with majority or mainstream society – a factor which is manifest in disaffection in second generation immigrants. A positive approach to discrimination would be to conceptualize this phenomenon as a default outcome resulting from under-developed policy and/or inefficient policy implementation processes. Strategy based on this understanding would render this long-standing problem directly amenable to policy and practice interventions.

In settlement societies, the organizing of diversity is increasingly along principles of multiculturalism, even though the term itself might not be used and the national policies might vary in different contexts. Multiculturalism has resonance with earlier approaches to pluralism before the supremacy of national culture became a prime force for asserting unity in societies. Multiculturalism of today diverges from the older ideas in that the incorporation of diversity calls for specific actions and measures by the state to work towards the inclusion of new groups into the arena of substantive and equal citizenship. It calls for a qualitative shift in policy-making.

Policy practice has been discussed as a key area of activity with immigrant and refugee communities. A heightened role in policy-making (and in the public discourse) would create stronger channels for influencing national immigration activity and growth. Immigration is being understood increasingly as a resource opportunity for receiving societies to enable them to sustain service sectors, and to renew and invigorate other labour market sectors that are being depleted as working populations come to retirement age. Immigration will continue to be a feature of societies in a globalized world. Social work is one of the professions most heavily engaged with the actors in the field – immigrants, families, communities, and their myriad informal, formal and institutional networks. The profession is well poised to make a significant contribution towards the recognition and realization of immigrant and refugee populations as a major resource for their countries of settlement.

Bibliography

Abele, F. (ed.) (1991), *How Ottawa Spends 1991–1992: The Politics of Fragmentation* (Ottawa: Carleton University Press).

Adams, R., Dominelli, L. and Payne, M. (eds) (1998), *Social Work: Themes, Issues and Critical Debates* (New York: Palgrave).

Adams, R., Dominelli, L. and Payne, M. (eds)(2001), *Social Work: Themes, Issues and Critical Debates* (London: Macmillan).

Adelman, H. (ed.) (1995), Legitimate and Illegitimate Discrimination: New Issues in Migration (Toronto: York Lanes Press).

Ager, A. (1993), *Mental Health Issues in Refugee Populations: A Review*, Working Paper of the Harvard Center for the Study of Culture and Medicine.

Ahearn, F.L. and Athey, J.L. (eds) (1991), *Refugee Children: Theory, Research, and Services* (Maryland: Johns Hopkins University Press).

Ahmad, W.I.U. (1996), 'The Trouble with Culture', in D. Kelleher and S. Hillier (eds), *Researching Cultural Differences in Health* (London: Routledge).

Akerman, S. and Granatstein, J.L. (eds) (1995), *Welfare States in Trouble* (Uppsala: Swedish Science Press).

Alba, R. and Nee, V. (1996), 'The Assimilation of Immigrant Groups: Concept, Theory, and Evidence', paper presented at the Social Science Research Council conference on Becoming American/America Becoming, Sanibel Island, February.

Alba, R. and Nee, V. (1999), 'Rethinking Assimilation Theory for a New Era of Immigration', in C. Hirschman, P. Kasinitz and J. DeWind (eds), *The Handbook of International Migration: The American Experience* (New York: Russell Sage Foundation).

Alexander, J.C. (1997), 'The Paradoxes of Civil Society', *International Sociology* 12(2), 115–33.

Alexander, J. (ed.) (1998), *Real Civil Societies: Dilemmas of Institutionalization* (London: Sage Publications Ltd).

Alford, J. (1997), 'Towards a New Public Management Model: Beyond "Managerialism" and its Critics', in M. Considine and M. Painter (eds), *Managerialism: The Great Debate* (Melbourne: Melbourne University Press).

Alitolppa-Niitamo, A. (2004), 'Somali Youth in the Context of Schooling in Metropolitan Helsinki: A Framework for Assessing Variability in Educational Performance', *Journal of Ethnic and Migration Studies* 30(1), 81–106.

Al-Krenawi, A. (2000), *Ethno-Psychiatry Among the Bedouin-Arab of the Negev* (Tel Aviv: Hakibbutz Hameuchad) (in Hebrew).

Al-Krenawi, A. and Graham, J.R. (1999), 'Gender and Biomedical/Traditional Mental Health Utilization among the Bedouin-Arab of the Negev', *Culture, Medicine, and Psychiatry* 23(2), 219–43.

Al-Krenawi, A. and Graham, J.R. (2001), 'The Cultural Mediator: Bridging the Gap Between a Non-Western Community and Professional Social Work Practice', *British Journal of Social Work* 31, 665–85.

Alund, A. and Schierup, C.-U. (eds) (1991), *Paradoxes of Multiculturalism* (Aldershot: Avebury).

Amin, A. and Thrift, N. (2002), 'Guest Editorial. Cities and Ethnicities', *Ethnicities* 2(3), 291–300.

Anderson, L.P. (1991), 'Acculturative Stress: A Theory of Relevance to Black Americans', *Clinical Psychology Review* 11, 685–702.

Andrews, G. (ed.) (1991), *Citizenship* (London: Lawrence and Wishart).

Anisef, P. and Lanphier, M. (2003), *The World in a City* (Toronto: University of Toronto Press).

Anthias, F. (1998), 'Evaluating "Diaspora": Beyond Ethnicity?', *Sociology* 2(3), 557–80.

Anthias, F. (2002), 'Diasporic Hybridity and Transcending Racisms: Problems and Potential', in F. Anthias and C. Lloyd (eds), *Rethinking Anti-racisms: From Theory to Practice* (London and New York: Routledge).

Anthias, F. and Lloyd, C. (eds) (2002), *Rethinking Anti-racisms: From Theory to Practice* (London and New York: Routledge).

Antonovsky, A. (1979), *Health, Stress and Coping* (California: Jossey-Bass Publishers).

Appleyard, R. (ed.) (1999), *Emigration Dynamics in Developing Countries Vol. IV: The Arab Region* (Aldershot: Ashgate).

Aronson Fontes, L. (2005), *Child Abuse and Culture: Working with Diverse Families* (New York: The Guilford Press).

Bacharach, S.B. and Lawler, E.J. (1980), *Power and Politics in Organizations* (San Francisco: Jossey-Bass).

Baldwin, M. (2000), Care Management and Community Care: Social Work Discretion and the Construction of Policy (Aldershot: Ashgate).

Balgopal, P.R. (ed.) (2000), *Social Work Practice with Immigrants and Refugees* (New York: Columbia University Press).

Banks, S. (1995), *Ethics and Values in Social Work* (Basingstoke: Macmillan).

Barker, R.L. (1995), *The Social Work Dictionary*, 3rd edition (Washington, DC: NASW Press).

Barot, R. (ed.) (1996), The Racism Problematic: Contemporary Sociological Debates on Race and Ethnicity (Lewiston: The Edwin Mellen Press).

Barth, F. (ed.) (1969), *Ethnic Groups and Boundaries* (Boston: Little, Brown and Company).

Barudy, J. (1989), 'A Programme of Mental Health for Political Refugees: Dealing with the Invisible Pain of Political Exile', *Social Science and Medicine* 28(7), 715–27.

Basch, L., Glick Schiller, N. and Szanton Blanc, C. (1994), Nations Unbound: Transnational Projects, Postcolonial Predicaments, and Deterritorialized Nation-States (Basel, Switzerland: Gordon and Breach).

Baubock, R. (1991), 'Migration and Citizenship', *New Community* 18(1), 27–48.

Baumann, G. (1996), Contesting Culture: Discourses of Identity in Multi-ethnic London (Cambridge: Cambridge University Press).

Baumeister, R.F., Faber, J.E. and Wallace H.M. (1999), 'Coping and Ego Depletion', in C.R. Snyder (ed.), *Coping: The Psychology of What Works* (Oxford: Oxford University Press).

Becker, G.S. (1962), 'Investment in Human Capital', *Journal of Political Economy* 70.

Bek-Pedersen, K. and Montgomery, E. (2006), 'Narratives of the Past and Present: Young Refugees' Construction of a Family Identity in Exile', *Journal of Refugee Studies* 19(1), 94–112.

Bereford, P. and Croft, S. (1993), *Citizen Involvement – A Practical Guide for Change* (Basingstoke: Macmillan).

Berry, J.W. (1988), 'Acculturation and Psychological Adaptation: A Conceptual Overview', in J.W. Berry and R.C. Annis (eds), *Ethnic Psychology: Research and Pratice with Immigrants, Refugees, Native Peoples, Ethnic Groups and Sojourners* (Amsterdam: Swets and Zeitlinger).

Berry, J.W. (1996), 'Prejudice, Ethnocentrism and Racism', *Siirtolaisuus – Migration* 2, 5–9.

Berry, J.W. and Annis, R.C. (eds.) (1988), Ethnic Psychology: Research and Pratice with Immigrants, Refugees, Native Peoples, Ethnic Groups and Sojourners (Amsterdam: Swets and Zeitlinger).

Bidney, D. (1953), 'The Concept of Culture and Some Cultural Fallacies', in D. Bidney, *Theoretical Anthropology* (New York: Columbia University Press).

Bidney, D. (1953), *Theoretical Anthropology* (New York: Columbia University Press).

Blalock, H. (1967), *Toward a Theory of Minority Group Relations* (New York: Jon Wiley and Sons).

Blau, J. (1992), *The Visible Poor: Homelessness in the United States* (New York: Oxford University Press).

Bloom, M. and Klein, W.C. (eds) (1997), Controversial Issues in Human Behavior in the Social Environment (Boston: Allyn & Bacon).

Blumer, H. (1958), 'Race Prejudice as a Sense of Group Position', *Pacific Sociological Review* 1, 3–7.

Borjas, G.J. (1990), Friends or Strangers: The Impact of Immigrants on the US Economy (New York: Basic Books).

Bourdieu, P. (1986), 'The Forms of Capital', in J.G. Richardson (ed.), *Handbook of Theory and Research for the Sociology of Education* (Westport, CT: Greenwood Press).

Bourdieu, P. (1991), *Language and Symbolic Power* (Cambridge: Polity Press).

Bourdieu, P. and Passeron, J.C. (1977), *Reproduction in Education, Society, Culture* (Beverly Hills, CA: Sage).

Bourdieu, P. and Wacquant, L.J.D. (1992), *An Invitation to Reflexive Sociology* (Chicago: Chicago University Press).

Bovenkerk, F., Miles, R. and Verbunt, G. (1990), 'Racism, Migration and the State in Western Europe: A Case for Comparative Analysis', *International Sociology* 5(4), 475–90.

Breton, R. (1992), *Report of the Academic Advisory Panel on the Social and Cultural Impacts of Immigration* (Canada: Research Division, Strategic Planning & Research, Immigration Policy Group, Employment and Immigration).

Briskin, L. and Eliasson, M. (eds) (1999), *Women's Organizing and Public Policy in Canada and Sweden* (Montreal: McGill-Queen's University Press).

Briskman, L. and Cemlyn, S. (2005), 'Reclaiming Humanity for Asylum Seekers: A Social Work Response', *International Social Work* 49(6), 714–24.

Brown, R. (1995), *Prejudice. Its Social Psychology* (Oxford: Blackwell).

Brubaker, R. (1992), *Citizenship and Nationhood in France and Germany* (Cambridge, MA: Harvard University Press).

Brubaker, R. (2001), 'The Return of Assimilation? Changing Perspectives on Immigration and its Sequels in France, Germany, and the United States', *Ethnic and Racial Studies* 24(4), 531–48.

Brubaker, R. (2003), 'Neither Individualism nor "Groupism": A Reply to Craig Calhoun', *Ethnicities* 3(4), 553–7.

Brubaker W.R. (ed.) (1989), Immigration and the Politics of Citizenship in Europe and North America (London: University Press of America).

Brysk, A. (2005), Human Rights and Private Wrongs: Constructing Global Civil Society (New York and London: Routledge).

Buijs, G. (ed.) (1993), Migrant Women: Crossing Boundaries and Changing Identities (Oxford: Berg Publishers Ltd).

Bullivant, B. (1981), *The Pluralist Dilemma in Education: Six Case Studies* (Sydney: George Allen & Unwin).

Bulmer, M. and Rees, A.M. (1996), *Citizenship Today: The Contemporary Relevance of T.H. Marshall* (London: UCL Press).

Calhoun, C. (1995), Critical Social Theory: Culture, History and the Challenge of Difference (Oxford: Blackwell Publishers Ltd).

Calhoun, C. (1999), 'Nationalism, Political Community and the Representation of Society; Or, Why Feeling at Home is not a Substitute for Public Space', *European Journal of Social Theory* 2(2), 217–31.

Calhoun, C. (2003), '"Belonging" in the Cosmopolitan Imaginary', *Ethnicities* 3(4), 531–68.

Calhoun, C., LiPuma, E. and Postone, M. (1993), *Bourdieu: Critical Perspectives* (Cambridge: Polity Press).

Canadian Employment and Immigration Commission (CEIC) (1982), *Affirmative Action: Technical Training Manual* (Ottawa: CEIC).

Cashmore, E. (1996), *Dictionary of Race and Ethnic Relations* (London: Routledge and Kegan Paul).

Castel, R. (1996), 'Work and Usefulness to the World', *International Labour Review* 135(6), 615–21.

Castles, S. (1995), 'How Nation States Respond to Immigration and Ethnic Diversity', *New Community* 21(3), 293–308.

Castles, S. and Miller, M. (1993), The Age of Migration: International Population Movements in the Modern World (Hampshire: The Macmillan Press).

Cetrez, Ö.A. (2005), Meaning-Making Variations in Acculturation and Ritualization: A Multi-Generational Study of Suroyo Migrants in Sweden (Uppsala University:Dept of Theology).

Chaliand, G. (ed.) (1989), *Minority Peoples in the Age of Nation-States* (London: Pluto).

Chamberlain, M. (2006), Family Love in the Diaspora: Migration and the Anglo-Caribbean Experience (Kingston: Ian Randle Publishers).

Clark, C.L. (2000), *Social Work Ethics* (Basingstoke, Hampshire: Macmillan Press Ltd).

Clark, K. (1953), 'Desegregation: An Appraisal of the Evidence', *Journal of Social Issues* 9(4).

Clark, K. (1955), *Prejudice* (Boston: Beacon Press).

Clark, K. (1965), *Dark Ghetto* (New York: Harper and Row).

Clarke, K. (2006), 'Producing Social Work Knowledge on Migrants in Finland: Complicit with Power or Committed to Empowerment?', paper presented at Trajectories of Commitment and Complicity Workshop, Amsterdam School for Cultural Analysis, 29–31 March 2006.

Clawson, J.G. (1999), *Level Three Leadership: Getting Below the Surface* (New Jersey: Prentice-Hall).

Coleman, J.S. (1990), *Foundations of Social Theory* (Cambridge, MA: The Belknap Press of Harvard University Press).

Compton, B.R. and Galaway, B. (1999), *Social Work Processes* (Pacific Grove, CA: Brooks/Cole Publishing Company).

Considine, M. and Painter, M. (eds), (1997), *Managerialism: The Great Debate* (Melbourne: Melbourne University Press).

Cox, D. and Pawar, M. (2006), *International Social Work: Issues, Strategies and Programs* (Thousand Oaks, CA: Sage Publications Inc.).

Cyrus, N., Gropas, R., Kosic, A. and Vogel, D. (2005), *Opportunity Structure for Immigrants' Active Civic Participation in the European Union. Sharing Comparative Observations*, University of Oldenburg, POLITIS Working Paper No. 2 <www.uni-oldenburg.de/politis-europe/webpublications>.

D'Andrade, R. (1984), 'Cultural Meaning Systems', in R.A. Schweder and R.A. Leine (eds), *Culture Theory* (Cambridge: Cambridge University Press).

Dannreuther R. (2007), 'War and Insecurity: Legacies of Northern and Southern State Formation', *Review of International Studies* 33, 307–26.

Das Gupta, T. (1996), *Racism and Paid Work* (Toronto: Garamond Press).

Davies, M. (ed.) (1991), *The Sociology of Social Work* (London: Routledge).

Davies, M. (ed.) (2005), *Blackwell Encyclopaedia of Social Work* (Oxford: Blackwell Publishing).

Davis, G. (1997), 'Towards a Hollow State: Managerialism and its Critics', in M. Considine and M. Painter (eds),*Managerialism: The Great Debate* (Melbourne: Melbourne University Press).

de Bernart, M. (1997), 'Where Does He/She, Where Do They, Come From?', paper presented at Inclusion and Exclusion: International Migrants and Refugees in Europe and North America, New School for Social Research, New York, 5–7 June 1997.

De Levita, D.J. (1965), *The Concept of Identity* (Paris: Mouton).

Delap, C. (1997), 'Social Work and Social Exclusion: Voices from the Front Line and Signals for the Makers and Shapers of Policy', *Social Work in Europe* 4(2), 28–31.

Derber, C. (1982), 'Managing Professionals: Ideological Proletarianization and Mental Labor', in C. Derber (ed.), *Professionals as Workers: Mental Labor in Advanced Capitalism* (Boston, MA: G.K. Hall).

Derber, C. (ed.) (1982), Professionals as Workers: Mental Labor in Advanced Capitalism (Boston, MA: G.K. Hall).

Devore, W.and Schlesinger, E.G. (1981), *Ethnic-Sensitive Social Work Practice* (St Louis: C.V. Mosby).

Dobbins, J.E. and Skillings, J.H. (2000), 'Racism as a Clinical Syndrome', *American Journal of Orthopsychiatry* 70(1), 14–27.

Dolgoff, R. (1999), 'What Does Social Welfare Produce?', *International Social Work* 42(3), 295–307.

Dominelli, L. (1988), Anti-racist Social Work: A Challenge for White Practitioners and Educators (London: The Macmillan Press Ltd).

Dominelli, L. (1994), 'Antiracist Social Work Education', paper given at the 27th Congress of the International Association of Schools of Social Work, Amsterdam, July.

Dominelli, L. (1996), 'Globalization and the Technocratization of Social Work', *Critical Social Policy* 47(16), 45–62.

Doyal, L. and Gough, I. (1991), *A Theory of Human Need* (Basingstoke: Macmillan).

Dunn, K.M. (1998), 'Rethinking Ethnic Concentration: The Case of Cabramatta, Sydney', *Urban Studies* 35(3), 503–27.

Dworkin, R. (1977), *Taking Rights Seriously* (Cambridge, MA: Harvard University Press).

Eberly, D.E. (ed.) (2000), *The Essential Civil Society Reader* (Maryland: Rowman & Littlefield Publishers, Inc.).

Edwards, R.L. (Ed.-in-Chief) (1995), *Encyclopedia of Social Work*, 19th edn (Washington, DC: NASW Press).

Eisenstadt, S.N. (1954), *The Absorption of Immigrants* (London: Routledge & Kegan).

Ervasti, H. and Kangas, O. (1995), 'Are Nordic Welfare States Still Distinct?', *European Journal of Political Research* 27(3), 347–67.

Esping-Andersen, G. (1990), *The Three Worlds of Welfare Capitalism* (Cambridge: Polity).

Esping-Andersen, G. (ed.) (1996), Welfare States in Transition: National Adaptations in Global Economies (London: Sage).

Esping-Andersen, G. (2005), 'Inequality of Incomes and Opportunities', in A. Giddens and P. Diamond, *The New Egalitarianism* (Cambridge: Polity Press).

Esser, H. (2004), 'Does the "New" Immigration Require a "New" Theory of Intergenerational Integration?', *International Migration Review* 38(3), 1126–59.

Ewen, M.J. (2006), *Public Policy: The Competitive Framework* (Oxford: Oxford University Press).

Ezell, M. (2001), *Advocacy in the Human Services* (Belmont, CA: Brooks/Cole/Thomson Learning).

Faist, T. (2000a), 'Transnationalization in International Migration: Implications for the Study of Citizenship and Culture', *Ethnic and Racial Studies* 23(2), 189–222.

Faist, T. (2000b), The Volume and Dynamics of International Migration and Transnational Social Spaces (Oxford: Oxford University Press).

Fennema, M. (2004), 'The Concept and Measurement of Ethnic Community', *Journal of Ethnic and Migration Studies* 30(3), 429–47.

Fennema, M. and Tillie, J. (1999), 'Political Participation and Political Trust in Amsterdam. Civic Communities and Ethnic Networks', *Journal of Ethnic and Migration Studies* 25(4), 703–26.

Fennema, M. and Tillie, J. (2002), 'The Paradox of Multicultural Democracy', paper presented at ECPR Joint Session of Workshops, Workshop 7: Rescuing Democracy: The Lure of the Associative Elixir, Turin, 22–27 March.

Fincher, R. (1997), 'Gender, Age, and Ethnicity in Immigration for an Australian Nation', *Environment and Planning* 29, 217–36.

Fleras, A. and Elliott J.L. (1996), Unequal Relations: An Introduction to Race, Ethnic and Aboriginal Dynamics in Canada (Ontario: Prentice-Hall Canada Inc.).

Flosser, G. and Otto, H.-U. (eds) (1998), *Towards More Democracy in Social Services: Models and Culture of Welfare* (Berlin and New York: Walter de Gruyter).

Foner, N. (1997), 'The Immigrant Family: Cultural Legacies and Cultural Changes', *International Migration Review* 31(4), 961–74.

Fong, R. (2001), 'Culturally Competent Practice: Past to Present', in R. Fong and S. Furuto (eds), Culturally Competent Practice: Skills, Interventions, and Evaluations (Boston: Allyn & Bacon).

Fong, R. (ed.) (2004), Culturally Competent Practice with Immigrant and Refugee Children and Families (New York: The Guildford Press).

Fong, R. and Furuto, S. (eds) (2001), Culturally Competent Practice: Skills, Interventions, and Evaluations (Boston: Allyn & Bacon).

Fook, J. (2003), 'Critical Social Work: The Current Issues', *Qualitative Social Work* 2(2), 123–30.

Forsander, A. (ed.) (2002), *Immigration and Economy in the Globalization Process: The Case of Finland*, Sitra Report Series 20 (Vantaa: Tummavuoren Kirjapaino Oy).

Foucault, M. (1977), *Discipline and Punish: The Birth of the Prison* (New York: Pantheon Books).

Foucault, M. (1982), Madness and Civilization: A History of Insanity in the Age of Reason (London: Tavistock).

Foweraker, J. and Landman, T. (1997), Citizenship Rights and Social Movements: A Comparative and Statistical Analysis (Oxford: Oxford University Press).

Franklin, M.I. (2003), 'I Define My Own Identity: Pacific Articulations of "Race" and "Culture" on the Internet', *Ethnicities* 3(4), 465–90.

Fraser, N. (1989), Unruly Practices: Power, Discourse and Gender in Contemporary Social Theory (Cambridge: Polity).

Freeman, G.P. (1986), 'Migration and the Political Economy of the Welfare State', *Annals of the American Academy of Political and Social Sciences* 485, 51–67.

Freire, P. (1970), *Pedagogy of the Oppressed* (New York: Seabury Press).

Furuto, S.B.C.L. (2004), 'Theoretical Perspectives for Culturally Competent Practice with Immigrant Children and Families', in R. Fong (ed.), *Culturally Competent Practice with Immigrant and Refugee Children and Families* (NewYork: The Guildford Press).

Gable, K. (1998), *Strategic Action Planning: A Guide for Setting and Meeting Your Goals* (Boca Raton, FL: St Lucie Press) HD 30.28 G318 1998.

Gal, J. (2001), 'The Perils of Compensation in Social Welfare Policy', *Social Service Review* 75(2), 225–44.

Gamble, D.N. and Weil, M.O. (1995), 'Citizen Participation', in R.L. Edwards (Ed.-in-Chief), *Encyclopedia of Social Work*, 19th edition (Washington, DC: NASW Press).

Gans, H.J. (1979), 'Symbolic Ethnicity: The Future of Ethnic Groups and Cultures in America', *Ethnic and Racial Studies* 2, 1–20.

Gans, H.J. (1999), 'Toward a Reconciliation of "Assimilation" and "Pluralism": The Interplay of Acculturation and Ethnic Retention', in C. Hirschman, P. Kasinitz and J. DeWind (eds), *The Handbook of International Migration: The American Experience* (New York: Russell Sage Foundation).

Geddes, A. (2003), 'Migration and the Welfare State in Europe', in S. Spencer (ed.), *The Politics of Migration: Managing Opportunity, Conflict and Change* (Oxford: Blackwell Publishing Ltd).

Geertz, C. (1971), 'The Integrative Revolution: Primordial Sentiments and Civil Politics in the New States', in C.E. Welch (ed.), *Political Modernization. A Reader in Comparative Political Change*, 2nd edition (Belmont: Duxbury Press).

Geertz, C. (1973), *The Interpretation of Cultures* (New York: Basic Books).

Gellis, Z.D. (2003), 'Kin and Non-kin Social Supports in a Community Sample of Vietnamese Immigrants', *Social Work* 48(2), 248–58.

Germain, C.B. (1973), 'An Ecological Perspective in Casework Practice', *Social Casework* 4, 323–30.

Germain, C.B. and Gitterman, A. (1995), 'Ecological Perspective', in R.L. Richards (Ed.-in-Chief), *Encyclopedia of Social Work*, 19th edition, Vol. 1 (Washington, DC: NASW Press).

Geyer, R., Ingebritsen, C. and Moses, J.W. (2000), *Globalization, Europeanization and the End of Scandinavian Social Democracy* (Basingstoke: Palgrave).

Gibelman M. (2000), 'Affirmative Action at the Crossroads: A Social Justice Perspective', *Journal of Sociology and Social Welfare* XXVII(1), 153–73.

Giddens, A. (1990), *The Consequences of Modernity* (Cambridge: Polity Press).

Giddens, A. (1998), 'Equality and the Social Investment State', in I. Hargreaves and I. Christie (eds), *Tomorrow's Politics: The Third Way and Beyond* (London: Demos).

Giddens, A. and Diamond, P. (2005), *The New Egalitarianism* (Cambridge: Polity Press).

Gil, D.G. (1998a), Confronting Injustice and Oppression: Concepts and Strategies for Social Workers (New York: Columbia University Press).

Gil, D.G. (1998b), 'Confronting Injustice and Oppression', in F.G. Reamer (ed.), *The Foundation of Social Work Knowledge* (New York: Columbia University Press).

Ginsberg, L. (1996), *Understanding Social Problems, Policies and Programs*, 2nd edition (Colombia, South Carolina: University of South Carolina Press).

Gitterman, A. and Shulman, L. (eds) (1994), *Mutual Aid Groups, Vulnerable Populations, and the Life Cycle* (New York: Columbia University Press).

Gladstone, A. with Wheeler, H., Rojot, J., Eyraud, F. and Ben-Israel, R. (eds) (1992), *Labour Relations in a Changing Environment* (Berlin and New York: Walter de Gruyter).

Glastra, F., Schedler, P. and Kats, E. (1998), 'Employment Equity Policies in Canada and The Netherlands: Enhancing Minority Employment between Public Controversy and Market Initiative', *Policy and Politics* 26(2), 163–76.

Goldberg, D. (1994), *Multiculturalism: A Critical Reader* (London: Blackwell).

Goldman, L. (1993), 'Misconceptions of Culture and Perversions of Multiculturalism', *Interchange* 24(4), 397–408.

Gordon, M. (1964), *Assimilation in American Life* (New York: Oxford University Press).

Gore, C. (1995), 'Introduction: Markets, Citizenship and Social Exclusion', in G. Rodgers, C. Gore and J.B. Figueiredo (eds), *Social Exclusion: Rhetoric, Reality, Responses* (Geneva: International Institute for Labour Studies, International Labour Organization).

Gottlieb, B.H. (ed.) (1981), *Social Networks and Social Support* (Beverly Hills: Sage).

Gould, K.H. (1995), 'The Misconstruing of Multiculturalism: The Stanford Debate and Social Work', *Social Work* 40(2), 198–205.

Gowricharn, R. (2002), 'Integration and Social Cohesion: The Case of the Netherlands', *Journal of Ethnic and Migration Studies* 28(2), 259–73.

Graham, M. (2002), 'Creating Spaces: Exploring the Role of Cultural Knowledge as a Source of Empowerment in Models of Social Welfare in Black Communities', *British Journal of Social Work* 32, 35–49.

Graham, M. and Soininen, M. (1998), 'A Model for Immigrants? The Swedish Corporate Model and the Prevention of Ethnic Discrimination', *Journal of Ethnic and Migration Studies* 24(3), 523–39.

Granovetter, M.S. (1973), 'The Strength of Weak Ties', *American Journal of Sociology* 78(6), 1360–81.

Green, J. (1982), *Cultural Awareness in the Human Services* (Englewood Cliffs, NJ: Prentice Hall).

Green, J. (1995), Cultural Awareness in the Human Services: A Multi-ethnic Approach (Englewood Cliffs, NJ: Prentice Hall).

Greene, R. (ed.) (2002), Resiliency: An Integrated Approach to Practice Policy and Research (Washington, DC: NASW Press).

Hadden, T. (2002), 'Integration and Autonomy: Legal and Political Approaches to Minority Issues', Working Paper presented at Danish Center for Human Rights.

Hagen, J.L. (2000), 'Critical Perspectives on Social Welfare: Challenges and Controversies', *Families in Society* 81(6), 555–6.

Hall, E.T. (1976a), 'How Cultures Collide', *Psychology Today* 10(2), 66–75.

Hall, E.T. (1976b), *Beyond Culture* (Garden City, New York: Anchor Press Doubleday).

Hall, S. (1992), 'The Question of Cultural Identity', in S. Hall, D. Held and T. McGrew (eds), *Modernity and its Futures* (Cambridge: Polity Press).

Hall, S., Held, D. and McGrew, T. (eds) (1992), *Modernity and its Futures* (Cambridge: Polity Press).

Hammar, T. (1990), Democracy and the Nation-State: Aliens, Denizens, and Citizens in a World of International Migration (Aldershot: Gower).

Hammar, T. (1991), '"Cradle of Freedom on Earth": Refugee Immigration and Ethnic Pluralism', *West European Politics* 14(3), 182–97.

Handlin, O. (1973), *The Uprooted*, 2nd edition (Boston: Little, Brown and Company).

Hargreaves, I. and Christie, I. (eds) (1998), *Tomorrow's Politics: The Third Way and Beyond* (London: Demos).

Harris, J. (1998), 'Personal Social Services: Changing Organizational Forms and Service User Participation. A British Perspective on the Democratization Debate', in G. Flosser and H.-U. Otto (eds), *Towards More Democracy in Social Services: Models and Culture of Welfare* (Berlin and New York: Walter de Gruyter).

Harris, M. (1974), *Cows, Pigs, Wars, and Witches* (New York: Random House).

Hatziprokopiou, P. (2003), 'Albanian Immigrants in Thessaloniki, Greece: Processes of Economic and Social Incorporation', *Journal of Ethnic and Migration Studies* 29(6), 1033–57.

Hawthorne, L. (1997), 'The Question of Discrimination: Skilled Migrants' Access to Australian Employment', *International Migration* 35(3), 395–417.

Haynes, K.S. and Mickelson, J.S. (1991), *Affecting Change: Social Workers in the Political Arena* (White Plains, NY: Longman).

Healy, K. (2005), Social Work Theories in Context: Creating Frameworks for Practice (New York: Palgrave Macmillan).

Healy, L. (2004), 'Strengthening the Link: Social Work with Immigrants and Refugees and International Social Work', *Journal of Immigrant and Refugee Services* 2(1/2), 49–67.

Henry, F., Tator, C., Mattis, W. and Rees, T. (2000), *The Colour of Democracy: Racism in Canadian Society*, 2nd edition (Toronto: Harcourt Brace & Company).

Hepworth, D.H. and Larsen, J.A. (1986), 'Employing Advocacy and Social Action', in D.H. Hepworth and J.A. Larsen (eds), *Direct Social Work Practice: Theory and Skills* (Chicago: Dorsey).

Hepworth, D.J., Rooney, R.H. and Larsen, J.A. (1997), *Direct Social Work Practice: Theory and Skills* (Pacific Grove, CA: Brook/Cole Publishing Limited).

Herberg, D.C. (1993), *Frameworks for Cultural and Racial Diversity* (Toronto: Canadian Scholars' Press Inc.).

Herberg, W. (1960), *Protestant, Catholic, Jew: An Essay in American Religious Sociology*, revised edition (Garden City, NY: Anchor Books).

Higham, J. (1975), Send These to Me: Jews and Other Immigrants in Urban America (New York: Atheneum).

Hill, M. (1996), *Social Policy: A Comparative Analysis* (London: Prentice Hall/ Harvester Wheatsheaf).

Hirschman, A. (1972), *Exit, Voice, Loyalty* (Cambridge, MA: Harvard University Press).

Hirschman, C. (2004), 'The Role of Religion in the Origins and Adaptation of Immigrant Groups in the United States', *International Migration Review* 38(3), 1206–33.

Hirschman, C., Kasinitz, P. and DeWind, J. (eds) (1999), *The Handbook of International Migration: The American Experience* (New York: Russell Sage Foundation).

Hitchcox, L. (1993), 'Vietnamese Refugees in Hong Kong: Behavior and Control', in G. Buijs (ed.), *Migrant Women: Crossing Boundaries and Changing Identities* (Oxford: Berg Publishers Ltd).

Hodges-Aeberhard, J. (1999), 'Affirmative Action in Employment: Recent Court Approaches to a Difficult Concept', *International Labour Review* 52(4,) 111–32.

Hugman, R. (1996), 'Professionalization in Social Work: The Challenge of Diversity', *International Social Work* 39, 131–47.

Hulewat, P. (1996), 'Resettlement: A Cultural and Psychological Crisis', *Social Work* 41(2), 129–35.

Hutchinson, J.F. (2005), *The Coexistence of Race and Racism: Can They Become Extinct Together?* (Boulder: University Press of America Inc.).

Hyde, C. (1998), 'A Model for Diversity Training in Human Service Agencies', *Administration in Social Work* 22(4), 19–33.

Ife, J. (2001), *Human Rights and Social Work: Towards Rights-based Practice* (Cambridge, England: Cambridge University Press).

Ivancevich, J.M. (2003), *Human Resource Management* (Boston: McGraw Hill).

Jack, G. (2005), 'Ecological Approach to Social Work', in Martin Davies (ed.), *Blackwell Encyclopaedia of Social Work* (Oxford: Blackwell Publishing).

Jackson-Elmore, C. (2005), 'Informing State Policymakers: Opportunities for Social Workers', *Social Work* 50(3), 251–61.

Jacobs, D. and Tillie, J. (2004), 'Introduction: Social Capital and Political Integration of Migrants', *Journal of Ethnic and Migration Studies* 30(3), 419–28.

Jacobs, R.N. (1998), 'The Racial Discourse of Civil Society: The Rodney King Affair and the City of Los Angeles', in J. Alexander (ed.), *Real Civil Societies: Dilemmas of Institutionalization* (London: Sage Publications Ltd).

Jain, H.C. (1992), 'Affirmative Action, Employment Equity and Visible Minorities in Canada', in A. Gladstone, with H. Wheeler, J. Rojot, F. Eyraud and R. Ben-Israel (eds), *Labour Relations in a Changing Environment* (Berlin and New York: Walter de Gruyter).

Jansson, B.S. (2003), *Becoming an Effective Policy Advocate: From Policy Practice to Social Justice* (Pacific Grove, CA: Brooks/Cole/Thomson Learning).

Jenkins, R. (1994), 'Rethinking Ethnicity: Identity, Categorization and Power', *Ethnic and Racial Studies* 17(2), 197–223.

Jenkins, R. (1996), '"Us" and "Them": Ethnicity, Racism and Ideology', in R. Barot (ed.), *The Racism Problematic: Contemporary Sociological Debates on Race and Ethnicity* (Lewiston: The Edwin Mellen Press).

Johnson, C.E. (2001), Meeting the Ethical Challenges of Leadership: Casting Light or Shadow (London: Sage Publications).

Johnson, D.W. and Johnson, R.T. (2000), 'The Three Cs of Reducing Prejudice and Discrimination', in S. Oskamp (ed.), *Reducing Prejudice and Discrimination* (New Jersey: Lawrence Erlbaum Associates).

Joly, D. (ed.) (2002), *Global Changes in Asylum Regimes* (Basingstoke: Palgrave Macmillan).

Jones, A. (2001), 'Child Asylum Seekers and Refugees: Rights and Responsibilities', *Journal of Social Work* 1(3), 253–71.

Jordens, A.-M. (1999), 'Australian Citizenship: 50 Years of Change', *ALRC Reform Issue* 74, Autumn, 24–8.

Joyce, P. (1999), *Strategic Management for the Public Services* (Buckingham: Open University Press).

Kabeer, N. (ed.) (2004), *Inclusive Citizenship* (London: Zed Books).

Kallen, E. (1995), *Ethnicity and Human Rights in Canada* (Toronto: Oxford University Press).

Kapferer, B. (1969), 'Norms and the Manipulation of Relationships in a Work Context', in J.C. Mitchell (ed.), *Social Networks in Urban Situations* (Manchester, UK: Manchester University Press).

Keane, J. (ed.) (1988), *Civil Society and the State* (London: Verso).

Kelleher, D. and Hillier, S. (eds) (1996), *Researching Cultural Differences in Health* (London: Routledge).

Kellner, D. (1989), *Critical Theory, Marxism, and Modernity* (Baltimore: Johns Hopkins University Press).

Kelson, G.A. and DeLaet, B.L.(eds) (1999), *Gender and Immigration* (Basingstoke: Macmillan Press Ltd).

Kernaghan, K. (1992), 'Choose Your Partners – Its Innovation Time!', *Public Sector Management* 3(2).

Kervinen, J., Korhonen, A. and Virtanen, K. (eds) (1996), *Identities in Transition: Perspectives on Cultural Interaction and Integration* (University of Turku: Publications of the Doctoral Program on Cultural Interaction and Integration).

Kivisto, P. (2001), 'Theorizing Transnational Immigration: A Critical Review of Current Efforts', *Ethnic and Racial Studies* 24(4), 549–77.

Kivisto, P. (2002), *Multiculturalism in a Global Society* (Oxford: Blackwell).

Kjaerum, M. (2002), 'Human Rights and the Formation of Refugees Regimes', in D. Joly (ed.), *Global Changes in Asylum Regimes* (Basingstoke: Palgrave Macmillan).

Kofman, E. (2004), 'Family-Related Migration: A Critical Review of European Studies', *Journal of Ethnic and Migration Studies* 30(2), 243–62.

Kohlberg, L. (1963), 'The Development of Children's Orientations toward a Moral Order I: Sequence in the Development of Moral Thought', *Vita Humana* 6, 11–35.

Kohlberg, L. (1981), *Essays on Moral Development* (San Francisco: Harper & Row).

Kothari, M. (1999), *Development and Social Action* (Oxford: Oxfam GB).

Kottak, C.P. (2000), *Anthropology: The Exploration of Human Diversity* (New York: McGraw-Hill Inc.).

Kritz, M.M., Lim, L.L. and Zlotnick, H. (1992), *International Migration Systems: A Global Approach* (Oxford: Clarendon Press).

Lang, N.C. and Sulman, J. (eds) (1986), *Collectivity in Social Group Work: Concept and Practice* (New York: The Haworth Press).

Lanphier, C.M. (1996), 'Welfare and Immigration: The Canadian Case', in J. Kervinen, A. Korhonen and K. Virtanen (eds), *Identities in Transition: Perspectives on Cultural Interaction and Integration* (University of Turku: Publications of the Doctoral Program on Cultural Interaction and Integration).

Law, L. (2002), 'Sites of Transnational Activism: Filipino Non-government Organizations in Hong Kong', in B.S.A. Yeoh, P. Teo and S. Huang (eds), *Gender Politics in the Asia-Pacific Region* (London: Routledge).

Lazarus, R.S. (1984), 'Puzzles in the Study of Daily Hassles', *Journal of Behavioral Medicine* 7, 375–84.

Lazarus, R.S. and Folkman, S. (1984), *Stress Appraisal and Coping* (New York: Springer).

Leadbetter, M. (1998), 'Empowerment and Advocacy', in R. Adams, L. Dominelli and M. Payne (eds), *Social Work: Themes, Issues and Critical Debates* (New York: Palgrave)..

Leonard, P. (1997), Postmodern Welfare: Reconstructing an Emancipatory Project (London: Sage).

Leonard, S.T. (1990), *Critical Theory in Political Practice* (Princeton, NJ: Princeton University Press).

Leonard, S.T. (1994), 'Knowledge/Power and Postmodernism: Implications for the Practice of a Critical Social Work Education', *Canadian Social Work Review* 11(1), 11–26.

Lepola, O. and Suurpaa, L. (2003), *In the Margin of Power? A Study of the Function of the Advisory Board for Ethnic Relations* (Helsinki: Ministry of Labour) (in Finnish).

Lewis, M.A. and Widerquist, K. (2001), Economics for Social Workers: The Application of Economic Theory to Social Policy and the Human Services (New York: Columbia University Press).

Lewis, W.A. (1955), *The Theory of Economic Growth* (London: George Allen & Unwin).

Lieberson, S. (1980), *A Piece of the Pie: Black and White Immigrants Since 1880* (Berkeley, CA: University of California Press).

Lin, N., Ensel, W.M. and Vaughn, J.C. (1981), 'Social Resources and Strength of Ties: Structural Factors in Occupational Status Attainment', *American Sociological Review* 46, 393–405.

Lindström, V. (1995), 'The Development of Multicultural Policy in Canada', in S. Akerman and J.L. Granatstein (eds), *Welfare States in Trouble* (Uppsala: Swedish Science Press).

Lippmann, W. (1922), *Public Opinion* (New York: Free Press).

Lorenz, W. (1998), 'Social Work, Social Policies and Minorities in Europe', in C. Williams, H. Soydan and M.R.D. Johnson (eds), *Social Work and Minorities* (London and New York: Routledge).

Lorenz, W. (2006), Perspectives on European Social Work – From the Birth of the Nation State to the Impact of Globalisation (Opladen: Barbara Budrich Publishers).

Lum, D. (1992), Social Work Practice and People of Colour: A Process-stage Approach (Monterey, CA: Brooks/Cole).

Lum, D. (1999), *Culturally Competent Practice* (Pacific Grove, CA: Brooks/Cole).

Lyons, K. (1999), *International Social Work: Themes and Perspectives* (Aldershot: Ashgate/ARENA).

Lyons, K. and Lawrence, S. (eds) (2006), *Social Work in Europe: Educating for Change* (Birmingham: Venture Press).

Lyons, K., Manion, K. and Carlsen, M. (2006), *International Perspectives on Social Work: Global Conditions and Local Practice* (Basingstoke, Hampshire: Palgrave Macmillan).

Macedo, D. and Gounari, P. (eds) (2006), *The Globalisation of Racism* (Boulder/London: Paradigm Publishers).

Macey, M. and Moxon, E. (1996), 'An Examination of Anti-Racist and Anti-Oppressive Theory and Practice in Social Work Education', *British Journal of Social Work* 26, 297–314.

MacLeod, J. (1987), Ain't No Making It: Leveled Aspirations in a Low-Income Neighborhood (Boulder, CO: Westview Press).

Manning, S.S. (2003), Ethical Leadership in Human Services: A Multidimensional Approach (Boston: Allyn & Bacon).

Marshall, T.H. (1950), *Citizenship and Social Class* (London: Pluto Press).

Marshall, T.H. (1963), *Sociology at the Crossroads and Other Essays* (London: Heinemann).

Marsiglia, F.F. and Menjivar, C. (2004), 'Nicaraguan and Salvadoran Children and Families', in R. Fong (ed.), *Culturally Competent Practice with Immigrant and Refugee Children and Families* (New York: The Guildford Press).

Massey, D.S. (1999), 'Why Does Immigration Occur? A Theoretical Synthesis', in C. Hirschman, P. Kasinitz and J. DeWind (eds), *The Handbook of International Migration: The American Experience* (New York: Russell Sage Foundation).

Matinheikki-Kokko, K., Koivumaki, K. and Kuortti, K. (2003), 'Developing Cross-cultural Careers Guidance', Labour Policy Studies No. 253 (Helsinki: Ministry of Labour).

Mayer, B. (2000), The Dynamics of Conflict Resolution: A Practitioner's Guide (San Francisco: Jossey Bass).

McAdam, D. (1995), '"Initiator" and "Spin-off" Movements: Diffusion Processes in Protext Cycles', in M. Traugott (ed.), *Reportoires and Cycles of Collective Action* (Durham, NC: Duke University Press).

McAdam, D., McCarthy, J.D. and Zald, M.N. (1988), 'Social Movements', in N. Smelser (ed.), *Handbook of Sociology* (Newbury Park, CA: Sage Publications).

McAll, C. (1990), *Class, Ethnicity, and Social Inequality* (Montreal and Kingston: McGill-Queen's University Press).

McCallin, M. (1992), 'The Impact of Current and Traumatic Stressors on the Psychological Well-being of Refugee Communities', in McCallin (ed.), *The Psychological Well-Being of Refugee Children: Research, Practice and Policy Issues* (Geneva: International Catholic Child Bureau).

McCallin, M. (ed.) (1992), The Psychological Well-Being of Refugee Children: Research, Practice and Policy Issues (Geneva: International Catholic Child Bureau).

McClelland, D.C. (1955), *Studies in Motivation* (New York: Appleton-Century-Crofts).

McInniss-Dittrich, K. (1994), *Integrating Social Welfare Policy and Social Work Practice* (Pacific Grove, CA: Brooks/Cole Publishing Company).

McLean, I. (1996), *The Concise Oxford Dictionary of Politics* (Oxford: Oxford University Press).

McKnight, J. (1995), The Careless Society: Community and its Counterfeits (New York: Basic Books).

McKnight, J.L. (2000), 'Professionalized Services: Disabling Help for Communities and Citizens', in D.E. Eberly (ed.), *The Essential Civil Society Reader* (Maryland: Rowman & Littlefield Publishers, Inc.).

Mead, M. (1978), Culture and Commitment: The New Relationship between the Generations in the 1970s (New York: Columbia University Press).

Midgley, J. (1995), *Social Development: The Development Perspective in Social Welfare* (London: Sage).

Miller, S.R. and Rosenbaum, J.E. (1997), 'Hiring in a Hobbesian World: Social Infrastructure and Employers' Use of Information', *Work and Occupations* 24(4), 498–523.

Mitchell, J.C. (ed.) (1969), *Social Networks in Urban Situations* (Manchester, UK: Manchester University Press).

Mizrahi, T. and Morrison, J. (eds) (1993), Community Organization and Social Administration: Advances, Trends and Emerging Principles (New York: Haworth Press).

Mizrahi, T. and Rosenthal, B.B. (1993), 'Managing Dynamic Tensions in Social Change Coalitions', in T. Mizrahi and J. Morrison (eds), *Community Organization and Social Administration: Advances, Trends and Emerging Principles* (New York: Haworth Press).

Modood, T. (1997), 'Culture and Identity', in T. Modood, R. Berthoud, J. Lakey, J. Nazroo, P. Smith, S. Virdee and S. Beishon (eds), *Ethnic Minorities in Britain: Diversity and Disadvantage* (London: Policy Studies Institute).

Modood, T. (2003), 'Muslims and the Politics of Difference', in S. Spencer (ed.), *The Politics of Migration: Managing Opportunity, Conflict and Change* (Oxford: Blackwell Publishing Ltd).

Modood, T. (2006), 'British Muslims and the Politics of Multiculturalism', in T. Modood, A. Triandafyllidou and R. Zapata-Barrero (eds), *Multiculturalism, Muslims and Citizenship* (London and New York: Routledge).

Modood, T., Berthoud, R., Lakey, J., Nazroo, J., Smith, P., Virdee, S. and Beishon, S.(eds) (1997), *Ethnic Minorities in Britain: Diversity and Disadvantage* (London: Policy Studies Institute).

Modood, T. and Kastoryano, R. (2006), 'Secularism and the Accommodation of Muslims in Europe', in T. Modood, A. Triandafyllidou and R. Zapata-Barrero (eds), *Multiculturalism, Muslims and Citizenship* (London and New York: Routledge).

Modood, T., Triandafyllidou, A. and Zapata-Barrero, R. (eds) (2006), *Multiculturalism, Muslims and Citizenship* (London and New York: Routledge).

Moore, S.T. (1990), 'A Social Work Practice Model of Case Management: The Case Management Grid', *Social Work* 35(5), 444–8.

Morris, P.M. (2002), 'The Capabilities Perspective: A Framework for Social Justice', *Families in Society: The Journal of Contemporary Human Services* 83(4), 365–73.

Mullaly, B. (1997), *Structural Social Work: Ideology, Theory and Practice* (Oxford: Oxford University Press).

Mullaly, B. (2002), *Challenging Oppression: A Critical Social Work Approach* (Oxford: Oxford University Press).

Myles, J. (1998), 'How to Design a "Liberal" Welfare State: A Comparison of Canada and the United States', *Social Policy & Administration* 32(4), 341–64.

Nash, M., Wong, J. and Trlin, A. (2006), 'Civic and Social Integration: A New Field of Social Work Practice with Immigrants, Refugees and Asylum Seekers', *International Social Work* 49(3), 345–63.

National Association of Social Workers (NASW) (1996), *Code of Ethics* (Washington, DC: NASW).

National Population Council (NPC) (1988), *The Accreditation of the Skills of Overseas Trained Workers* (Australia: National Population Council).

Nazroo, J.Y. and Karlsen, S. (2003), 'Patterns of Identity Among Ethnic Minority People: Diversity and commonality', *Ethnic and Racial Studies* 26(5), 902–30.

Needleman, M. and Needleman, C. (1974), Guerrillas in the Bureaucracy: The Community Planning Experiment in the US (New York: Wiley).

Neymare, K. (1998), 'OECD Proceedings: Immigrants, Integration and Cities: Exploring the Links' (OECD).

Northouse, P.G. (2004), *Leadership: Theory and Practice* (London: Sage Publications).

Nussbaum, M.C. (1999), 'Women and Equality: The Capabilities Approach', *International Labor Review* 138(3), 227–51.

Nussbaum, M.C. (2006), *Frontiers of Justice: Disability, Nationality, Species Membership* (Cambridge, MA: The Belknap Press of Harvard University Press).

Nyamu-Musembi, C. (2004), 'Towards an Actor-oriented Perspective on Human Rights', in N. Kabeer (ed.), *Inclusive Citizenship* (London: Zed Books).

Odmalm, P. (2004), 'Civil Society, Migrant Organisations and Political Parties: Theoretical Linkages and Applications to the Swedish Context', *Journal of Ethnic and Migration Studies* 30(3), 471–89.

Office of Multicultural Affairs (OMA) (1989), Towards a National Agenda for a Multicultural Australia – A Discussion Paper (Canberra: AGPS).

Ohmae, K. (1990), The Borderless World: Power and Strategy in the Interlinked Economy (New York: Harper).

Olson, J.M., Herman, C.P. and Zanna, M.P. (eds) (1986), *Relative Deprivation and Social Comparison*, The Ontario Symposium, Vol. 4. (New Jersey: Lawrence Erlbaum Associates).

O'Melia, M. and Miley, K. (2002), Pathways to Power: Readings in Contextual Social Work Practice (Boston: Allyn & Bacon).

Orum, A.M. (1998), 'The Urban Imagination of Sociologists: The Centrality of Place', *The Sociological Quarterly* 39(1), 1–10.

Oskamp, S. (ed.) (2000), *Reducing Prejudice and Discrimination* (New Jersey: Lawrence Erlbaum Associates).

Ostrom, E. (1990), Governing the Commons: The Evolution of Institutions for Collective Action (Cambridge: Cambridge University Press).

Papademetriou, D.G. (2003), 'Managing Rapid and Deep Change in the Newest Age of Migration', in S. Spencer (ed.), *The Politics of Migration: Managing Opportunity, Conflict and Change* (Oxford: Blackwell Publishing Ltd).

Parekh, B. (1997), 'Foreword', in T. Modood, R. Berthoud, J. Lakey, J. Nazroo, P. Smith, S. Virdee and S. Beishon (eds), *Ethnic Minorities in Britain: Diversity and Disadvantage* (London: Policy Studies Institute).

Parekh, B. (2006), 'Europe, Liberalism and the "Muslim Question"', in T. Modood, A. Triandafyllidou and R. Zapata-Barrero (eds), *Multiculturalism, Muslims and Citizenship* (London and New York: Routledge).

Park, R. and Burgess, E. (1921/24), *Introduction to the Science of Sociology* (Chicago: University of Chicago).

Parker, S., Fook, J. and Pease, B. (1999), 'Empowerment: The Modern Social Work Concept Par Excellence', in B. Pease and J. Fook (eds), *Transforming Social Work Practice: Postmodern Critical Perspectives* (London: Routledge).

Payne, M. (2001), 'Knowledge Bases and Knowledge Biases in Social Work', *Journal of Social Work* 1(2), 133–46.

Pease, B. (2002), 'Rethinking Empowerment: A Postmodern Appraisal for Emancipatory Practice', *British Journal of Social Work* 32, 135–47.

Pease, B. and Fook, J. (eds) (1999), Transforming Social Work Practice: Postmodern Critical Perspectives (London: Routledge).

Peillon, M. (1998), 'Bourdieu's Field and the Sociology of Welfare', *Journal of Social Policy* 27(2), 213–29.

Pennington, M. and Rydin, Y. (2000), 'Researching Social Capital in Local Environmental Policy Contexts', *Policy & Politics* 28(2), 33–49.

Perlmutter, F.D. and Crook, W.P. (2004), *Changing Hats While Managing Change: From Social Work Practice to Administration* (Washington, DC: NASW Press).

Phillips, A. (1991), 'Citizenship and Feminist Theory', in G. Andrews (ed.), *Citizenship* (London: Lawrence and Wishart).

Phillips, S.D. (1991), 'How Ottawa Blends: Shifting Government Relations with Interest Groups', in F. Abele (ed), *How Ottawa Spends 1991–1992: The Politics of Fragmentation* (Ottawa: Carleton University Press).

Pierik, R. (2004), 'Conceptualizing Cultural Groups and Cultural Difference: The Social Mechanism Approach', *Ethnicities* 4(4), 523–44.

Pinto, J.K., Thoms, P., Trailer, J., Palmer, T. and Govekar, M. (1998), *Project Leadership: From Theory to Practice* (Pennsylvania: Project Management Institute; HD 69 P75 P726 1998).

Pojman, L. and Westmoreland, R. (eds) (1997), *Equality Selected Readings* (Oxford: Oxford University Press).

Pollitt, C. (1993), *Managerialism and the Public Service*, 2nd edition (Oxford: Blackwell).

Porter, J. (1979), The Measure of Canadian Society: Education, Equality, and Opportunity (Toronto: Gage).

Portes, A. (1994), 'Introduction: Immigration and Its Aftermath', *International Migration Review* xxviii(4), 632–9.

Portes, A. (1998), 'Social Capital: Its Origins and Applications in Modern Sociology', *Annual Review of Sociology* 2, 1–24.

Portes, A. (1999), 'Conclusion: Towards a New World: The Origins and Effects of Transnational Activities', *Ethnic and Racial Studies* 22(2), 463–77.

Portes, A., Guarnizo, L.E. and Landholt, P. (1999), 'The Study of Transnationalism: Pitfalls and Promise of an Emergent Research Field', *Ethnic and Racial Studies* 22(2), 217–37.

Portes, A. and Rumbaut, R. (1990), *Immigrant America. A Portrait* (Berkeley: University of California Press).

Portes, A. and Zhou, M. (1993), 'The New Second Generation: Segmented Assimilation and its Variants', *The Annals of the American Academy of Political and Social Science* 530 (November), 74–97.

Pratkanis, A.R. and Turner, M.E. (1996), 'The Proactive Removal of Discriminatory Barriers: Affirmative Action as Effective Help', *Journal of Social Issues* 52(4), 111–32.

Prilleltensky, I. and Prilleltensky, O. (2005), 'Beyond Resilience: Blending Wellness and Liberation in the Helping Professions', in M. Ungar (ed.), *Handbook for Working with Children and Youth: Pathways to Resilience Across Cultures and Contexts* (Thousand Oaks, CA: Sage).

Proehl, R.A. (2001), *Organizational Change in the Human Services* (Thousand Oaks, CA: Sage).

Przeworski, A. (1995), *Sustainable Democracy* (Cambridge: Cambridge University Press).

Putnam, R., Leonardi, R. and Nanette, R.Y. (1993), *Making Democracy Work: Civic Traditions in Modern Italy* (Princeton, NJ: Princeton University Press).

Puuronen, V., Hakkinen, A., Pylkknen, A., Sandlund, T. and Toivanen, R. (eds) (2002), *New Challenges for the Welfare Society* (Joensuu: University of Joensuu, Karelian Institute).

Quillian, L. (1995), 'Prejudice as a Response to Perceived Group Threat: Population Composition and Anti-immigrant and Racial Prejudice in Europe', *American Sociological Review* 60, 586–611.

Ramakrishnan, K.R. and Balgopal, P.R. (1995), 'Role of Social Institutions in a Multicultural Society', *Journal of Sociology and Social Welfare* 22(1), 11–27.

Rappaport, J. (1990), 'Research Methods and the Empowerment Agenda', in P. Tolan, F. Cherntak and L. Jason (eds), *Researching Community Psychology* (Washington: D.S.L. American Psychological Assocation).

Rawls, J. (1971), *A Theory of Justice* (Cambridge, MA: Harvard University Press).

Rawls, J. (1973), *A Theory of Justice* (Oxford: Oxford University Press).

Raz, J. (1994), Ethics in the Public Domain: Essays in the Morality of Law and Politics (Oxford: Oxford University Press).

Reamer, F.G. (ed.) (1998), *The Foundation of Social Work Knowledge* (New York: Columbia University Press).

Reisch, M. (2002), 'Defining Social Justice in a Socially Unjust World', *Families in Society* 83(4), 343–54.

Reisch, M. (2005), 'American Exceptionalism and Critical Social Work: A Retrospective and Prospective Analysis', in I. Ferguson, M. Lavalette and E. Whitmore (eds), *Globalisation, Global Justice and Social Work* (London and New York: Routledge).

Reisch, M. and Gambrill, E. (eds) (1997), *Social Work in the 21st Century* (Thousand Oaks: Pine Forge Press).

Reisman, D. (2005), Democracy and Exchange: Schumpeter, Galbraith, T.H. Marshall, Titmuss and Adam Smith (Cheltenham: Edward Elgar Publishing Limited).

Richards, R.L. (Ed.-in-Chief) (1995), *Encyclopedia of Social Work*, 19th edition, Vol. 1 (Washington, DC: NASW Press).

Richardson, J.G, (ed.) (1983/86), *Handbook of Theory and Research for the Sociology of Education* (Westport, CT: Greenwood Press).

Richmond, A.H. (1994), *Global Apartheid: Refugees, Racism, and the New World Order* (Toronto: Oxford University Press).

Rodgers, G., Gore, C. and Figueiredo J.B. (eds) (1995), *Social Exclusion: Rhetoric, Reality, Responses* (Geneva: International Institute for Labour Studies, International Labour Organization).

Roer-Strier, D. (1996), 'Coping Profiles of Immigrant Parents: Directions for Family Therapy', *Family Process* 35, 363–76.

Roer-Strier, D. (1997), 'In the Mind of the Beholder: Evaluation of Coping Styles of Immigrant Parents', *International Migration* 35(2), 271–86.

Roer-Strier, D. and Rosenthal, M.K. (2001), 'Socialization in Changing Cultural Contexts: A Search for Images of the "Adaptive Adult"', *Social Work* 46(3), 215–28.

Rogers, G. (1995), 'Practice Teaching Guidelines for Learning Ethnically Sensitive, Anti-Discriminatory Practice: A Canadian Application', *British Journal of Social Work* 25(4), 441–57.

Room, G. (ed) (1991), *Towards a European Welfare State?* (Bristol: SAUS).

Room, G. (ed) (1995), Beyond the Threshold: The Measurement and Analysis of Social Exclusion (Bristol: The Polity Press).

Rooth, D-O. and Ekberg, J. (2003), 'Unemployment and Earnings for Second Generation Immigrants in Sweden. Ethnic Background and Parent Composition', *Journal of Population Economics* 16, 787–841.

Rosanvallon, P. (1988), 'The Decline of Social Viability', in J. Keane (ed.), *Civil Society and the State* (London: Verso).

Ross, M., Eyman, A. and Kishchuk, N. (1986), 'Determinants of Subjective Well-Being', in J.M. Olson, C.P. Herman and M.P. Zanna (eds), *Relative Deprivation and Social Comparison*, The Ontario Symposium, Vol. 4. (New Jersey: Lawrence Erlbaum Associates).

Rueschemeyer, D., Stephens, E.H. and Stephens, J.D. (1992), *Capitalist Development and Democracy* (Cambridge: Polity Press).

Rumbaut, R.G (1991), 'The Agony of Exile: A Study of the Migration and Adaptation of Indochinese Refugee Adults and Children', in F.L. Ahearn and J.L. Athey (eds), *Refugee Children: Theory, Research, and Services* (Maryland: Johns Hopkins University Press).

Rumbaut, R. (1999), 'Assimilation and Its Discontents: Ironies and Paradoxes', in C. Hirschman, P. Kasinitz and J. DeWind (eds), *The Handbook of International Migration: The American Experience* (New York: Russell Sage Foundation).

Rydgren, J. (2004), 'Mechanisms of Exclusion: Ethnic Discrimination in the Swedish Labour Market', *Journal of Ethnic and Migration Studies* 30(4), 697–716.

Saleebey, D. (1997), 'Is It Feasible to Teach HBSE from a Strengths Perspective, In Contrast To One Emphasizing Limitations and Weaknesses? Yes', in M. Bloom and W.C. Klein (eds), *Controversial Issues in Human Behavior in the Social Environment* (Boston: Allyn & Bacon).

Sashkin, M. and Sashkin, M.G. (2003), *Leadership that Matters* (San Francisco: Berrett-Koehler Publishers).

Satka, M. and Karvinen, S. (1999), 'The Contemporary Reconstruction of Finnish Social Work Expertise', *European Journal of Social Work* 2(2), 119–29.

Schaar, J.H. (1997), 'Equality of Opportunity, and Beyond', in L. Pojman and R. Westmoreland (eds), *Equality Selected Readings* (Oxford: Oxford University Press).

Schierup, C.-U. (1991), 'The Puzzle of Trans-ethnic Society', in A. Alund and C.-U. Schierup (eds), *Paradoxes of Multiculturalism* (Aldershot: Avebury).

Schinke, S.P. (1997), 'Prospects for Prevention', in M. Reisch and E. Gambrill (eds), *Social Work in the 21st Century* (Thousand Oaks: Pine Forge Press).

Schnapper, D. (1991), *La France de l'integration* (Paris: Galimard).

Schweder, R.A. and Leine, R.A. (eds) (1984), *Culture Theory* (Cambridge: Cambridge University Press).

Sen, A. (1985), *Commodities and Capabilities* (Amsterdam: North-Holland).

Sen, A. (1997), 'Inequality, Unemployment and Contemporary Europe', *International Labour Review* 136(2), 155–72.

Sennett, R. (2003), Respect: The Formation of Character in an Age of Inequality (London: Penguin Books).

Shapiro, B.Z. (1986), 'The Weak-Tie Collectivity: A Network Perspective', in N.C. Lang and J. Sulman (eds), *Collectivity in Social Group Work: Concept and Practice* (New York: The Haworth Press).

Sheafor, B.W., Horejsi, C.R. and Horejsi, G.A. (2000), *Techniques and Guidelines for Social Work Practice* (Needham Heights, MS: Allyn & Bacon).

Sheffer, G. (1995), 'The Emergence of New Ethno-National Diasporas', *Migration* 28/9, 5–28.

Shields, J. and Evans, B.M. (1998), Shrinking the State: Globalization and Public Administration 'Reform' (Halifax: Fernwood Publishing).

Shils, E. (1997), The Virtue of Civility: Selected Essays on Liberalism, Tribalism and Civil Society, edited by Steven Grosby (Indianapolis: Liberty Fund).

Silver, H. (1994), 'Social Exclusion and Social Solidarity: Three Paradigms', *International Labour Review* 133(5–6), 531–7.

Simon-Barouh, I. and Simon, P.J. (1990), *Les etrangers dans la ville* (Strangers in the City) (Paris: L'Harmattan).

Skegg, A.-M. (2005), 'Human Rights and Social Work: A Western Imposition or Empowerment to the People?', *International Social Work* 48(5), 667–72.

Smelser, N. (ed.) (1988), *Handbook of Sociology* (Newbury Park, CA: Sage Publications).

Smolicz, J. (1981), 'Core Values and Cultural Identity', *Ethnic and Racial Studies* 4(1), 75–90.

Snyder, C.R. (ed.) (1999), *Coping: The Psychology of What Works* (Oxford: Oxford University Press).

Sogren, M. (2004), *The Status of the Institution of the Family in Trinidad and Tobago*, report prepared for the Office of the Prime Minister (OPM), Trinidad and Tobago.

Solomos, J. (1998), 'Beyond Racism and Multiculturalism', *Patterns of Prejudice* 32(4), 45–62.

SOPEMI (2000), 'Comparative Analysis of the Legislation and the Procedure Governing the Immigration of Family Members in Certain OECD Countries', *Trends in International Migration* (Paris: OECD), 105–26.

Soysal, Y. (1994), Limits of Citizenship: Migrants and Postnational Membership in Europe (Chicago: University of Chicago Press).

Spencer, S. (ed.) (2003), The Politics of Migration: Managing Opportunity, Conflict and Change (Oxford: Blackwell Publishing Ltd).

Spicker, P. (1991), 'Solidarity', in G. Room (ed.), *Towards a European Welfare State?* (Bristol: SAUS).

Spicker, P. (1993), 'Understanding Particularism', *Critical Social Policy* 39, Winter 1993/4, 5–20.

Stahl, C.W. and Bradford, W. (1999), 'Conceptualizing and Simulating Emigration Dynamics', in R. Appleyard (ed.), *Emigration Dynamics in Developing Countries Vol. IV: The Arab Region* (Aldershot: Ashgate).

Stanfield, J.H. II and Dennis, R.K. (eds) (1993), *Race and Ethnicity in Research Methods* (London: Sage Publications).

Stein, B.N. (1986), 'The Experience of Being a Refugee: Insights from the Research Literature', in C.L. Williams, and J. Westermeyer (eds), *Refugee Mental Health in Resettlement Countries* (Washington, DC: Hemisphere Publishing).

Stern, M.J. (2000), 'Back to the Future? Manuel Castells, The Information Age and the Prospects for Social Welfare', *Cultural Studies* 14(1), 99–116.

Stern, M.J. (2004), 'Back to the Future? Manuel Castells, The Information Age and the Prospects for Social Welfare', in F. Webster and B. Dimitriou (eds), *Manuel Castells: Masters of Modern Social Thought*, Vol. III (London: Sage).

Stiglitz, J. (2002), *Globalization and its Discontents* (London: Penguin).

Stocke, V. (1999), 'New Rhetorics of Exclusion in Europe', *Social Science Journal* 159, 25–36.

Strauss, C. and Quinn, N. (1997), *A Cognitive Theory of Cultural Meaning* (New York: Cambridge University Press).

Suarez-Orozco, C. and Suarez-Orozco, M. (2001), *Children of Immigration* (Cambridge, MA: Harvard University Press).

Sue, S. and Okazaki, S. (1990), 'Asian American Educational Achievements: A Phenomenon in Search of an Explanation', *American Psychologist* 45(8), 913–20.

Sumner, W.G. (1907), *Folkways* (Boston: Ginn).

Swank, D. (2000), 'Social Democratic Welfare States in a Global Economy: Scandinavia in Comparative Perspective', in R. Geyer, C. Ingebritsen and J.W. Moses (eds), *Globalization, Europeanization and the End of Scandinavian Social Democracy* (Basingstoke: Palgrave).

Taylor M.C. (2000), 'Social Contextual Strategies for Reducing Discrimination' in S. Oskamp (ed.), *Reducing Prejudice and Discrimination* (New Jersey: Lawrence Erlbaum Associates).

Taylor, O.W. (2002), 'Cultural Considerations for Social Workers in the Jamaican Inner City: A Sociological Perspective', *Caribbean Journal of Social Work* 1, 48–59.

Teitelbaum, M.S. (1980), 'Right Versus Right: Immigration and Refugee Policy in the United States', *Foreign Affairs* 59(1), 21–59.

Thomas-Hope, E.M. (1992), *Explanation in Caribbean Migration* (London: The Macmillan Press Limited).

Thompson, N. (1997), *Anti-Discriminatory Practice*, 2nd edition (London: Macmillan).

Thompson, N. (1998), Promoting Equality: Challenging Discrimination and Oppression in the Human Services (London: Macmillan).

Thompson, N. (2002), *People Skills* (Basingstoke: Palgrave Macmillan).

Tilly, C. (1998), *Durable Inequality* (Berkeley and Los Angeles: University of California Press).

Tilly, C. and Tarrow, S. (2006), *Contentious Politics* (Boulder: Paradigm Publishers).

Titmuss, R. (1958), *Essays on the Welfare State* (London: Allen and Unwin).

Tolan, P., Cherntak, F. and Jason, L. (eds) (1990), *Researching Community Psychology* (Washington: D.S.L. American Psychological Assocation).

Torpey, J.A. (2000), The Invention of the Passport: Surveillance, Citizenship and the State (Cambridge: Cambridge University Press).

Traugott, M. (ed.) (1995), *Reportoires and Cycles of Collective Action* (Durham, NC: Duke University Press).

Triandafyllidou, A., Modood, T. and Zapata-Barrero, R. (2006), 'European Challenges to Multicultural Citizenship: Muslims, Secularism and Beyond', in T. Modood, A. Triandafyllidou and R. Zapata-Barrero (eds), *Multiculturalism, Muslims and Citizenship* (London and New York: Routledge).

Tsang, K.T. and George, U. (1998), 'Towards An Integrated Framework For Cross-Cultural Social Work Practice', *Canadian Social Work Review* 15(1), 73–90.

Tsui, M. and Cheung, F.C.H. (2004), 'Gone with the Wind: The Impacts of Managerialism on Human Services', *British Journal of Social Work* 34, 437–42.

Tully, J. (1995), *Strange Multiplicity* (Cambridge: Cambridge University Press).

Ungar, M. (ed.) (2005), Handbook for Working with Children and Youth: Pathways to Resilience Across Cultures and Contexts (Thousand Oaks, CA: Sage).

United Nations General Assembly (1948), *Universal Declaration of Human Rights* (New York: United Nations).

Valtonen, K. (1996,) 'East Meets North: The Finnish-Vietnamese Community', *Asian and Pacific Migration Journal* 5(4), 471–89.

Valtonen, K. (1998), 'Resettlement of Middle Eastern Refugees in Finland: The Elusiveness of Integration', *Journal of Refugee Studies* 11(1), 38–59.

Valtonen, K. (1999), *The Integration of Refugees in Finland in the 1990s* (Helsinki: Ministry of Labour).

Valtonen, K. (2002), 'Transnationalism and Its Significance to the Vietnamese Community in Finland', in V. Puuronen A. Hakkinen, A. Pylkknen, T. Sandlund and R. Toivanen (eds), *New Challenges for the Welfare Society* (Joensuu: University of Joensuu, Karelian Institute).

Valtonen, K. (2004), 'From the Margin to the Mainstream: Conceptualizing Refugee Settlement Processes', *Journal of Refugee Studies* 17(1), 70–96.

Van Hear, N. (1994), *Migration, Displacement and Social Integration*, Occasional Paper No. 9, World Summit for Social Development (Geneva: UNRISD United Nations Research Institute for Social Development).

Van Hear, N. (1998), New Diasporas: The Mass Exodus, Dispersal and Regrouping of Migrant Communities (Seattle: University of Washington Press).

Van Soest, D. (1992), *Incorporating Peace and Social Justice into the Social Work Curriculum* (Washington, DC: National Association of Social Workers).

Vander Zanden, J.W. (1983), *American Minority Relations* (New York: Alfred A. Knopf).

Vertovec, S. (2003), 'Migration and Other Modes of Transnationalism: Towards Conceptual Cross-Fertilization', *International Migration Review* 37(3), 641–65.

Viviani, N. (1996), 'Vietnamese Concentrations: A Response', *People and Place* 4(3), 20–23.

Vogel, D. and Triandafyllidou, A. (2005), *Civic Activation of Immigrants – An Introduction to Conceptual and Theoretical Issues*, University of Oldenburg, POLITIS Working Paper No. 1.

Wahlbeck, Ö. (1998), 'Community Work and Exile Politics: Kurdish Refugee Associations in London', *Journal of Refugee Studies* 11(3), 215–30.

Wahlbeck, Ö. (1999), Kurdish Diasporas: A Comparative Study of Kurdish Refugee Communities (London: Macmillan Press).

Wahlbeck, Ö. (2002), 'The Concept of Diaspora as an Analytical Tool in the Study of Refugee Communities', *Journal of Ethnic and Migration Studies* 28(2), 221–38.

Waldinger, R. and Feliciano, C. (2004), 'Will the New Second Generation Experience Downward Assimilation? Segmented Assimilation Reassessed', *Ethnic and Racial Studies* 27(3), 376–402.

Walzer, M. (1983), *Spheres of Justice* (New York: Basic Books).

Washington, J. and Paylor, I. (1998), 'Europe, Social Exclusion and the Identity of Social Work', *European Journal of Social Work* 1(3), 327–38.

Waters, M.C. (1994), 'Ethnic and Racial Identities of Second-Generation Black Immigrants in New York City', *International Migration Review* xxviii(4),795–819.

Weaver, H.N. (2000), 'Culture and Professional Education: The Experience of Native American Social Workers', *Journal of Social Work Education* 36, 415–28.

Weick, A., Rapp, C., Sullivan, W.P. and Kisthardt, W. (1989), 'A Strengths Perspective for Social Work Practice', *Social Work* 35 (July), 350–54.

Weinbach, R. (2003), *The Social Worker as Manager* (Boston: Allyn & Bacon).

Weiss, A. (2006), 'The Racism of Globalisation', in D. Macedo and P. Gounari (eds), *The Globalisation of Racism* (Boulder/London: Paradigm Publishers).

Welch, C.E. (ed.) (1971), *Political Modernization. A Reader in Comparative Political Change*, 2nd edition (Belmont: Duxbury Press).

Wellman, B. (1981), 'Applying Network Analysis to the Study of Support', in B.H. Gottlieb (ed.), *Social Networks and Social Support* (Beverly Hills: Sage).

Williams, C. (1999), 'Connecting Anti-racist and Anti-oppressive Theory and Practice: Retrenchment or Reappraisal?', *British Journal of Social Work* 29, 211–30.

Williams, C., Soydan, H. and Johnson, M.R.D. (eds) (1998), *Social Work and Minorities* (London and New York: Routledge).

Williams, C.L. and Westermeyer J. (eds) (1986), *Refugee Mental Health in Resettlement Countries* (Washington, DC: Hemisphere Publishing).

Wimmer, A. (2004), 'Does Ethnicity Matter? Everyday Group Formation in Three Swiss Immigrant Neighbourhoods', *Ethnic and Racial Studies* 27(1), 1–36.

Woo, D. (2000), Glass Ceilings and Asian Americans: The New Face of Workplace Barriers (New York: Altamira Press).

Wrench, J. (1996), *Preventing Racism at the Workplace: A Report on 16 European Countries* (Dublin: European Foundation for the Improvement of Living and Working Conditions).

Wrench, J. and Solomos, J. (1993), *Racism and Migration in Western Europe* (Oxford: Berg).

Wronka, J.M. (1992), Human Rights and Social Policy in the 21st Century: A History of the Idea of Human Rights and Comparison of the United Nations Universal Declaration of Human Rights with United States Federal and State Constitutions (Lanham, MD: University Press of America).

Wu, D.T.L. (1997), *Asian Pacific Americans in the Workplace* (Walnut Creek, CA: Altamira Press).

Yeoh, B. and Huang, S. (1999), 'Spaces at the Margins: Migrant Domestic Workers and the Development of Civil Society in Singapore', *Environment and Planning* A, 31, 1149–67.

Yeoh, B.S.A., Teo, P. and Huang, S. (eds) (2002), *Gender Politics in the Asia-Pacific Region* (London: Routledge).

Yeoh, B.A., Willis, K.D. and Abdul Khader Fakri, S.M. (1999), 'Introduction: Transnationalism and its Edges', *Ethnic and Racial Studies* 26(2), 207–17.

Yeung, H.W.-C. (1998), Transnational Corporations and Business Networks: Hong Kong Firms in the ASEAN Region (London: Routledge).

Young, I.M. (1990), *Justice and the Politics of Difference* (Princeton, NJ: Princeton University Press).

Young-Bruehl, E. (1996), *The Anatomy of Prejudices* (Cambridge, MA: Harvard University Press).

Yuval-Davis, N. (1997), *Gender and Nation* (London: Sage Publications Ltd).

Zastrow, C. and Kirst-Ashman, K.K. (2001), *Understanding Human Behavior and the Social Environment* (Belmont, CA: Wadsworth/Thomson Learning).

Zhou, M. (1997), 'Segmented Assimilation: Issues, Controversies, and Recent Research on the New Second Generation', *International Migration Review* 31(4), 975–1008.

Zolberg, A.R., Suhrke, A. and Aguayo, S. (1989), *Escape from Violence: Conflict and the Refugee Crisis in the Developing World* (New York: Cambridge University Press).

Index